QMW Library

23 0959118 3

CW01183424

DATE DUE FOR RETURN		
2 7 MAR 1996	- 4 MAY 2007	
	1 1 JAN 2008	
- 8 MAY 1996		
2 8 NOV 1996	2 - MAY 2008	
10 JAN 1997		
1 0 JAN 1997		
16 JAN 1998		
- 1 JUN 1998		
- 7 FEB 2000		
1 9 JAN 2001		
- 7 FEB 2001		
0 5 APR 2001		

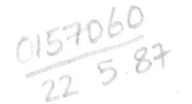

Rousseau, Nature, and History

Asher Horowitz offers in this study a new interpretation of Rousseau's major works and a stirring re-evaluation of his cultural and intellectual achievement. Where conventional readings have seen in Rousseau's critique of civilization the standard Enlightenment opposition of nature and artifice, Horowitz describes the development in the second *Discourse* of a new, historical view of human nature and society. He argues for Rousseau's discovery there of the possibility of a dialectical and historical anthropology, and he demonstrates its importance as a context for the mingled and evolving psychoanalytic, moral, and political concerns of the later works.

In Horowitz's Rousseau individuality itself, the private as well as the public, has become a product and a problem of history. Through works often viewed as contradictory Horowitz traces a persistent focus on the network of further problems revealed by this understanding – in *La Nouvelle Héloïse*, which explores the relationship between the pathologies of society and the pathologies of the modern conscience; in the *Social Contract*, which attempts a resolution of the conflicts of public and private virtue. The conclusion of his study treats the education of Emile as Rousseau's more complete attempt to distinguish between necessary and excessive denaturation, and to overcome modern alienation.

In each of these settings Horowitz's own sure grasp of interpretative problems and possibilities yields a Rousseau both complex and richly coherent, whose writings are vital in our time and condition.

This work in its original thesis form won the American Political Science Association's 1984 Leo Strauss award for the best dissertation in political philosophy.

ASHER HOROWITZ is a post-doctoral fellow in the Department of Political Science, York University.

ASHER HOROWITZ

Rousseau, Nature, and History

UNIVERSITY OF TORONTO PRESS
Toronto   Buffalo   London

© University of Toronto Press 1987
Toronto   Buffalo   London
Printed in Canada

ISBN 0-8020-5681-4

COVER ILLUSTRATION *Rosseau âgé*, by Houdon.
Reproduced from André Legarde and Laurent Michard, eds.,
Les Grands Auteurs français, vol. 4, *XVIIIe siècle*
(Paris: Bordas 1970)

Canadian Cataloguing in Publication Data

Horowitz, Asher, 1950–
Rousseau, nature, and history

Bibliography: p.
Includes index.
ISBN 0-8020-5681-4

1. Rousseau, Jean-Jacques, 1712-1778 – Criticism
and interpretation. I. Title.

PQ2053.H67 1987   848'.509   C86-094607-X

This book has been published with the help of
a grant from the Social Science Federation of Canada,
using funds provided by the Social Sciences and
Humanities Research Council of Canada,
and a grant from the Andrew W. Mellon Foundation
to University of Toronto Press.

For my parents

CONTENTS

Acknowledgments / ix
Abbreviations / xi

1 Introduction / 3
2 On the Concept of Nature / 36
3 Rousseau's Historical Anthropology / 50
4 Anthropology as History: Pre-modern Social Forms / 86
5 Anthropology as History: The Critique of Bourgeois Society / 108
6 *Julie* and the Pathology of Conscience / 135
7 'A Masterpiece of Modern Policy': The *Social Contract* / 166
8 *Emile*: The Reconciliation of Art and Nature / 207

Bibliography / 255
Index / 265

ACKNOWLEDGMENTS

For their help in all its varieties I would like to thank the following teachers and friends: Alkis Kontos, C.B. Macpherson, Christian Bay, Gad Horowitz, Ross Rudolph, Christian Lenhardt, David Kettler, Rick Matthews, Mark Warren, Margaret Paternek, Bob Gallagher, Sue Golding, and Marte Misiek.

For their patience and support I would like to thank my editors at University of Toronto Press, R.I.K. Davidson and Susan Kent.

This project would not have been possible without the generous assistance of the Canada Council and the Social Sciences and Humanities Research Council of Canada.

ABBREVIATIONS

Translations of passages from French texts are my own.

CG *Correspondance générale de Jean-Jacques Rousseau*, ed. T. Dufour (Paris: Armand Colin 1924–34). References are to volume and page.
CPC *Constitutional Project for Corsica*, in Rousseau, *Political Writings*, trans. F. Watkins (London: Thomas Nelson 1953)
DAS *Discourse on the Arts and Sciences*, in *The Social Contract and Discourses*, trans. G.D.H. Cole (London: Dent 1968)
DI *Discours sur l'inégalité*, in *Oeuvres complètes de Jean-Jacques Rousseau*, ed. Bernard Gagnebin and Marcel Raymond, vol. 3 (Paris: Gallimard 1964)
DOI *Discourse on the Origin of Inequality*, in *The Social Contract and Discourses*, trans. G.D.H. Cole (London: Dent 1968)
DOIC *Discourse on the Origin of Inequality*, in *The Social Contract and Discourse on the Origin of Inequality*, ed. L.G. Crocker (New York: Simon and Schuster 1967)
E *Emile*, trans. Barbara Foxley (New York: Dutton 1976)
EC *Ebauches des Confessions*, in *Oeuvres complètes de Jean Jacques Rousseau*, ed. B. Gagnebin and M. Raymond, vol. 1 (Paris: Gallimard 1959)
EF *Emile. Ms. Favre*, in *Annales de la Société Jean-Jacques Rousseau*, t 8
EG *L'Etat de guerre*, in *The Political Writings of Jean-Jacques Rousseau*, ed. C.E. Vaughan, vol. 1 (Cambridge: Cambridge University Press 1915)

Abbreviations / xii

EMF   *Emile (Manuscript Favre)*, in *Oeuvres complètes de Jean-Jacques Rousseau*, ed. B. Gagnebin and M. Raymond, vol. 4 (Paris: Gallimard 1969)

EOL   *Essay on the Origin of Languages*, in J.H. Moran and Alexander Gode, *On the Origin of Languages* (New York: Ungar 1966)

EP   *Epitre à Parisot*, in *Oeuvres complètes de Jean-Jacques Rousseau*, vol. 6 (Paris: Librairie Hachette 1911)

GMS   *On the Social Contract (First Version)*, in *On the Social Contract*, ed. R.D. Masters, trans. Judith R. Masters (New York: St Martin's Press 1978)

GP   *The Government of Poland*, trans. Willmoore Kendall (New York: Bobbs-Merrill 1972)

LA   *Letter to M. d'Alembert on the Theatre*, trans. Allan Bloom (Ithaca: Cornell University Press 1960)

LCB   *Letter to Christopher de Beaumont*, in *Miscellaneous Works of Jean-Jacques Rousseau*, vol. 3 (1767; repr. New York: Lennox Hill 1972)

LM   *Lettres morales*, in *Oeuvres complètes de Jean-Jacques Rousseau*, ed. B. Gagnebin and M. Raymond, vol. 4 (Paris: Gallimard 1969)

LMF   *Lettre à M. de Franquières*, in *Oeuvres complètes de Jean-Jacques Rousseau*, ed. B. Gagnebin and M. Raymond, vol. 1 (Paris: Gallimard 1959)

LNH   *La Nouvelle Héloïse*, in *Oeuvres complètes de Jean-Jacques Rousseau*, ed. B. Gagnebin and M. Raymond, vol. 2 (Paris: Gallimard 1964)

LP   *Lettre à Philopolis*, in *Oeuvres complètes de Jean-Jacques Rousseau*, ed. B. Gagnebin and M. Raymond, vol. 3 (Paris: Gallimard 1964)

LV   *Letter to Voltaire on Optimism*, in *The Indispensable Rousseau*, ed. John Hope Mason (London: Quartet Books 1979)

NH   *La Nouvelle Héloïse*, trans. Judith H. McDowell (University Park: Pennsylvania State University Press 1968). References are to part and letter.

OCI   *Oeuvres et correspondance inédites de Jean-Jacques Rousseau*, ed. Streckeisen-Moultou (Paris 1861)

PC   *Projet de constitution pour la Corse*, in *Oeuvres complètes de Jean-Jacques Rousseau*, ed. B. Gagnebin and M. Raymond, vol. 3 (Paris: Gallimard 1964)

PE   *Discourse on Political Economy*, in *The Social Contract and Discourses*, trans. G.D.H. Cole (London: Dent 1968)

PF   *Profession de foi du vicaire savoyard*, ed. Masson (Fribourg 1914)

PN   *Preface to Narcissus*, in *Miscellaneous Works of Jean-Jacques Rousseau* (1767; repr. New York: Lennox Hill 1972)

Abbreviations / xiii

RJ   *Rousseau juge de Jean-Jacques, Oeuvres complètes de Jean-Jacques Rousseau*, vol. 9 (Paris: Librairie Hachette 1911)

RPS *Rêveries du promeneur solitaire*, in *Oeuvres complètes de Jean-Jacques Rousseau*, ed. B. Gagnebin and M. Raymond, vol. 1 (Paris: Gallimard 1959)

RW   *Reveries of the Solitary Walker*, trans. Peter France (Harmondsworth: Penguin 1979)

SC   *The Social Contract*, in *The Social Contract and Discourses*, trans. G.D.H. Cole (London: Dent 1968). References are to page and, where necessary, note numbers.

SGP *Sur le gouvernement de Pologne*, in *Oeuvres complètes de Jean-Jacques Rousseau*, vol. 1 (Paris: Librairie Hachette 1911)

Rousseau, Nature, and History

CHAPTER ONE

Introduction

This essay attempts to intervene in a complex and many-sided debate on the question of Jean-Jacques Rousseau, who after more than two hundred years still manages to command a virtually inexhaustible fascination. More than most literary and philosophical figures of the eighteenth century Rousseau appeals to modern readers as practically their contemporary. On the bicentennial of his death, for example, the American Academy of Arts and Sciences devoted one entire issue of its journal, *Daedalus*, to an exploration of 'Rousseau for Our Time.'[1] The essays produced included studies of Rousseau as a theorist of utopias, a political philosopher, a theorist of the drama, an innovator of the first rank in the philosophy of education, an anthropologist, and a founder of the modern literary genre of autobiography. Yet it is not the variety of subjects in his writing that has made that writing of compelling interest. It is rather the perception that Rousseau's problems are still our own problems, perhaps more so than ever.

Most of the contributors to 'Rousseau for Our Time' chose to treat Rousseau's dilemmas as symptomatic of an inability on his part to face the demands of modern social life squarely.[2] The Rousseau problem has, since its inception in the eighteenth century, also constituted a debate about the value and viability of an urban, industrial, economically expansive and complex society. In the late twentieth century it seems

1 *Daedalus*, Proceedings of the American Academy of Arts and Sciences 107, no 3 (summer 1978)
2 Notable exceptions were the articles by A. Bloom, 'The Education of Democratic Man: *Emile*,' ibid., 135–53, and J. Featherstone, 'Rousseau and Modernity,' ibid., 167–92.

something of a foregone conclusion that our civilization will, barring nuclear or ecosystemic catastrophe, continue in this mode into the indefinite future. At the same time, the twentieth century has seen and continues to see the tremendous strains and costs in human suffering imposed by the continuing rationalization of the world, in a light much more stark than that afforded by the haze of optimism that characterized much of the nineteenth century. In the late twentieth century the question of civilization once more looms as a potentially explosive issue on the political agenda. In these circumstances it is understandable that Rousseau should come under a scrutiny both severe and anxious. As the *locus classicus* of criticism directed at many, if not most, of our hallowed rationalist and liberal values, Rousseau is the perfect foil for our own anxieties. In finding him wanting we may reassure ourselves that the continuation of our efforts in much the same direction is justified. The Rousseau problem, as it appears in the huge and varied literature of comment and criticism, thus reflects some of the most important political and philosophical divisions of post-Enlightenment Western civilization.

What is startling in this connection is not that the interpretative literature on Rousseau should be so highly charged with political purpose but that among all the various understandings of Rousseau there should not be present a left-Freudian reading.[3] This perspective, exemplified in Herbert Marcuse's efforts to join Marx and Freud in a grand critical renewal of utopian thought, invites obvious comparison with Rousseau's critique of civilization.[4]

It would be more than anachronistic to suggest that Rousseau and Marcuse share the same arsenal of concepts. Nor is it the purpose of this Marcusean reading of Rousseau to suggest that Marcuse's thought draws heavily upon Rousseau as a historical source.[5] Yet it is evident

---

3 William Kessen, 'Rousseau's Children,' ibid., 155–66, wonders at the paucity of Freudian comment on Rousseau, who 'looks like a treasure trove of psychoanalytic ore' (163). Featherstone, 'Rousseau and Modernity,' sees Rousseau as the 'great-grandaddy' of 'Freudians of the Left and Right,' among other 'maturationalist' psychologists (176).

4 See David Kettler's lengthy and thoughtful essay on Marcuse in *Contemporary Political Philosophers*, ed. A. de Crespigny and K. Minogue, 1–48. For Kettler, Marcuse's work as a whole can be fruitfully understood as a revival of the type of eighteenth-century social criticism that undertook the critical analysis of the strain and possibilities emerging in bourgeois civilization.

5 There is very little direct reference to Rousseau in Marcuse's major works. He is named, for example, in *Eros and Civilization*, as a 'theorist of educational dictatorship' along with Plato (40); in *Studies in Critical Philosophy* he is briefly mentioned as a contract theor-

Introduction / 5

that many of Rousseau's successors are some of the central figures in Marcuse's critical theory. The debt that Kant's philosophy owes to Rousseau is by now firmly established. We know that, at least as a young man, Hegel neglected his university studies at Tübingen in order to immerse himself in *Emile*, the *Social Contract*, and the *Confessions*.[6] In his mature political philosophy Hegel still reserved a special place for Rousseau's supposed understanding of the will, 'a principle which has thought for both its form and content,' as an essential moment in the realization of rational freedom.[7] Schiller conceived of Rousseau as a martyr to wisdom, comparing his fate to the fate of Socrates.[8] There is in Marx's early writings what one recent Kantian reading of the *Social Contract* calls 'an obvious, though largely unacknowledged, debt to Rousseau's moral vision of the world, a profound conceptual affinity.'[9] Engels, in a moment of enthusiastic exaggeration, was still not without cause in asserting that in the *Discourse on the Origins of Inequality* 'we find not only a sequence of ideas which corresponds exactly with the sequence developed in Marx's *Capital*, but that the correspondence extends also to details, Rousseau using a whole series of the same dialectical developments as Marx used: processes which in their nature are antagonistic, contain a contradiction, are the transformation of one

---

ist (112). Yet even a cursory reading of many of Marcuse's works reveals a profoundly Rousseauist strain. Take, for example, in *An Essay on Liberation*, his idea of a 'moral radicalism' organically founded, an 'instinctual foundation for solidarity among human beings' (10), or the appeal to a break in the chain linking generations (25), and compare with chapter 8 below, or his call, not for a 'regression to a previous stage of civilization, but a return to an imaginary *temps perdu* in the real life of mankind' (90).

6 Walter Kauffman, *Hegel: A Re-Interpretation*, 7-8
7 G.W.F. Hegel, *Philosophy of Right*, sec. 258, p 159. Comparisons are sometimes made even between Rousseau's writings and Hegelian method. See, eg, Victor Goldschmidt, *Anthropologie et Politique*, 774-5; Jean Starobinski, *Jean-Jacques Rousseau: La Transparence et l'Obstacle*, 27; also A. Bloom, 'Education,' 135, who calls *Emile* 'a *Phenomenology of Mind* posing as Dr. Spock'; also Andrew Levine, *The Politics of Autonomy: A Kantian Reading of Rousseau's Social Contract*, 24, 27.
8 This judgment appears in his poem 'Rousseau,' quoted by Peter Gay, introduction to Cassirer, *The Question of Jean-Jacques Rousseau*, 5.
9 Levine, *Autonomy*, vii. Levine indicates that this affinity rests largely on Rousseau's attempt in the *Social Contract* to overcome the alienation of man's essence, moral autonomy, which alienation, however, Rousseau understood as a historical product of social relations. For the extent of my disagreement with Levine, see chapter 8 below. Part of my purpose is to show that Rousseau cannot be fully grasped as an 'essentialist' in the manner of Feuerbach and of Althusser's readings of the early Marx. For a different critique of Levine see Howard Cell, 'Breaking Rousseau's Chains.'

extreme into its opposite; and, finally, as the kernel of the whole process, the negation of the negation.'[10]

The line of influence connecting Rousseau with Freud is more tenuous but has not gone unnoticed.[11] Jean Starobinski, in his own right-Freudian treatment of Rousseau, has left the question open as to the extent of the affinity between the two. Paraphrasing Eric Weil's statement that 'il fallait Kant pour penser les pensées de Rousseau,' Starobinski adds that 'il fallait Freud pour penser les sentiments de Rousseau.'[12] The implication is that not only does psychoanalytic theory provide a key to understanding the emotional dynamic propelling Rousseau's theoretical effort, but something of what became with Freud a conscious theory of the unconscious was present in Rousseau as pre-conscious knowledge. Freud's 'distinctive contribution ... to our concept of civilization' was the idea that progress in civilization has inextricably meant an increase in mental suffering.[13] In the contrast that Rousseau draws, for example, between the Caribbean native and the European cabinet minister, he wishes us to see in the 'mental afflictions that prey on us, the violent passions that waste and exhaust us ... how dearly nature makes us pay for the contempt with which we have treated her lessons' (*DOI* 224-5).[14]

An exercise in the history of ideas that attempts to show the degree to which Rousseau might have anticipated or influenced any of these thinkers is not my purpose here. Such studies, undertaken systematically, would be quite rewarding and, I believe, add significantly to our understanding of crucial or formative influences upon some of the major shapers of modern thought. My purpose has been to use concepts developed by Marcuse and, more broadly, by other thinkers in the Western Marxist

10 Engels, *Herr Eugen Duhring's Revolution in Science*, 153-4. I am grateful to Professor Benjamin Barber for first pointing out this passage to me. It may also be conveniently located in R.M. Lemos, *Rousseau's Political Philosophy: An Exposition and Interpretation*, 177.
11 Kessen, 'Rousseau's Children,' finds only four references to Rousseau in Freud's entire corpus, and 'none of the references is beguiling' (163; see also 167 n 27). Judith Shklar, *Men and Citizens: A Study of Rousseau's Social Theory*, 142, notices in *La Nouvelle Héloïse* an anticipation of psychoanalytic technique on Rousseau's part, but no anticipation of psychoanalytic theory.
12 Starobinski, *Transparence*, 223
13 Gad Horowitz, *Repression: Basic and Surplus Repression in Psychoanalytic Theory: Freud, Reich, Marcuse*, 154ff
14 Freud, 'Civilized Sexual Morality and Modern Nervousness'; a definition of man as the 'neurotic animal' is of course not the only point of similarity. See, eg, F. Jameson, *Marxism and Form*, who sees the 'source of Rousseau's political speculations in undisguised erotic reverie and sexual daydreaming (as in the 9th book of the *Confessions*)' (91).

Introduction / 7

tradition to attempt to illuminate certain dimensions of Rousseau's thought that, although broached by some of his critics and commentators, have remained largely underdeveloped. These are not only often tacit features of his texts but notions that would tend to recommend themselves largely, if not exclusively, to other radical modern critics of modernity.[15] It has not been my concern to criticize Rousseau; but if this study has some merit, one of my hopes would be that it might help to raise Rousseau criticism to an even higher level. Beyond that, I believe that current radicalism, Marxian and non-Marxian, has something most valuable to rediscover in this 'petit-bourgeois' neurotic, not merely a theorist of democratic movements but a utopian political philosopher with a powerful vision of 'what nature permits the species to become' (*EMF* 62).

Something about Rousseau's writings has permitted, if not authorized, an astonishing number of disparate interpretations. Peter Gay once wrote that 'many thinkers have suffered at the hands of commentators, but few have had to endure as much as Rousseau.'[16] To a great extent, whether innocently or with guilty foreknowledge, Rousseau brought this upon himself. Not only are his writings unsystematic, but the concepts he employs are often only cursorily defined, while their usage shifts from place to place; he alludes a great deal without referring specifically to other writings (including his own); and above all he loves to shock and perplex. One of his most judicious and restrained commentators has observed that his work 'habitually contains statements which appear to be at one moment astonishing syntheses, and at the next, unhappy and unresolved paradoxes.'[17] Consequently, 'Rousseauist criticism ... has been characterized by continuing fundamental disagreement and wildly conflicting scholarship ever since the eighteenth century.'[18]

If we ignore the early tendency to place Rousseau in terms of his putative influence upon political actors and thinkers during the era of the French Revolution,[19] there have been, broadly speaking, two types

---

15 Readers familiar with the writings of Georg Lukács, Max Horkheimer, Theodor W. Adorno, and Alfred Schmidt as well as Marcuse will recognize my indebtedness. Were I to attempt to describe that debt in any detail, I should, in the words of one recent interpreter of Rousseau, referring to the literature of interpretation, 'undoubtedly become so mired in digression that I should be prevented from presenting systematically my own interpretation and assessment of his position' (Lemos, *Rousseau's Political Philosophy*, viii).
16 Gay, introduction, 4
17 David Cameron, *The Social Thought of Rousseau and Burke*, 81
18 Ibid., 76
19 Gay, introduction, 1–8

of methodological approach to Rousseau interpretation. Various contextualizations of Rousseau's writings have been pursued with a view to ferreting out his intended meaning. But even though historical research has succeeded both in dispelling many crude misconceptions and in raising the level of sophistication in subsequent debates, there has been little in the way of fundamental agreement or conclusive demonstration concerning the specific content of the notions Rousseau intended to communicate.[20] Agreement seems to exist only on the fact that Rousseau does not fit well or consistently into a neat set of recognizable or stable categories. He is neither straightforwardly an individualist nor a collectivist;[21] he cannot be consigned to either the school of natural rights

20 It would be out of place to expand at length upon even some of the most important disagreements. But as an indication of the extent of the controversies, one might contrast Robert Derathé's extremely well-informed study of Rousseau's dependence on the 'school of the law of nature and the law of nations,' *Jean-Jacques Rousseau et la science politique de son temps*, with D. Cameron's quite cogent arguments that Rousseau belongs neither to the tradition of natural law nor to its sixteenth- and seventeenth-century offshoot, the theory of natural right (*Social Thought*, esp. 70-6), that his thought rather is a 'flowing away from the rationalist and empiricist forms of social and political inquiry and towards the idealist forms' (168). Yet this raises a certain number of unanswered questions. Is Derathé's work an effort to place Rousseau *within* the tradition of natural law or, as Peter Gay reads it, an attempt to demonstrate that 'Rousseau belongs, in spirit, with the rationalist individualists whom he is supposed to have overcome and denied' (Gay, introduction, 26)? Furthermore, is not the German idealism to which Cameron points as the direction in which Rousseau is moving also deeply indebted to that 'transcendental realism' (Cameron, *Social Thought*, 20) that Rousseau is moving away from? One of the most perplexing problems, after all, of Hegel scholarship is the extent and nature of his transcendental realism.

Rousseau has also been understood in the context of 'classical natural law' by Leo Strauss in *Natural Right and History* and by commentators depending heavily on him. Strauss sees Rousseau as undermining the 'modern natural right teaching' on the basis of the modern scientific understanding of nature. But if Cameron is right in disputing the 'decisive break between traditional natural law and the school of natural rights' so characteristic of Strauss's approach (77-8), then would Rousseau also be undermining the entire natural-law tradition – classical, Christian, and modern? This seems to be the position of at least one of those who follow Strauss closely. See Marc F. Plattner, *Rousseau's State of Nature: An Interpretation of the Discourse on the Origins of Inequality*, 44, 50-1, and esp. 106. Yet this is not the opinion of most of those who follow Strauss and prefer to see in Rousseau the radical critic of modernity, something of a Platonist *manqué*, holding a position of ambivalence between Hobbes and Plato.

Disagreeing implicitly with all of these is Lemos, *Political Philosophy*, who presents a rather sophisticated reading of Rousseau as a translator of Christian natural law into modern terms.

21 C.E. Vaughan in the introduction to his edition of *The Political Writings of Jean-Jacques Rousseau*, 1-117, made the classic case for Rousseau's transition from one extreme to the other. But see Peter Gay's appreciation of Vaughan: 'Vaughan's edition shows

or the school of utility;[22] he is much closer to Burke as a traditionalist than is commonly believed by those who tend to see him sharing the radical rationalism of the later Enlightenment.[23] One of the difficulties is that the sources upon which Rousseau draws are themselves extremely various.[24] When the philosophical context includes not only the major figures of the French Englightenment but also Montesquieu, Hobbes, Locke, the 'juriconsultes,' such as Grotius, Puffendorf, Althusius, Burlamaqui, and Barbeyrac, and Descartes and Malebranche, Machiavelli, the Cambridge Platonists, Lucretius, Plutarch, Aristotle, and Plato – then sorting out what Rousseau accepts, rejects, or transforms, *after* one determines what in the first place he recognized, threatens to become, at least in the long run, something of a Sisyphean labour. And this list does not by any means exhaust the possible permutations and combinations of the contexts in which Rousseau's writings, in full or in part, could be placed.[25]

The second broad methodological approach has been to attempt the educated but imaginative reconstruction of the significance of Rousseau's thought. This has also been undertaken in a variety of ways, ranging from Cassirer's reliance upon Dilthey in his own attempt at *Verstehen* to Starobinski's existential psychoanalysis and Burgelin's apparently intuitively guided systematic reconstruction of Rousseau's thought as an existential dialectic of religious enlightenment.[26] This second type of

---

unwittingly that the critic who wants to understand Rousseau must transcend political categories and consider his work as a whole' (introduction, 13).

22 Alfred Cobban, *Rousseau and the Modern State*, and 14–17 below
23 This included, of course, Burke himself. See Cameron, *Social Thought*, esp. 119–27; see also Strauss, *Natural Right*, 255–63.
24 And, of course, a historical-contextualist interpretation would seem to depend upon a prior interpretation of the many figures who make up the context. Thus, for example, Strauss's Rousseau inevitably depends upon a prior reading of Plato that is itself contestable. See M.F. Burnyeat, 'Sphinx without a Secret,' 30–6. The contextualist approach seems, in general, to hold a realistic epistemological stance, urging that the meaning of the text is prior to it and its adequate significance. This is in itself a notion that current literary and philosophical post-structuralism is contesting quite adamantly. In any case, one cannot help but wonder whether the historical realism of this approach often depends upon so many tacit assumptions that it is rendered quite as constructivist as the various forms of anachronism it seems to hope to replace.
25 The impressive number of figures whom Rousseau read, read about, could have read, and probably heard mentioned is one of the factors that makes it very difficult, in the context of his style, to judge the depth of his learning. R.D. Masters, *The Political Philosophy of Rousseau*, ix, calls him 'an enormously learned man.' Harold Laski, *The Rise of European Liberalism*, 80, calls him an autodidact and a 'magnificent sciolist.'
26 Louis Althusser's 'symptomatic reading' of the *Social Contract*, in *Politics and History: Montesquieu, Rousseau, Hegel and Marx*, 111–60, could also be included in this list.

approach aims on the whole not at the historical interpretation of Rousseau's *intentions* but at a systematic reading, a reconstruction of the thought appearing in the writings. To a great extent, therefore, the methodological strictures that are appropriate to the historical effort to elicit a thinker's conscious intentions, although possibly helpful to the reconstructionist, should not unduly restrain the creative use of the ideas of later periods and thinkers as heuristic and expository devices.[27] As such as they do not simply amount to an anachronistic importation of later (or earlier) thoughts to a historically improper context.

The approach I have just termed reconstructionist tends to consider Rousseau as important for having discovered territories that other, later thinkers have explored more extensively or profoundly but not necessarily as broadly. It also tends to recognize what Andrew Levine has very aptly called the 'polyvalence' of Rousseau's thoughts.[28] Polyvalence, of course, is a chemical and biological term denoting the ability of an element to combine with many other different elements and produce an effect on them. Rousseau's writings have this quality not only with respect

27 The most prominent statement of the strict historical-contextualist view is to be found in the recent writings of Quentin Skinner. For a critical discussion of some of the issues raised see 'Political Thought and Political Action: A Symposium on Quentin Skinner,' *Political Theory* 2 (1974): 251-303. In this symposium Skinner denies that his method, which aims at decoding the actual intention of a particular writer, refuses the possibility of studying genres and traditions of discourse (287). He furthermore distinguishes between the intended meaning of an act or utterance and the significance this might have for an observer, in 'Meaning and Understanding in the History of Ideas,' 49, and makes this distinction more explicit in 'Motives, Intentions and the Interpretation of Texts,' 405. Skinner also makes a number of other major concessions. See the excellent critique on the part of Michael Freeman in his volume on Burke, *Burke and the Critique of Political Radicalism*, 5-14. Burke, of course, not only shares a similar linguistic and historical context with Rousseau but presents similar stylistic difficulties for the interpreter. Freeman concludes that 'these concessions seem to grant a great deal to the ... doctrines Skinner opposes. There are traditions of political discourse. We may conceive of them in terms of our own philosophical interests. We may write about them with our own concepts ... In his reply to his critics, Skinner states that he never sought to deny that a classic political theorist may have had the intention to speak "transhistorically." He also says that we must be prepared to make some crucial decisions at the outset about what deserves to be studied and what is best ignored ... and they must be our own decisions, arrived at by applying our own criteria for judging what is rational and significant' (12-13). These considerations, among others, led me to classify Strauss earlier as among the 'contextualists,' even though from Skinner's point of view he should not be. They also indicate the ultimate inadequacy of a sharp dichotomy between contextualist and non-contextualist approaches.
28 Levine, *Autonomy*, 197; to the psychoanalytic ear the notion of polyvalence also suggests important features of 'primary process thinking,' ie, condensation and displacement.

to a plurality of other thinkers and traditions of discourse but also internally, with respect to his own writings.

There are at least two further characteristics of Rousseau's writings that to my mind make this sort of approach of continuing value and importance in his case. Even in his most systematic efforts, such as the *Social Contract*, there are a number of voices or characters present, suggesting, as in a dramatic production, the author's less than full identification with any one of them.[29] Second, and perhaps more important, is that Rousseau 'thought new thoughts in old concepts, "imported concepts" (to use Kant's expression), concepts inadequate to the thought expressed through them.'[30] One of the unavoidable consequences of recognizing that Rousseau did put some remarkably new wine in old bottles is that no reconstructionist reading will be interested in exhausting the text. It also leaves open the significance that future generations may find in Rousseau's writings. This reading therefore takes as one of its

---

29 See Pierre Burgelin, *La Philosophie de l'existence de Jean-Jacques Rousseau*, 2-13. Cameron, *Social Thought*, 29, describes this feature as follows: 'Rousseau's most famous political text, then, the *Contrat Social*, must be recognized as a multi-purpose composition, extremely varied in its context and in its styles of argumentation; and this observation is no less applicable to his other social and political writings.' From his consideration of the methodological issues Cameron concludes that 'a single word, a single passage, a single sentence in ... his writings is often irreducibly equivocal ... and is enough to show that no final resolution of the problem can be hoped for ... A good ear is to be preferred to any analytic technique, but the best ear in the world cannot provide conclusive proof for accuracy' (32-3). This is especially remarkable from a fairly strict contextualist who, although he argues that Rousseau's politics is a break with earlier traditions and to some degree an anticipation of Hegel's *Philosophy of Right*, refuses to use Hegel or Kant 'as a foil for understanding' because this would lead to the 'likely result' that Rousseau's writings would be 'interpreted at a higher level of generality than the evidence warranted, and ... applauded or faulted for the success and failure in an enterprise which ... he had not undertaken' (169).

30 Levine, *Autonomy*, 6; Rousseau used, for example, according to Levine, 'the contractarian idiom to express his own thought. But Rousseau's adherence to this tradition is problematical, for he did in effect break with the substance of contractarianism.' In Strauss and his followers this gap between Rousseau's thought and its means of expression quickly becomes a conscious intention on Rousseau's part to convey two different meanings to two distinct audiences, a vulgar and a philosophic audience. See esp. R.D. Master, *Political Philosophy*, 106-11. Masters goes so far as to arrange his books in numerological correspondence to the substance of his reading, placing his comments on Rousseau's first *Discourse*, his 'most defensible work' and his most essential one, in the centre of the book to correspond to the episode of the cave in Plato's *Republic*. Cf Cameron, *Social Thought*, 11, 114-15, and esp. 173: 'these words nature and artifice are as much on his lips as on anyone's else's, but it can be seen that when he does employ them he is very often attempting to develop new ideas within an old terminological framework.'

aims not the resolution of the Rousseau problem but the rendering of that problem even more complex. Rousseau discovered even more territory than that more fully explored by Kant, Hegel, and Marx.

Rousseau's use of imported concepts, the polyvalence of many of his ideas, together with the political use-values that are regularly assigned to his writings make the literature of interpretation, at least in its general outlines, an important part of the context for any new interpretation. Although readers versed in the literature should find the following discussion familiar at many points, the non-expert reader (to whom this study is also addressed) may also find it useful, not only as something of an overview of the state of the recent debates on Rousseau but also in understanding why this reading took the direction it did. Both groups may also, in postponing a more direct descent into Rousseau's writings, be spared a study that, in the words of one recent scholar, 'cannot take a step without leaving a footnote.'[31]

Rousseau was both a great precursor and a great throwback. His thought reaches forward towards Kant's moral idealism, Hegel's state of universal recognition, to romanticism, and to Darwinian evolution. It also resonates with echoes of Montesquieu's virtuous democracy, Machiavelli's republicanism, Aristotle's citizenship, Stoic autarky, and Platonic sublimation. Yet all of these notions and more, whether germs or vestiges, are stations in a unique theoretical undertaking. Rousseau was a transitional figure; but more than that, like a crucible in which many elements can be thrown together to be recast in different form, he seems in the heat of his profound discontent with the life in and around him to have recast the shape of much of our own self-understanding, the shape of the self-knowledge of modern bourgeois society.

The Rousseau problem has not only been indelibly stamped with the opinions of later scholarship but has also been formulated differently in terms of the problems of a variety of philosophical or ideological movements. It is therefore possible to find students of Rousseau grouped in galaxies.[32] Each tends to emphasize a limited number of debates, and each strives to define the Rousseau problem in the terms through which

---

31 Masters, *Political Philosophy*, viii
32 This discussion of the literature does not aim to be exhaustive, complete, or 'objective.' It concentrates on relatively recent contributions and offers only one of many possible ways of organizing a vast array of material. For excellent discussions of the older literature see Gay, introduction, 3-32, as well as his bibliographical essay in *The Enlightenment: An Interpretation*, vol. 2, *The Science of Freedom*, 694-700; also J. Chapman, 'Rousseau,' in the *Critical Bibliography of French Literature*, vol. 4, *Supplement*, 142-64; also Cobban, *Modern State*, 14-31.

it structures its theoretical universe in general. Each also tends to use Rousseau positively or negatively in its general debates with the other clusters. In the universe of Rousseau scholarship there are galaxies in which some luminaries shine more brightly than others; there is some communication, mutual attraction and repulsion, among galaxies. But among them there are also, in many cases, vast gulfs.

Among liberal thinkers Rousseau's character as a throwback has been briefly but forcefully pointed out by Sir Ernest Barker. Rousseau is seen as a true precursor of German idealism since he again conceived of the state in terms of its moral mission, reintroduced a fundamentally Aristotelian concept of citizenship, and thus prepared the way for Hegel, who restored to political philosophy its native tongue, the language of ethics.[33] But Barker was one of the first among liberal political thinkers to speak of Rousseau with sympathy. Most of the debate among Liberals has concerned the degree to which Rousseau's political and social thought can be accommodated to the liberal and liberal-democratic traditions. In the nineteenth century Hippolyte Taine already condemned Rousseau for totally sacrificing the individual to a state constructed after the model of Sparta or Rome. Others, like Benjamin Constant, saw in Rousseau's egalitarianism nothing but an equality of mistreatment.[34] In their reaction to the French Revolution they framed the Rousseau problem in terms that were to preoccupy other nineteenth-century figures like Tocqueville. To such men the Rousseau problem presented itself as a stark dichotomy between egalitarianism and individuality, conformity versus creativity, the imposition of external moral authority through the force of the state as opposed to the unbroachable moral autonomy of the individual, mediocrity and mass culture versus excellence.

Over a century later the same debate goes on, in slightly different terms but if anything more acrimoniously. The question is now posed whether Rousseau is a totalitarian or democrat. A generation ago the answers were framed in largely political terms. J.L. Talmon argued that Rousseau, in his formulation of the sovereignty of the general will and the need for a Legislator, was preparing the way for the totalitarian democracy of Robespierre and Saint-Just and, by implication, all of their followers.[35] L.G. Crocker took this charge a number of steps further. He accused Rousseau of having no trust in the 'unguided individual' and of substituting a model of totalitarian society headed by a charismatic

---

33 Sir Ernest Barker, *The Political Thought of Plato and Aristotle*, 520ff
34 See Cobban, *Modern State*, 27.
35 J.L. Talmon, *The Origins of Totalitarian Democracy*

leader, holding ideals of organic community, striving after unanimity ultimately fortified by techniques of social mobilization and mind control.[36] More recently the debate has shifted slightly to psychological grounds. Judith Shklar sees in Rousseau's personal failures and disappointments the causes of an overwhelming *ressentiment* against a complex, urban, cosmopolitan society. Rousseau's resentment motivated his self-serving image of himself as an outsider, a stranger, yet one obsessed with the need of acceptance. As an authoritarian personality who could not settle down with one master, Rousseau becomes the 'Homer of the losers.'[37] Rousseau was a utopist who, from the depths of his psychic malaise, constructed two mutually exclusive utopias, equally far removed from the equipoise demanded of the free and authentic individual: one is a heroic dream of the reign of virtue, in which men are entirely given up to the 'moi commun'; the other is the dream of a Golden Age in which the individual is sheltered and stifled in the warmth and intimacy of the family. Both are deemed typical fantasies of the authoritarian personality.[38] Rousseau has even been labelled a case of pathological narcissism.[39] Yet there is, as it seems there must be, something disturbingly circular in this type of psycho-biographical approach to Rousseau's thought: evidence for the meaning of his thought is found in his psychic life, while his psychic life is arrived at through his thought.

The diagnostic judgment of totalitarianism or authoritarianism has not, of course, gone uncontested by other liberal scholars. Alfred Cobban sets out to test Rousseau's work against a number of the central tenets of liberal democracy and does not find him terribly wanting, especially when set in the context of the thought of his contemporaries and associates. In opposition to the rest of the philosophes, Rousseau was never prepared to arrive at any compromise with despotism, enlightened or otherwise. Casting him in the role of a moralist, Cobban sees an individualist who could not utterly reject the utilitarian justification of society yet found it insufficient in and of itself and wished to make of it an aspect of a larger conception of social justice. The notion of the sovereignty of the general will loses its terroristic overtones as Cobban realizes that it is limited by the terms of its own definition. The *Social Contract* is only another attempt to justify the rule of law philosophically. Cobban

---

36 Lester G. Crocker, *Rousseau's Social Contract: An Interpretive Essay*, esp. 12–13, 16, 46, 47, 60, 163–4
37 Judith Shklar, 'Jean-Jacques Rousseau and Equality'
38 Shklar, *Men and Citizens*
39 Kessen, 'Rousseau's Children,' 166 n 28

even finds in it an insistence on the separation of powers and anything but a mistrust of the people, who are made the only possible source of a law not perverted to selfish ends. If there is anything illiberal in Rousseau, it is his plan for a civil religion, together with the first stirrings of nationalism in his critique of cosmopolitanism. But these are secondary or subsidiary themes when seen in their proper context, Rousseau's correction of Locke. Whereas Locke grants his abstract individual an innate knowledge of moral truth, Rousseau rediscovers the importance of the community to the individual's moral life. The good man and the just state are once again placed in a relation of deep reciprocal dependence, and Rousseau thus opens the door to the German idealists.[40]

Thus we have two substantially different, if not diametrically opposed, visions of Rousseau that begin from political premises that are quite similar. And it does not seem that this debate could be resolved through more careful and thorough examination of the texts. There is, however, another way of posing what is essentially the same problem, one that does not so much issue in its solution but in its displacement. If scholarship finds itself in contradiction, we may be able to attribute this to the disunity of Rousseau. Not as many commentators have taken this route. It holds that there are actually two Rousseaus. The first, the author of the *Social Contract*, recommends his totalitarian state to us denatured men transformed by civil society. Rousseau the man of nature, recognizing the unredeemable corruption of the social state but remaining uncorrupted himself, chooses to remain on the fringes of society, enjoying whatever happiness he may find, his relations with others regulated only by his innate *bonté* rather than by the coercive force in civil society. Two Rousseaus correspond to two human types: citizens and men, social beings and autonomous individuals. Rousseau is both liberal and totalitarian,

---

40 Cobban, *Modern State*; the issue of Rousseau's 'totalitarianism' is still far from moot. A recent sophisticated restatement is to be found in David Gauthier, 'The Politics of Redemption,' 71–98. Levine has presented a strong defense of Rousseau (*Autonomy*, 72–9) and claims that the theoretical illiberalism of the *Social Contract* is liberal in its consequences and that the absoluteness of Rousseau's sovereign in fact gives rights a firmer foundation than liberalism can provide. Levine finds Rousseau's real illiberalism at the 'level of customs and opinion' and, unlike Cobban, thinks of this as anything but a subsidiary theme. Cameron, *Social Thought*, sees in Rousseau not only a radical democrat but a 'rank tory' (178), not so much because of the need for an apparatus of moral reform that accompanies the contract but because he does not see in the principles governing the formation of the general will any necessity for 'democratic decision making' (177).

since for him the state in its very essence is necessary, but necessarily illiberal.[41]

It may be, however, that the source of the contradiction lies not in Rousseau or the nature of the relationship between society and the individual but in the terms of the debate. It is a debate between two forms of liberalism. The one takes its stand on the natural right of the abstract individual, whose nature is taken as given within himself; the other, to a certain extent issuing from Rousseau, acknowledges the abstract nature of the individual that the first accepts but grants to society or the state the function of ennobling the very same individual by presenting him with the opportunity or necessity to act morally. The second form thus results in a sort of dualism in which the very *same* individual, still taken abstractly, is possessed of two natures: a lower and a higher, an active and a passive, a particular and a universal, a material and a spiritual, a phenomenal and a noumenal nature.[42]

Receiving its most influential expression in the work of Ernst Cassirer, the neo-Kantian interpretation attempts to recover the unity of Rousseau's work but does so only tenuously. For Cassirer, following Kant, Rousseau is the great critic of utilitarian and hedonist moralities. The state functions primarily to create citizens, while remaining fundamentally unconcerned with their happiness and welfare.[43] These are presumably left to the sphere of private initiative. Yet Cassirer insists that Rousseau's entire work is motivated by the problem of the relation of virtue to happiness.[44] Virtue, expressed in obedience to a universal law derived from the active, spontaneous ethical will, is by no means easily united with happiness, which remains subjective and passive. A life governed by mere feeling would be aimless and shapeless, a meaningless subjection to nature, while the civil life of practical reason is too 'high' an ideal for Rousseau to maintain consistently.[45] The final resolution will be left up to Kant, who had less sensitivity, perhaps, to the problem of human happiness but

---

41 See J. McManners, 'The Social Contract and Rousseau's Revolt against Society.' For a similar view within a more comprehensive treatment, see R. Grimsley, *The Philosophy of Rousseau*, as well as his 'Rousseau and the Problem of Happiness.' Vaughan tried to solve this problem by finding not two Rousseau's but one Rousseau moving from individualism to collectivism; see chap. 1, n 21, above.
42 In some loose sense these two types of liberalism seem to correspond to continental liberalism versus Anglo-American liberalism (at least that not heavily influenced by continental philosophies), or to C.B. Macpherson's 'protective' versus 'developmental' strains in liberal-democracy. See Macpherson, *The Life and Times of Liberal Democracy*.
43 Cassirer, *Question*, 63; see also his *The Philosophy of the Enlightenment*, 258–73.
44 Cassirer, *Question*, 70
45 Ibid., 126–7

for whom the 'dignity of man' remained primary (see below, chapter 2). Robert Derathé, while sharing Cassirer's opinion of Rousseau's opposition to much eighteenth-century thought on ethics and politics and his affinity to Kant concerning the primacy of practical reason, cannot go to the same lengths in affirming the unity of Rousseau's thought along idealist lines. According to Derathé, there remain in Rousseau two moralities, one a morality of instinct, the other a victory of reason over the natural penchants. Society is preferable to nature because it raises man to a superior moral level in forcing him to be virtuous. But virtue remains a practically unrealizable ideal concerning which Rousseau was always sceptical and which he opposed to a *bonté* at once available to all and more reliable.[46] To Derathé, therefore, the neo-Kantian Rousseau is far too much of an 'intellectualist.'[47] But is Rousseau then forced back into the position of a utopian dreamer, a merely negative thinker, as Shklar would have him? Does an idealistic liberalism rescue Rousseau from the charge of totalitarianism only to allow him to sink helplessly into a different dilemma: virtue versus *bonté*, duty versus happiness?

Although the idealist position does not completely surrender to the abstract notion of the individual, it generally limits its understanding of the social formation of genuine individuality by adopting a static opposition of nature and society. In this schema a static nature is opposed to a static society; they are considered only 'in themselves,' or abstractly. What the natural individual, the creature of mere passions (whether perverted or wholesome), gains through freely submitting himself to the law is a moral and rational mode of being, dignity through the pursuit of virtue. Through this acquisition he is raised above 'mere nature,' but perhaps at the cost of sacrificing a part of himself that he cannot do without. What the neo-Kantian interpretation does not adequately address is the historicity and variability of both the individual and society. The relationship between the two can only be fully understood in Rousseau by attending to the history of both, not as separate things but in their internal relations. If Cassirer over-assimilates Rousseau to Kant, it is at the cost of forcing something substantial into an alien mould, as Derathé subtly and skilfully points out; yet if Derathé is right in attempting to recover Rousseau the 'defender of nature,' it is at the cost of once again splitting him in two.

46 Robert Derathé, *Le Rationalisme de Jean-Jacques Rousseau*, esp. 115–23
47 Ibid., esp. appendix, 182–90; for other, more recent critiques of the neo-Kantian Rousseau see G.A. Kelly, 'Rousseau, Kant and History,' who finds an enormous distance between Kant's 'liberal progressivist' view of history and Rousseau's 'fatalism'; see also N. Keohane, '"The Masterpiece of Policy in Our Century": Rousseau on the Morality of the Enlightenment.'

Of all the schools of interpretation it is the conservative that stresses most the importance of history to Rousseau. This was not at first the case. Burke's well-known critique of Rousseau as ideological source of the French Revolution tended to oppose a Rousseauan rationalism to a conservative respect for history, prescription, and organic development.[48] Bonald and de Maistre centred their critiques in the position that law cannot be based on human will alone but must issue from a higher source.[49] More recently, Leo Strauss has formulated a very influential version of Rousseau in which history stands at the centre of his thought. Rousseau becomes the first modern critic of 'modernity,' the vehicle of the upstart passions, which now acquire the temerity to judge reason's errors. Unreconciled to modern bourgeois society, Rousseau launches a critique at first based upon a retreat to the classical idea of virtue. But this is merely a way-station in a regression to nature, from which point of view Rousseau deems himself able to reject both the philosophy of the ancient polis and bourgeois society. In retreating to nature, however, Rousseau has not really transcended what for Strauss is modernity, since he will begin from the same premises as Descartes and Hobbes. Rousseau's work demonstrates the incompatibility of 'modern theoretical science' and the 'good society.' Accepting Hobbes' premise that natural law must have its roots in principles anterior to reason – that is, in the common animal passions – Rousseau nevertheless deviates from Hobbes in introducing a 'natural history of the passions.' In this way he arrives at the notion that there is no human nature in the exact sense (presumably in neither the exact teleological or the mechanistic senses). This discovery forces the abandonment of the modern theory of natural right. Because for Rousseau the historical process of humanization begins with 'accidental causation,' Strauss sees Rousseau's twist on 'modern theoretical science' as a kind of initiation of historical materialism. Struggling under the yoke of a blind necessity, the crude and stupid savage is gradually humanized, acquiring at the penultimate moment, Rousseau's historical moment, sufficient rationality to assume command over a history that up to that point had been governed by laws identical with the laws of mechanical causation.

Surprisingly, however, at least for us if not for Strauss, Rousseau balks at this precise juncture. Not content with following the road of a historical materialism into the era of emergent nihilism, Rousseau searches for some transhistorical standard of public right without which the approaching era of *human* history will remain meaningless. According to Strauss,

48 Edmund Burke, *Reflections on the Revolution in France*, 279-84, 181-4
49 Cobban, *Modern State*, 24

Introduction / 19

Rousseau once again finds himself faced with a choice between the teleology of the Platonic tradition and the mechanism of Hobbes and his followers. Once again Rousseau chooses Hobbes. Rousseau's standard of public right, the general will, is desire subject only to the test of generalization. And for Strauss this is far too much a merely formal test of rationality. This conception of right is one that follows directly from Rousseau's fundamental error, the determination of the human essence as freedom rather than reason. The great opportunity for a return to classical philosophy is missed and the rest is a rather disappointing dénouement. Outside of the central concept of the general will, Rousseau's theory of civil society is an attempt to clarify its problems rather than to offer a practicable solution. Despairing of a real solution to the problems of civil society, Rousseau retreats to the 'noblest' concerns of the bourgeois, the family and romantic love, and beyond this to the solitary bohemian artist. He ends up as a bourgeois with a bad conscience.[50]

This vision of Rousseau has been amended slightly by one of Strauss's students.[51] Allan Bloom has found in Rousseau's

50 Leo Strauss, *Natural Right*, 252-93
51 The last two decades have, in fact, seen a steady and growing stream of writing on Rousseau by those who rely heavily on Strauss. See Masters, *Political Philosophy*, and also his 'The Structure of Rousseau's Political Thought,' 'Jean-Jacques Is Alive and Well: Rousseau and Contemporary Sociobiology,' and 'Nothing Fails like Success: Development and History in Rousseau's Political Teaching.' See also A.M. Melzer, 'Rousseau and the Problem of Bourgeois Society'; H. Gilden, *Rousseau's Social Contract: The Design of the Argument*; and Bloom, 'Education'; for the most part they add little of substantial originality to what was already contained in Strauss's terse and stimulating chapter in *Natural Right and History*. Plattner, eg, states that he has 'not heavily relied on the work of modern commentators on Rousseau, with one important exception: the chapter on Rousseau in Leo Strauss's *Natural Right and History*' (x). Masters's indebtedness is plain throughout his book but is revealed most openly in the concluding chapter (esp. 418-25). Goldschmidt, although he produced his massive study of the first and second *Discourses* before having read Masters, but not Strauss, states that the former's book lent 'une confirmation précieuse et imprévue à mon travail, et j'ai tenu à m'y referer (quoi qu'il en soit des divergences de detail) aussi souvent qu'il m'était possible' (131). The major divergences that appear seem to centre around the degree to which Rousseau might have been aware of his failure to follow through his critique of the theory of modern natural right and the degree to which he therefore belongs to the philosophic few. Plattner, eg, concentrating on the second *Discourse*, finds in Rousseau an attack not merely on the theory of modern natural right, exemplified in Hobbes, but also a seemingly thoroughgoing rejection of the classical past. For Masters and Goldschmidt, however, Rousseau's thought is throughout informed by the tension between a non-teleological concept of nature and the desideratum, at least, of a teleological concept of human nature. The latter, they believe, is the only adequate ground of a political philosophy capable of distinguishing between virtue and the common animal passions.

Emile[52] a stronger foundation for a specifically Rousseauan solution to the problems of civil society. Bloom finds in *Emile* both a psychology and a myth meant to rival Plato's. The myth is a bourgeois substitute for the 'great human type' supplied by the traditions of classical antiquity and Judeo-Christian religion. The psychology is a version of Platonic sublimation ending not in an ascent from the cave to the realm of ideas but in an ascent from sexual desire and egoism to love and compassion. These are meant to temper the conflicts inherent in civil society and serve as a bridge between the particular will and the general will. Rousseau completes Machiavelli's project of abandoning the old morality through a two-fold cunning of the imagination. The poetic construct of the natural man ironically leads to very realistic techniques of manipulating the imagination, which, through its ability to represent and substitute for instinct, achieves the partial self-transcendence of bourgeois egoism.[53] There are dark hints at a higher teaching lurking behind this recommendation to make the best of democracy, presumably reserving the eternal life of ideas for the philosophic few, as opposed to the ideals of self-satisfaction that Rousseau legitimates and moderates for the many.

If the conservative reading surpasses the other treatments mentioned, it is in its sensitivity to the importance of history to Rousseau and in its understanding that in grappling with the problems of civil society, Rousseau stood outside of that society more than is often presumed. Yet the historical vision attributed to him is framed in the terse opposites of a latter-day Platonism. Reason and history stand apart and irreconcilable. There is no resolution possible within history, only an accommodation or compromise that, in Rousseau's case even more than in the case of Machiavelli, Hobbes, or Locke, points to the real and forgotten solution: 'the necessity of returning to [the] classics themselves ... our predicament requires, as for Rousseau, a confrontation of the scientific optimism of modern opinion with the political pessimism of ancient philosophy.'[54]

Regrettably, although they often see in Rousseau an interesting precursor, most Marxists, curiously at home with the liberals in this, abstract the 'contractarian' Rousseau of the *Social Contract* for serious consideration. The rest of Rousseau, if not ignored, is often assigned to the historical waste-bin of pre-Romanticism or made to fit with an

---

52 Bloom at first follows Strauss much more closely (in 'Jean-Jacques Rousseau,' 514-35), but in 'Education' he seems to diverge somewhat, at least with respect to Rousseau's doctrine of civil society.
53 Bloom, 'Education'; see esp. 148.
54 Masters, *Political Philosophy*, 443

interpretation of the history of social thought that can grant only to Marx the role of seeing through bourgeois society. This is done not simply on the grounds of Marx's genius. Rather, the development of capitalist relations of production is considered, up to his historical moment, to have not yet sufficiently matured to allow such an achievement. Historical materialism must ground itself, as much as its analysis of any other form of knowledge, in history. But when this injunction is taken in a narrow sense, it sometimes produces more of a gap between Marx and all that precedes him than might be warranted.

Marx himself, although he owes a great deal to Rousseau, at least according to the eminent Marxist scholar Lucio Colletti,[55] never seems to acknowledge that debt.[56] Engels, in *Anti-Dühring*, sees in the second *Discourse* a call to revolution and in the *Social Contract* an attempt to transcend civil society in a higher synthesis of society and the individual.[57] Lukács, sensitive to the real protest in romanticism, saw in Rousseau's concept of nature a radical departure from the bourgeois concept of nature. Nature in bourgeois philosophy had been identified with the formal system of laws governing phenomena and opposed to the artifice and arbitrariness of a declining feudal absolutism. Rousseau's appeal to nature sounded like an appeal (albeit in alienated form) on behalf of a human essence submerged by capitalism and reification.[58] Yet for Lukács, Rousseau's concept of nature appeared as an ahistorical abstraction, in opposition to the 'artificial structures of *human* civilization' (emphasis added). It would have been impossible for him, given the state of knowledge at the time (and therefore also the economic conditions or the degree of the 'socialization of society'), to see the two concepts of nature in their social unity, 'namely capitalist society with its dissolution of every natural bond.'[59] Curiously, this is what Strauss indicates Rousseau did manage to see, if not in 'capitalist' society then at least in bourgeois society.[60]

Taking the *Social Contract* as something of Rousseau's summa sociologica, others have gone on to stress his limitations in economic matters.

55 Lucio Colletti, introduction to Karl Marx, *Early Writings*, 41, 46
56 At one point, in *On the Jewish Question*, Marx does praise Rousseau's description of the abstraction of the political man (in *Early Writings*, 234).
57 For a critical discussion of Engels's reading of Rousseau, see Starobinski, *Transparence*, 33-4.
58 Georg Lukács, *History and Class Consciousness*, 136
59 Ibid., 237
60 This also happens to be very similar to what Althusser, *Politics and History*, esp. 118-22, and Levine, *Autonomy*, following him, do see, at least in the state of nature as it is described in the *Social Contract*.

C.B. Macpherson places Rousseau squarely in the ranks of petit-bourgeois democrats, as vehemently opposed to the right of unlimited accumulation of private property in productive resources as he was insistent on a society of working proprietors associated through a market system.[61] Yet this interpretation, in addition to stopping with the Rousseau of the *Social Contract*, overlooks indications that Rousseau conceived of going beyond private property in both the *Social Contract* and *Emile*. Louis Althusser, even more insistent on classifying Rousseau as a petit-bourgeois, has presented a subtle analysis of the dynamic structure of tensions in the *Social Contract*. Rousseau's sleight of hand in constructing a contract with only one 'recipient party' Althusser exposes as an ideological veil behind which the real, fundamental, determining, and continuous struggle among social groups is concealed. Rousseau's inability even to conceive of socialized production forces him into a constant 'flight forward in ideology' – the construction of the whole apparatus of moral reform, which will, Rousseau hopes, cancel out the competition of interests in the individual conscience as the source of legislation – and into a 'regression in the economy,' that is, a continual reform of property holdings in favour of independent petty producers. Flight and regression presuppose each other if they are to be successful, but of course they cannot be. For Althusser, therefore, Rousseau is forced in reality to offer a legitimation of the false contract of the second *Discourse*, a contract in which the 'rich' take the initiative, only this time with a far more adequate ideological justification ready to hand.[62]

61 Macpherson, *Life and Times*, 16-17; Macpherson places Rousseau in the class of 'one-class democrats,' notably along with Jefferson. For a revisionist view of Jefferson, on largely Macphersonian grounds, as an anti-market theorist, see R.J. Matthews, *The Radical Politics of Thomas Jefferson*. A similar understanding of Rousseau is presented at greater length by I. Fetscher, *Rousseau's Politische Philosohipie*. Others have seen in the *Social Contract* the possibility, at least, of an appeal for a 'classless' society; see Levine, *Autonomy*, 188-90; Lemos, *Political Philosophy*, 178.
62 Althusser, *Politics and History*, 111-60; Levine, *Autonomy*, although he subtitles his book 'A Kantian Reading of Rousseau,' is as much an Althusserian in this work as a Kantian. It nicely fills out the argument adumbrated by Althusser and, in the process, exposes some of the weaknesses of the latter's reading. Rousseau, according to Levine, must, as a part of the effort at moral reform, 'suppress' all particular associations. But Rousseau states that they must either be suppressed or that one should leave 'as many as possible and prevent them from being unequal' (*sc* 23, II, III). For Levine this suppression takes place because Rousseau can only conceive of particular wills as the wills of individuals, not 'group wills' (103ff, 188) – this, even though he recognizes that Rousseau does not ontologize the individual will but conceives of it as 'explicitly ... a historical product, a consequence of antagonistic social relations ... the product of self-love in civil society' (102). Rousseau has a 'political ontology' that is fundamentally

Occupying a very different position in the debate among Marxist scholars is Lucio Colletti, who, while admitting the backwardness of Rousseau's economic ideas, attributes to that very deficiency his acuity as a critic of bourgeois society.[63] Rousseau could not accept the emerging liberal view of social relations as inherently competitive exchange relations; the 'invisible hand' and the 'harmony of competing interests' were for him chimeras, but also dangerous ones, mystifying the inequality and oppression inherent in civil society. From this follows Rousseau's rejection of the liberal–natural-law view of the state as a means for the preservation of a truncated version of the merely negative freedom of an insubstantial state of nature. For Rousseau freedom is no longer freedom from society but in and through society. This understanding of freedom Rousseau carries into the *Social Contract* in the doctrine of popular sovereignty. Relying on von Gierke's useful distinction, Colletti sees in the resolution of the pact of subjection into the pact of society, together with Rousseau's critique of parliamentary representation, a resumption of belief in popular power that amounts to the suppression of the theoretical split between civil society and the state, between bourgeois and citizen, and foreshadows Marx's notion of the withering away of the state. For Colletti this reading of Rousseau is premised on the increasing recognition of the 'supremacy' of politics in his writings, over against the image of Rousseau as expressing a romantic sensibility or the interiority of the moral subject. Yet Colletti tends to see the liberation of the individual one-sidedly, in terms of the 'liberation of society,' forgetting that for Rousseau as for at least the early Marx this depends in turn on the development of 'radical needs' in the individual.[64] This reading of Rousseau also opts for a rejection of the view that his idea of history is a translation into secular terms of the Christian ideal of the Fall, that history is degradation and, like sin, a falling away from an original condition of perfection. But Colletti does not follow up on this insight.

Perhaps Rousseau's most advanced position in Colletti's eyes is his

---

individualist, according to Levine; social groups are less 'real' and less important. Yet following Althusser, he understands Rousseau, even in the *Social Contract*, as historicizing and sociologizing Hobbes's state of nature (22). This points very strongly at what Carol Gould has called a 'social ontology.' Another Marxian reading that sees the route from Rousseau to Marx leading through a Kantian essentialism is G. della Volpe, *Rousseau and Marx*.

63 Lucio Colletti, *From Rousseau to Lenin: Studies in Ideology and Society*, 144–93
64 See, eg, Agnes Heller, *The Theory of Need in Marx*; Herbert Marcuse, 'The Foundation of Historical Materialism' in *Studies*, 1–48.

critique of Christianity. Relying on Karl Löwith,[65] Colletti sees in Rousseau's attack on Christianity for the sake of a civil religion the beginnings of a critique of ideology. For Löwith, Rousseau's work is the first clear statement of the 'human problem of bourgeois society' – that is, that in it man is not whole but a citizen over against a private individual. Like the rest of the philosophes Rousseau attacks the Church as 'another society,' but he adds the idea that as an abstract and unreal society it is only the negative communal image of the atomized society of private egoism, and as such reflects the internal contradiction that divides the bourgeois individual into private, egoistic agent and citizen. Rousseau's call for a civil religion would then be a demand for the suppression of this real division, and with it the illusion of an unreal heavenly community. Such an understanding of Rousseau as expressing critically but not necessarily fully thematizing the contradictions of bourgeois society opens up a most promising avenue for reinterpreting not only the *Social Contract* but its place in Rousseau's work as a whole.[66]

Most recent emphasis upon the subjective sources of Rousseau's theoretical work has come from existentialist writers or those heavily influenced by them. Pierre Burgelin, stressing above all the influence upon Rousseau of Plato and Christian Platonizers, has interpreted his work *in toto* as formulating a philosophy of existence in terms of a dialectical ascent from an immediate experience of incoherence, via the mediation of love, the family, and the city, to an intuition of an order in the world issuing from the will of a benevolent deity. According to Burgelin, Rousseau considers existence not necessarily an unhappy condition of being thrown into a world without meaning or objective value, but the route to the knowledge of God. This knowledge becomes in turn the foundation of a harmonious order in society and the individual. Rousseau's existentialism is, Burgelin argues, unique in stressing the importance to society of this fundamentally individual and religious quest.[67] Burgelin's Rousseau, in a curious inversion of Kant before the fact, makes the existence of God into the condition of morality, where Kant made the existence of morality into evidence for the existence of God.

Much more influential than Burgelin's lengthy attempt at a total and

65 Karl Löwith, *From Hegel to Nietzsche*, 232-7
66 For a similar view, only in existentialist terms, of Rousseau's self-consciousness as 'la contradiction connaissante,' see B. Muntéano, 'Les "Contradictions" de Jean-Jacques Rousseau,' 111; a more recent view of Rousseau's work that develops partly in this direction is L. Layton, 'Rousseau's Political and Cultural Revolution.'
67 Burgelin, *Existence*; see also 'Kant lecteur de Rousseau.'

comprehensive reading of Rousseau has been Jean Starobinski's Freudian existentialist version of Rousseauan romanticism.[68] In Starobinski's brilliant treatment all of Rousseau's writings may be seen as issuing from his particular psychological dilemma. Presenting Jean-Jacques as a case of development arrested at some stage of narcissistic object-relations, Starobinski unravels the secret of Rousseau's theoretical development and its contradictions on the basis of his overwhelming sense of guilt and need for self-justification. Rousseau's claim to innocence is not, however, a simple personal claim; in order to prove it he must first undermine the concept of original sin. The origin of evil and the source of guilt and unhappiness Rousseau assigns to 'mediation' taken in its widest sense – as speech, as instrumental action in the world, as reflection and reasoning, as history. Innocence, man's original and natural state, is identical with the absence of all mediation. Therefore, what Rousseau desires above all is the recovery, at least in fantasy if not in reality, of immediate communion among pure souls. Rousseau's vision is profoundly anti-political because it does not recognize the real world of human existence as being necessarily a realm of intersubjectivity. Rousseau therefore becomes the author of public utopias and private apologies. The *Social Contract* is, for example, a utopia of virtue in which all the members are transparent to each other, where there is nothing more pernicious than the immersion of an individual in his particular will. All of Rousseau's oscillations between man and citizen concern only the place where transparency, immediacy, spontaneity, and recovery of innocence are to be sought. If it should turn out that innocence and political society are incompatible, then he will seek it in the sociability of 'beautiful souls,' in a golden age of the extended family, which *La Nouvelle Héloïse* supposedly represents. And with the collapse of this daydream Rousseau will retreat even further into himself, as in the *Rêveries du Promeneur Solitaire*, where complete isolation is the necessary condition of a static, mystical, and timeless state of unity.

Starobinski's Rousseau is the epitome of inauthenticity. Driven by the unconscious compulsion to shun all efforts to transform the world instrumentally in either speech or action, Rousseau insists upon magically overcoming all obstacles in the path of transparent relations. Moving from existentialist to Hegelian terms, Starobinski takes Rousseau to represent subjectivity that refuses to alienate itself in exterior activity.[69]

---

68 Starobinski, *Transparence*; see also 'The Accuser and the Accused,' and esp. 'Jean-Jacques Rousseau et les pouvoirs de l'imaginaire.'
69 Starobinski, *Transparence*, esp. 222-3 n 1

Yet Starobinski maintains that in the case of this extraordinary man, pathological regression did lead to progress in thought. He is not wrong to call upon Freud for an 'explanation' of Rousseau, but this Freud seems to be inextricably enmeshed in a dichotomy of authenticity and immediacy. For Starobinski, it seems, there can be no lessening of guilt and no overcoming of alienation. The timeless existential choice is that of living in bad faith or else of taking upon oneself the guilt inevitably accruing to a being who always acts in freedom – that is, of living authentically.[70] His analysis of Rousseau, far from entertaining aims of clinical neutrality, therefore tends towards a moralizing condemnation. In spite of claiming to see in Rousseau progress in thought that follows from the regression, Starobinski fails to see in Rousseau any suggestion of the historical return of the repressed and, especially by de-emphasizing *Emile*, ignores Rousseau's idea of a regression in the service of the ego not aimed at an illusory aesthetic redemption but at the radical transformation of civilization.

As though in response to Starobinski, Marshall Berman has attempted a reading of Rousseau as a radical individualist struggling with the problem of authenticity.[71] For this Rousseau the personal is the political and the search for authenticity is a potentially liberating political force of the first order. Before the rise of a modern market society, selfhood and authenticity are apparently not at issue. For men in traditional society, identified narrowly with a unified and coherent set of roles, the question never arises. It emerges as an increasingly pressing problem, according to Berman, only from the matrix of bourgeois society, which replaces ascribed with achieved identity. Achieved identity, however, always turns out in bourgeois society to be relative to the place that one is assigned by others, in a manner analogous to the determination of value in a free market. A self thus wholly mediated by others is not a self, and bourgeois society feeds on the continual crisis of inauthenticity. Rousseau's response to this was to explore, in *Emile*, the possibilities for an 'authentic morality' and, in the *Social Contract*, for an 'authentic politics.' Yet these do not appear to be authentic solutions. Also, and ironically, the very

70 Marcuse's critique of this brand of existentialism can be found in 'Sartre's Existentialism,' *Studies*, 157–90.
71 Marshall Berman, *The Politics of Authenticity*. Berman's concept of authenticity is both more vague and 'essentialist' than Starobinski's; thus, they do not lend themselves very well to direct comparison. Yet both treatments share a striking similarity in making authenticity, rather than, say, freedom, happiness, or virtue, Rousseau's central problem. This problem is much closer to consciousness in Berman's Rousseau than it is in Starobinski's.

pressures of the search for authenticity create the anxious urge to flee from freedom and give rise in Rousseau to the 'perverse' project of a politics of inauthenticity, a denial of selfhood in submission to a totalitarian authority (as, for example, in *La Nouvelle Héloïse*). Self-surrender is not, however, Rousseau's final world. Rather than having Rousseau offer one, Berman chooses to ascribe to Rousseau the creation of a new language, one that has provided an agenda for all the radical movements of the past two centuries. Berman's analysis ultimately fails not because he wishes to link the psychological and the political or because he begins to sociologize and historicize the problem of individuality. In themselves these are quite salutary advances over Starobinski's approach. It fails in the end because for Berman 'selfhood' and 'psychological conditioning' are radically distinct and contradictory. Transferring this notion to Rousseau, and here Berman is in good company, he claims that Rousseau believed that men were born with a 'unity of self' that 'radical education' could preserve. Authentic politics would then be the creation of natural individuals; the task of radical critics would only be to point to what is already there, 'every man's sense of his own unique, irreducible self.' What lies between liberation and authenticity is a simple matter of bringing to consciousness what is easily available for all to see.[72]

One of the most persistent themes in the literature on Rousseau is thus the need to account for his 'failure' to face squarely the fundamental problems of modern civilization. Cassirer traces this failure to a reluctance to valorize categorically the dignity of the autonomous moral agent over the happiness that belongs to the simple, unconscious, and passive life of the senses. Strauss must account Rousseau a failure in that, after demonstrating the insufficiency of the modern theory of natural right in its own terms, he retreats not to the strategic stronghold even of ancient practice, let alone classical philosophy, but remains imprisoned in the foundations of the theory of modern natural right – 'nature' in the sense of the common animal passions. Marxist treatments tend to see Rousseau not, like Strauss, as having descended too far into history to be able to extricate himself but, in failing to comprehend both the liberating potential of capitalist economic development and the inadequacy of a

---

72 Berman sees in urban life a training in penetrating one's own and others' inauthenticity that Rousseau did not. Modern urbanity teaches us to separate role and self and thus to acknowledge the reality of self in ourselves and others. I would tend to agree with C. Wright Mills on this question, who sees in the transferability of roles that urban anonymity encourages more of an opportunity to achieve a profound psychological ignorance concerning others and ourselves.

moralistic and methodologically individualistic approach to politics, as not having descended far enough. Starobinski's work has the great merit of tracing these and other related failures to a fundamental refusal on Rousseau's part to accept what he himself recognized to be an inextricable part of the human condition. Rousseau's inauthenticity is not a transcendence of but a flight from time and history.

The importance of the history of society to the structure of Rousseau's thought has been suggested by many,[73] but by none so appositely as Lionel Gossman. According to him, Rousseau is 'the prophet of history far more than he is the prophet of the Romantic escape from it. His

---

73 See the discussion of Strauss, above, 18-20; Masters, *Political Philosophy*, goes so far as to assert that 'the development of what has come to be called a "philosophy of history" by Kant, Hegel and Marx merely elaborates what is suggested by Rousseau's criticism of previous philosophy ... Rousseau's own conception of the historical causes of social life led him to emphasize the creative role of human reason; man's capacity to form ideas is a capacity to change the universe in which he lives. Social man has a "second nature," for the creation of property law and the mechanical arts results in the creation of a new nature (or rather, the creation of ideas and things which have their own nature)' (202-3). Colletti, *From Rousseau to Lenin*, recognizes the importance of the 'philosophy of history' that stands behind the second *Discourse* but sees as unsatisfactory the widespread view of Rousseau as a rationalist echoing the Christian ideas of the Fall and redemption, a view exemplified by Starobinski, *Transparence*, and also his introduction to *Jean-Jacques Rousseau: Oeuvres completes*, ed. B. Gagnebin and M. Raymond, vol. 3 (Paris: Gallimard 1964), xlii-lxx. Cameron, *Social Thought*, recognizes that the second *Discourse* clearly implies that man's 'humanity' is a product of society and social relations (58, 82, 92) but like Cassirer seems to think that this humanity amounts largely to moral perfection (67-8). A similar view of human individuality as largely the production of social construction, only from an anarchist point of view, is offered by Stephen Ellenburg, *Rousseau's Political Philosophy: An Interpretation from Within*, esp. 51-82. Cameron holds that Rousseau, though, even more strongly than Burke, 'grasped the notion that the historical process shapes and forms human beings and produces a second nature fully as important and "natural" as the first' (83). He sees, however, along with E.H. Wright, *The Meaning of Rousseau*, no particularly profound or difficult problem in bringing the first and second natures into harmony: 'There is a condition which is appropriate to man at each point in the history of the species, but it is up to man to choose whether or not he will accept it or strive to achieve it' (92-3). Both Cameron (92) and Lionel Gossman, 'Time and History in Rousseau,' 316, insist that Rousseau's historicization of human nature goes far beyond asserting its 'plasticity'; and in this they are far closer to the crux of the issue than Cassirer, *Question*, esp. 60, or Lemos, *Political Philosophy*, 6. The latter, for example, holds that the plasticity of human nature gives way, in society, to the constancy of human nature as a permanent, trans-historical struggle between 'self-love' and 'moral freedom' (183). Most of these interpretations treat Rousseau's view of history as a basis for his moralism, rather than seeing his understanding of the historicity of human nature as throwing into question moralism itself. The exception to this is Gossman, 'Time and History'; see n 79, below.

problem is not that of man and time ... it is the problem of the prophet of history who despaired of history.'[74] Fundamental to Rousseau's thought is his acute awareness of history as 'the mode of being of all things.'[75] This awareness is visible not only in his anthropology – notable above all as an early example of and stimulus to 'an evolutionary concept of human history'[76] – but even in his theory of music and especially in his autobiography.

The *Confessions* should be understood as the application of the 'historical method' to individual personality. Unlike Montaigne, who paints a static portrait of himself, Rousseau follows a 'melodic model' in order to allow the reader to grasp his individuality 'in its historicity'[77]: 'the very act of self-narration [is itself] part of that living and changing being that is to be understood.'[78] Rousseau's understanding of the historicity and contradictory dynamism of human personality leads to an abandonment of moralism. His idea of personality 'implies that there are contradictions in men that defy the old categories of virtue and vice as we are accustomed to apply them to fixed, stable and independent things.'[79]

Accompanying the profound awareness of history is a deep pessimism concerning it. Any real overcoming of the predicament that Rousseau diagnosed in modern European civilization[80] must take place within history, not as flight to a transcendent reality, whether religious or philosophical.[81] The devolution of society to 'happier times' is impossible. Yet the future is blocked. As a critic of both the liberal philosophes and

74 Gossman, 'Time and History,' 348-9
75 Ibid., 312
76 Ibid., 328
77 Ibid., 315
78 Ibid., 317
79 Ibid., 318. Gossman adds, in a way that parallels the notion of Rousseau working with imported concepts, that this results in a conflict in his work between the 'universal categories of his time' upon which he had to rely and his vision of a historical universe to which 'a-historical categories of moral judgement are inappropriate.' Yet Gossman seems to succumb to the same sort of moralism in a later article, 'The Innocent Art of Confession and Reverie,' esp. 73.
80 This Gossman summarizes as the alienation of the individual, the atomization of society, the division of labour, and the commercial exploitation of man and nature ('Time and History,' 338).
81 He is quite right, I believe, in pointing out that Rousseau's quest for a totality in which to seek submersion is restricted to 'nature' and is therefore an 'immanent one' (346). But it is unclear whether or not it was Rousseau who recognized that nature 'can never be more than the form of totality, since she stands above and beyond history, ignoring rather than resolving historical contradiction' (347).

the traditionalist upholders of feudal privilege, Rousseau could not have had in his time any practical program to oppose to both groups. The 'existential' quality Gossman detects in his work, both autobiographical and theoretical, is thus also a function of history. As a result Rousseau's pessimism often is transformed into despair and the idea of development becomes an impasse. The unhappiness and alienation that Rousseau observed and experienced Gossman comes to understand as the 'inevitable consequence of a historical dialectic.'[82] All that is left in these moments is flight from time: 'Time appears as the absolute enemy ... emotion, passion, love, those very things in which Rousseau discerned man's glory – appear as that which has to be transcended.'[83]

That in this impasse Rousseau contrives to remain more the prophet of history than the prophet of romantic escape is puzzling. Yet by historicizing Rousseau's pessimism Gossman has taken one essential step beyond Starobinski. Rousseau is no longer a failure or a success, nor are we warranted in judging him 'inauthentic,' because authenticity is an ahistorical category that begs the question of its own validity. As a result Gossman is able to discern the central ambiguity and the central problem in Rousseau's work with considerably greater clarity than Starobinski's latent moralism allows. For Starobinski, Rousseau lives out an impossible absolute rejection of mediation as such. Starobinski has fully grasped in all its implicit seriousness the meaning of Voltaire's anxious barb that Rousseau wishes us to return to the forest and walk upon all fours. Gossman, although he discerns this tendency in Rousseau, recognizes that the 'rejection' of mediation is not necessarily fundamental, that first of all Rousseau rejects the 'prevailing forms of mediation.'[84] This implies in turn that the absence of a practical program, especially for a thoroughly historical thinker, does not mean final despair over the possibility of a practical and historical transcendence. That alienation is the 'inevitable consequence of an historical dialectic' does not mean, even for Rousseau, that it is the final consequence of history. Rousseau's 'flights' to nature are then, for Gossman, psychological solutions that Rousseau knows are for him alone, not answers to the problems of the second *Discourse*.

Gossman's analysis of Rousseau's ambiguity suggests the possibility of a reconsideration of the relationship between nature and history in Rousseau's theoretical works. That relationship might possibly provide

82 Ibid., 343
83 Ibid., 344
84 Ibid., 341

some of the necessary if not the sufficient grounds for a theoretical advance beyond Rousseau's practical impasse. For Rousseau not only possessed an understanding of human personality as historical, as evidenced in the *Confessions*, but began to develop a historical theory of human nature. It is difficult to accept that his appeal to nature was purely an individual solution to the historical impasse. In beginning with the second *Discourse* – according to Strauss, Rousseau's most philosophical work – and moving to a reading of *Emile* as an equally serious philosophical work, we may be able to discern the crucial role that Rousseau assigns to nature as the condition for *undoing* the historical impasse rather than escaping it.

Rousseau's most important shift away from the Enlightenment and the theory of natural law lies in his transformation of the concept of human nature. In abandoning the abstract opposition between nature and artifice, he undertook the elaboration of a historical and dialectical theory of human nature. As a biological species, humanity is the product of a process of evolution. The evolution of the human species is inseparable from the inauguration of its history, and humanity's biological evolution is a result of its own historical activity. Rousseau's thought is, in a sense, so thoroughly imbued with an awareness of history that history predates the human species properly so called. Humanity as a biological species gradually constitutes itself, its nature, in a social-labour process. And the forms of social labour, the specific sets of relationships in which social labour is undertaken, continue to affect deeply the directions in which a social human nature develops.

Humanity is for Rousseau inconceivable apart from society and labour. Labour itself, however, is not simply a neutral instrument, abstracted from and then added on to human desire. It is more than a mere substitute for instinctually governed behaviour in securing the objects of human desire. It is not the general term under which a human 'essence' is conceived, yet it is treated as negativity, as separation from and, initially, as opposition to that which is simply given. This distinguishes human beings from all other forms of being and bestows upon them the necessity of continuous collective self constitution. In beginning to produce the means of his subsistence the natural man creates culture, transforms external nature, and begins to transform his own internal nature too. In making a social humanity the product as well as the agent of its own history and in making labour in this sense the primordial form of historical activity, Rousseau must abandon the notion of the abstractly autonomous individual that informs and suffuses previous and subsequent liberalism. This is what makes possible both a distorted reading that makes him seem so illiberal as to be totalitarian and an alternative reading that makes him the first exponent, although not historically the founder, of a critical and materialist humanism.

Although Rousseau ceases to oppose nature to artifice in an essential way, he never thoroughly conflates the two. Nature remains a limit upon which artifice intrudes only at the peril of the species. The freedom and happiness of the state of nature also in some way contrive to remain standards – but standards that are immanent in the process of living matter itself. The theory of political life for Rousseau must be grounded not only in an awareness of the historical evolution of society but also in a theory of the historical development of human nature. The central, crucial dimension of being human is not simply temporality but a wider historicity that encompasses the social. The historicity of human nature entails a further transformation of our understanding of human biology, psychology, and society, all of which are intimately interrelated.

Rousseau's rejection of the theory of natural right meant not a return to the ancients but an entrée to history. In discovering the historicity of human nature, however, Rousseau found not only a vantage point from which to envision the transcendence of classical liberalism but also a whole network of further problems and dilemmas. History itself seemed to involve an increasingly difficult, painful, and contradictory set of demands upon human nature as biological desire. A historical existence is one in which the spontaneity and immediacy of the instinctual impulses of the savage man give way increasingly to the fetters, constraints, and compulsions of the artifice governing not only modern European culture but culture itself. At the same time, history apparently involves increasing alienation of man from his labour, from community, and from himself. Not only is history such a calamitous spectacle, but the two processes are linked in a self-supporting and expanding vicious circle. The repression of nature – as the animal 'sentiment of existence' and *pitié* – supports the social processes in which alienation takes place, while alienation enforces and requires repression to be carried out inside the individual. Philosophy conspires in this either by making repression invisible or by making it appear salutary to man's 'higher ends.'

Yet Rousseau never does recommend a return to nature, for the problem is even more complicated. Whatever pathological regression he himself suffered is not generalized into a prescription for the species. For Rousseau the necessity of repression follows directly, if not immediately, from human historicity. Repression in some mode or measure he regarded as being necessary for humanization and individuation. He could not advocate a real return to nature without advocating the destruction of the species. But neither could he rest content with a simple reliance on reason to deliver mankind from its self-imposed calamities. Reason had too much of a share in them already. Reason would not suffice since, among other things, it was no longer embedded in history as providence or as the latter's sister, progress. Nor was man any longer to be conceived as the *rational* animal. Reason and passion were no longer distinct substances vying for the will of man. There is implicit in Rousseau's writings an attack on the narcissistic Western evaluation of the self as a potentially transcendent rational ego, as radical in its implications as that which was to issue from Darwin and Freud. Rousseau could not look to reason for deliverance since, to the extent that reason was in its nature instrumental, he deemed its consequences to deny human nature in so far as this entailed fredom from the compulsion to perform and produce. Yet the consequences of the older view of a cosmic reason, the reason that identifies duty and happiness, morality and fulfilment, seemed to deny human nature in so far as this was unself-conscious play and display, eros, desire, pleasure, happiness. How Rousseau came to pose and solve these problems, to the extent that he did solve them, is the main theme of this essay.

The first half of the book, dealing largely with the *Discourse on the Origins of Inequality*, lays the theoretical foundations upon which the political and psychological speculations of the second half are developed. The remaining chapters, which explore three key texts serially, *La Nouvelle Héloïse*, the *Social Contract*, and *Emile*, are based upon that understanding of how Rousseau's historical anthropology generates his critique of human civilization. Yet the latter works are not simply superstructural. They not only depend upon the historical anthropology but elaborate, amplify, and extend it and, especially in the case of *Emile*, aim at a resolution of the deepest problems Rousseau discerned within the structure of human historicity.

Chapter 2 is concerned with setting the stage for Rousseau's break with the Enlightenment's concept of nature. A brief sketch of certain aspects of the historical development of that concept and closely related notions in the half-century or so immediately preceding the second *Discourse* is followed by a discussion of the traditional interpretation of Rousseau's amendment of that idea, as represented in the work of Ernst Cassirer.

Chapter 3 is devoted to elucidating Rousseau's philosophical anthropology, his view of the human essence as constituted within the history of social labour. Rousseau presents this notion only within a theory of human evolution, which is itself embedded in the rhetoric of social-contract theory. Before Rousseau's positive efforts in this regard can be directly approached, therefore, it is necessary to examine two problems that have historically hindered the understanding of the content and function of Rousseau's thought as an evolutionist: the first is the persistent image of his biological thought as non-transformist, while the second is the related assumption that, in reaction to eighteenth-century materialism, he reverted philosophically to a Cartesian spiritualism modified by Locke. This discussion prepares the way for a different understanding of his ideas concerning the relations between biology and history and also serves as a foundation for much of his psychology.

Chapters 4 and 5 address themselves to reconstructing Rousseau's implicit dialectic of the social formations of human nature. Chapter 4 is devoted to pre-bourgeois social forms, to primitive society and the polis, the two social forms most important to Rousseau in offering a critical perspective on modern civilization. Chapter 5 presents Rousseau's critique of bourgeois society and its political theory, and concludes with a discussion of the general pattern of human history as one in which the increasing freedom of the abstract and instrumentally rational individual is seen to amount to increasing alienation and repression.

Chapter 6 analyses Rousseau's views on conscience, the supposed *deus ex machina* through whose ostensible preservation of nature humanity may be able to transcend its civilized misery and degradation. It presents an understanding of Rousseau's conception of conscience as highly ambivalent rather than straightforward, not as the voice of a transcendent nature within human nature but as passion turned against itself. The novel *La Nouvelle Héloïse* is analysed as a case history of excessive denaturation or surplus repression resulting in the development of a punitive superego functioning in the interests of social domination.

Chapter 7 presents the *Social Contract* as the founding document of political emancipation in something very much like Marx's sense of the term, but discovers in the way in which the problem of the contract is posed and in the solution itself the groundwork of a critique of political emancipation as general human emancipation.

Based upon Rousseau's critique of conscience and of purely political emancipation, chapter 8 returns to the broadest concerns of Rousseau's historical anthropology by examining *Emile*, not as a handbook for the education of the natural man but as the vehicle for Rousseau's final theoretical resolution of his own ambivalence concerning the potentialities within human history. *Emile* makes the necessary and crucial distinction between basic and surplus repression and between alienation and objectification, and begins to carry these distinctions through to a vision of a non-austere democracy, together with a transcendence of the unhappiness that was for Rousseau previously bound up in an essential manner with a historical and social existence.

CHAPTER TWO

On the Concept of Nature

Experience and the Emancipation of Nature

Rousseau's central and ultimately durable achievement has been the reorientation of social and political theory to include at the core the concept of history. Rousseau, however, is supposed to be, for all his doubts and second thoughts about it, a man of the Enlightenment, one who at most anticipates further developments in the 'historical sense' that was to come into full flower in both the social and natural sciences during the nineteenth century and one who at best accommodates himself to history with a great deal of unease.[1] Even when he stands adamantly in opposition to the Enlightenment, that opposition seemingly rests upon a fundamentally similar cast of mind. Perhaps the single most important concept that unifies the thought of the Enlightenment and ostensibly also serves to join Rousseau irrevocably to that movement is its concept of nature.[2] Rousseau's transformation of the problematic of the Enlight-

---

[1] In two recent treatments of the philosophy of history, for example, of the type from which one might expect some treatment of Rousseau, he does not appear; see Karl Löwith, *Meaning in History*, and Frank E. Manuel, *Shapes of Philosophical History*. Where Rousseau does appear as a historical philosopher, as in Jean Ehrard, *L'idée de la nature en France dans la première moitié du xviiie siecle*, vol. 2, 749ff, the import of his philosophical history is, in an otherwise sensitive treatment, largely emasculated because it is seen as simply a fatalism.

[2] On the philosophical history of the concept of nature, R.G. Collingwood's *The Idea of Nature* supplies one of the few overviews available. For the specific period with which we are concerned Ehrard's monumental two-volume study is extremely useful. It teases

enment depends upon a thoroughgoing historicization of human nature and a naturalization of history. But in order to begin to grasp the full import of Rousseau's transformation of the notions of human nature and history, it is necessary at least to sketch briefly the development of the concept of nature during the Enlightenment. Although the specific content of the concept varies from figure to figure, all are united in opposing the rationality and immanent order of nature to the authority of the Church, tradition, and the absolutist state.

All human and divine authority could, in the mind of the Enlightenment, be replaced by the ultimate authority of unmediated experience. Nature itself, in its observable and precisely describable order and regularity, would henceforth be the ultimate and only source of truth and authority. In taking over Locke's idea of experience, the Enlightenment believed it had inherited the key to the universe, a key that would allow knowledge to dispense with all human and divine forms of authority

out the essence of the ambivalent role that the idea of nature played in the French Enlightenment: 'La bourgeoisie montante, qui n'a pas encore pris la première place dans la société française, a besoin d'ériger ses aspirations en lois universelles; dans sa lutte contre les survivances du passé, elle ne peut s'accommoder d'une vision de l'histoire qui paralyserait sa critique des "abus" présents. C'est le côté positif de l'idée de Nature, système de normes intemporelles, qui, bien avant 1750, oriente et guide le combat des "philosophes": parfois contre l'insolence des grands, plus surement contre le despotisme du Dieu chrétien et l'arbitraire du monarque de droit divin. Pour soulever la société le bourgeois a besoin du point d'appui que lui fournit la Nature. Mais cette nécessité prouve sa faiblesse autant que sa force. Incapable d'inventer des valeurs totalement nouvelles, il trouve dans l'idée d'un ordre naturel, pale substitute de l'ordre de la grace, à la fois un stimulant et une sécurité. Cette Nature immuable, à l'abri de laquelle il voudrait se menager un bonheur exempt de peril, ne lui permet de concevoir que des espérances limitées: *idée-force* de siècle, la nature est aussi une *idée-freine* . . . A cette dualité opportune l'idée de la nature doit au xviiie siècle son succès et son prestige' (vol. II, 785-6). Although he does not address the question of nature directly, Cassirer's *The Philosophy of the Enlightenment*, esp. chaps. 1-3, remains one of the few truly indispensable works. Also of particular value are Kingsley Martin, *French Liberal Thought in the Eighteenth Century*; Carl L. Becker, *The Heavenly City of the Eighteenth-Century Philosophers*; Laski, *Rise*; Norman Hampson, *The Enlightenment*; Paul Hazard, *European Thought in the 18th Century*. Peter Gay's two volumes of *The Enlightenment: An Interpretation* are useful for purposes of comparison with Ehrard. Gay tends to take the Enlightenment at its word, that is, that it is the movement of emancipation from myth. Gay does not see what Ehrard so forcefully evokes, that the Enlightenment replaces a religious myth with its own 'scientific' myth of nature. An extremely insightful treatment of the development of 'natural history' is to be found in John C. Greene, *The Death of Adam; Evolution and its Impact on Western Thought*; see also Stephen Toulmin and June Goodfield, *The Discovery of Time*. Finally, if only for the critical perspective that it lends to earlier versions of the idea of nature, see Alfred Schmidt, *The Concept of Nature in Marx*.

and to transform an unjust and arbitrary social order. But unwittingly, it had also inherited the very source of its own philosophical demise.

In challenging the Cartesian system Locke and Newton did not simply replace one theory of the physical and spiritual universe with another. They appeared to have decisively removed the need for any divine guarantee of the truths of reason. In Descartes's philosophy the guarantee of the correspondence of the concepts of knowledge with their object was achieved by a fundamental reduction of both to one underlying substratum. The correspondence of the order of clear and distinct innate ideas with the order of the phenomenal world followed from the goodness of God, the ultimate source of both: 'Reason, as the system of clear and distinct ideas, and the world, as the totality of created beings, can nowhere fail to harmonize; for they merely represent different expressions of the same essence. The "archetypal intellect" of God thus becomes the bond between thinking and being ... There is no union between soul and body, between our ideas and reality except that which is given or produced by the being of God.'[3] As a result of both Locke's critique of innate ideas and Newton's achievements in physics, the Enlightenment was able to emancipate simultaneously both nature and the human knowledge of nature from the vestiges of theology in Cartesianism. From then on sense experience would be the sole foundation of knowledge; no idea that had not passed the test of Lockean analysis would be admitted to the corpus of legitimate knowledge.

At first no threat was felt from this quarter to the notion of an inherently necessary, divinely ordained, and therefore stable natural order. Indeed, Newton's discovery of universal physical laws by means of a method compatible with Lockean empiricism was taken to herald the beginning of a new philosophical era in which not only the problems of physics but also those of biology and human society would yield to the 'experimental method' – the method of inductive generalization. Experience, especially sense-experience, the raw and unimpeachable data of nature, did not deceive. The goodness of God, which required a long and fallible chain of reasoning for its establishment, was to be replaced by the guilelessness of nature. For a moment it seemed that in principle all that was necessary was to turn away from the past with its inherited and tainted traditions in order to gaze with fresh eyes on the spectacle of a nature ready to reveal its universal patterns to human reason.

This simultaneous emancipation of both nature and the 'natural light' from a transcendent source of truth was a tremendous stimulus to the

---

3 Cassirer, *Enlightenment*, 95

various sciences but also to the self-assertion of the forces critical of the *ancien régime*. Lockean psychology seemed to guarantee the fundamental equality of men, since human differences were not innate but the results of different environments. It was not original sin but erroneous associations of ideas that were at the root of moral evil and antisocial behaviour. Society itself seemed to be open to fundamental reform through the wise regulation of material conditions. On this basis the Physiocrats, for example, sought to identify a natural order in the economic sphere, according to which the granting of individual property rights and the establishment of freedom to exchange would necessarily lead to the greatest social well-being. The pursuit of self-interest in its enlightened form was no longer to be considered the mortal sin of avarice but guaranteed to be good by nature. Nature itself guarantees the harmony of competing interests.

But this emancipation of nature and the knowledge of nature from God did not completely dispense with him. On the contrary, it was asserted that he was more firmly ensconced in the heavens than before. The keystone of the natural philosophy of the eighteenth century was the God of the deists. This God both had his existence demonstrated by the rational order of nature and was the source of the persistence and value of this same static order. As Voltaire, one of the chief architects of the prospective synthesis, put it: 'If matter gravitates, as has been proved, it does not do so by virtue of its very nature, as it is extended by reason of its nature. Therefore it received gravitation from God.'[4] The observable order of the behaviour of created beings in the world, its appropriateness as a habitation for all its creatures, also proclaimed the existence of a God standing outside of a nature that was still his product. This God no longer intervened in the affairs of men, took no part in their history; his task was completed by the creation of a nature that was for all intents and purposes self-sufficient. Outside of this remote and inscrutable divinity the entire universe was basically part and parcel of one all-encompassing, fundamentally benevolent and rational whole: the realm of nature, including the physical, biological, social, and moral worlds, which were to be grasped in one unified system of natural law. Between nature and society there was no gap, as there was none between nature and its reflection in the human mind. The reason that had found out with mathematical precision the universal laws of physics had also determined that society was a natural system.

For some, the eternal and fundamental laws of political society were

---

4 Voltaire, cited in Hampson, *Enlightenment*, 79

to be derived from the moral laws embedded in the rational faculty of each individual. These ethical laws had the validity of axioms even when, as with Locke, they were found out in or occasioned by experiences. Although their content, which was largely an inheritance from Hobbes as well as Locke, was the pursuit of enlightened self-interest, it was assumed that the harmony inherent in nature providentially guided the superficial clash of wills towards the greatest good of all. Thus in Locke's system the right to unlimited accumulation of property was equated with increasing wealth and comfort for even the propertyless subjects of political society. The meaning and validity of the rationale for absolute government seemed to recede into the mists of medieval darkness, bound up with a discredited theology. The laws of nature, which were also ultimately the laws of God, revealed that the state was merely an instrument of civil society and like any human instrument subject to the limitations dictated by its purpose. The ends and limitations of the state followed directly from the purposes of any rational individual, that is, the preservation of life, liberty, and estate.

Thus, before mid-century a grand new natural philosophy seemed to be taking shape, according to which emancipated reason, secure in its potential knowledge of the natural laws of physical and biological phenomena, would proceed to the natural laws of social phenomena and then, by adjusting human conduct to these laws, bring forth a 'happy society instead of an unnatural and therefore unhappy one.'[5] Challenges were of course offered to this emerging outlook from without, but the most serious challenges seemed to develop within the movement itself. From within the camp of the Enlightenment doubts concerning the idea of a single, static, harmonious, benevolent order of nature, issuing from and maintained by God, came from a number of sources. First of all the deistic philosophy of nature could not avoid a confrontation with the problem of evil. Voltaire's *Candide* signalled a recognition of the seriousness of the problem without giving it a really satisfactory solution. The later turn to the idea of a unilinear progress of reason in history, as in the thought of Condorcet, can be seen as in part a response to this dilemma.

Perhaps more serious were developments in natural science itself. Newton's cosmos required its God to keep the solar system in harmony, to correct the observed arbitrary irregularities in the planetary orbits. D'Alembert, however, soon demonstrated that these were periodic and self-correcting. Newton had believed that to account for the existence

---

[5] Martin, *French Liberal Thought*, 118

of all the planetary orbits in a single plane, divine purpose and intervention was a necessary postulate. But Buffon's theory of the formation of the solar system through the near-collision of a comet with the sun showed the possibility of dispensing with the need for the deity in yet another sphere. Geological investigations began to reveal the tremendous antiquity of the earth and to indicate the existence of extensive and continuous change, a theory that was almost as difficult to reconcile with the deistic conception of the order of nature as it was with the Christian idea of creation. Such developments in the science of nature introduced a shift in theoretical orientation increasingly hostile to the idea of a static order and ready to recognize revolutionary transformations of nature over vast periods of time.[6]

The most crucial challenge, however, to the Enlightenment's philosophy of nature came from a continuing reflection on the central concept of that very outlook. The Enlightenment took its most central task to be the elimination of all transcendence in the relation between nature and knowledge. Experience was to be the bedrock upon which both a theory of knowledge and a theory of nature would be erected. And experience was taken to mean the direct impression or influence of nature on the mind. Any other relation of subject and object would only reinstate 'a mock solution, an explanation of the unknown in terms of that which is still less known.'[7] But the continuing analysis of experience led to unforeseen and disturbing consequences for any theory that hoped to establish an objective knowledge of nature. The persistent drive to ground all ideas in experience, using Locke's genetic, or 'plain historical method,' ends up seemingly destroying all possibility of an objective knowledge of nature. In the philosophy of Condillac not only are all of what Locke had called innate operations of the mind or ideas of reflection reduced to the status of precipitates of experience, but their very order and apparent logic do not objectively mirror nature; rather, knowledge follows the

---

6 A brief but incisive treatment of the beginnings of the crumbling of the Newtonian-Voltairean system of nature is to be found in Hampson, *Enlightenment*, 88-94: 'The new attitude emphasized the complexity of matter and its apparent capacity to generate life, the existence of anomalies in nature and the revolutionary transformation of nature itself over an immense period of time. Science, in other words, seemed to have dispensed with the need for God as a necessary factor in its explanation of the universe. Diderot in his *Interprétation de la nature* (1754) observed that if gravitation were inherent in matter, chaos was an impossibility since matter would automatically arrange itself in an ordered way' (91); cf Cassirer, *Enlightenment*, 65-80. More extensive treatments of this shift are contained in Greene, *Death of Adam*, and Ehrard, *L'Idee de la nature*.

7 Cassirer, *Enlightenment*, 97

biologically rooted desire for self-preservation: 'The will is not founded on the idea, but the idea on the will.'[8] This transvaluation of the roles of reason and passion was completed in the work of Hume. In reducing causation to habit, to the combined operation of sensibility and the imagination, all objective knowledge of rationality in nature was uprooted. What had appeared to be rational knowledge was now revealed to be the work of an instinct that although necessary to the preservation of life, is blind.

The heritage of Locke and Newton, which had seemed so promising in immediate results, had thus, shortly after mid-century, arrived at a complete impasse. The only alternatives, barring a return to the Christian tradition, seemed to be on the one hand Humean scepticism, which with its turn towards empirical anthropology threatened the heritage of that natural law that was being pressed into such good service in the struggle with absolutism; or, on the other, the developing materialism that in d'Holbach and Helvétius was to turn into a complete determinism. 'By the middle of the century the efforts of scientists and philosophers to discover the purpose of nature and the rights and duties of man, by the light of unaided human reason, seemed to have led to a choice between the inscrutable and the intolerable.'[9]

Rousseau's Experience of Nature as Duty

It is in the context outlined above that Rousseau is customarily seen as having attempted to found a politico-moral theory that would avoid the impasse towards which the thought of the century as a whole was headed. Like his contemporaries and in fundamental agreement with the thought of the Enlightenment, Rousseau founds his theory on nature and experience. Except the experience to which Rousseau is referring is the sensitivity of the mind to the duty outlined in the voice of conscience, and the nature that is invoked is the direct and immediate source of this same 'moral instinct.'[10] According to this interpretation Rousseau opposes conscience not only to any hedonistic calculus but also to the ossified and arbitrary conventions of traditional society. Conscience, which is the voice of nature, 'never deceives us; she is the true guide of man; it is to the soul what instinct is to the body; he who obeys his conscience

8 Ibid., 103, 97ff
9 Hampson, *Enlightenment* 126
10 The role of conscience as irreducible to passive sensation is, whatever their other differences, central to the interpretations of Cassirer, *Question*, Derathé, *Rationalisme*, and Burgelin, *Existence*.

... need not fear that he will go astray' (*E* 250). Conscience, unlike reason, which can deceive (*E* 249), is an 'innate principle of justice and virtue' (*E* 252) remaining ultimately beyond the reach of education and social influence (*E* 249ff). Far from being the mere product of custom and prejudice, they are really the worst antagonists of conscience, threatening at times its effective disappearance from the social world (*LM* 1112).[11] Awareness of the voice of conscience is dependent on a disciplined retreat from social relations, a retreat into the self, where its essential autonomy can be reasserted (*LM* 1113). At the same time that the veracity and autonomy of the moral life is thus asserted, it is made to depend on a direct experience of unmediated nature. But the nature appealed to is not at all of the order of sense experience, which has been revealed to be, because of its variability and subjectivity, unreliable; it is of a higher order. Rousseau calls it the 'divine instinct.' It is an instinct that is active, forming, prehensive, and fundamentally unlike passive and receptive sensation.[12]

This interpretation grasps Rousseau's thought as an attempt to sidestep the dilemma of the Enlightenment while preserving its fundamental concepts. In the moral realm a sure and objective knowledge of nature based on experience is preserved. Both experience and nature remain outside although not untouched by the passage of time, the historical variability of the social order, and the human sense-experience enclosed within it. The moral law therefore owes nothing to the external authority of ecclesiastical dogma or to the material pressures of environmental influence. The morally reformed individual, dependent in his will and his activity only on the voice of conscience, is essentially autonomous, and autonomy itself becomes the essence of morality. Politics, in turn, is the problem of the collective self-regulation of a number of autonomous egos, and it is a problem amenable to solution in the *self*-surrender of the ego to the rule of law. The general will of the community, which

---

11 'La conscience est timide et craintive, elle cherche la solitude, le monde et le bruit l'épouvantent, les préjugés dont on la dit être l'ouvrage sont ses plus mortels ennemis, elle fuit ou se tait devant eux, leur voix bruyante étouffe la sienne et l'empeche de se faire entendre. A force d'être econduite elle se rebute à la fin, elle ne nous parle plus, et après un si long mépris pour elle il en coute autant de la rappeller qu'il en coutta de la bannir.' Cf *E* 254-5.
12 Rousseau, *E* 232-4, refers to an 'active' power in the human mind that is not reducible to sensation: 'This power of my mind which brings my sensations together and compares them may be called by any name; let it be called attention, meditation, reflection, or what you will; it is still true that it is in me and not in things, that it is I alone who produce it when I receive an impression from things. Though I am compelled to feel or not to feel, I am free to examine more or less what I feel' (234).

can only find expression in the law – that is, in a formal and universal rule – accordingly becomes essential to the moral destiny of the individual. The community, which is only a genuine community when it scrupulously eschews the expression in law of an exclusive or one-sided interest, becomes the condition and guarantee of personal virtue. The community, in calling upon the individual to overcome both his immediate and his longer-term, 'enlightened' self-interest does not act coercively. Rather, in pointing away from the arbitrariness of mere desire, it offers its citizens the only proper arena for the exercise of their freedom.

In this dominant, Kantian interpretation of Rousseau, his thought would therefore represent the emergence of a third force within the Enlightenment itself, departing from both the empiricism that ends in the thoroughgoing scepticism of Hume and from the materialist utilitarianism that was beginning to be seen as the emerging alternative to it. Yet what supposedly keeps Rousseau within the bounds of the Enlightenment is the appeal to a timeless nature and the conviction that this nature is directly accessible to experience. There is moreover no retreat from the position that the Enlightenment had won for itself, no appeal to a transcendent source of truth as there had been in the system of Descartes. And, at the same time, by splitting experience into inner and outer, into the inner experience of conscience, which shares the autonomy of will, and sense-experience, which does not (but does threaten to overwhelm the former), Rousseau in this view manages to save the objectivity of the moral law even though scepticism may triumph in physics.

This orientation to the interpretation of Rousseau, which has not lost its primary place, suffers from a number of problems. It must suppress or abstract from opposing tendencies in Rousseau that are evident even in the surface texture of his writing. I will mention here only two examples. In the first place there is the emphasis that Rousseau places in his political theory on the role of the Legislator and of the civil religion in the creation of suitable subjects of true civic responsibility. The political experience of the citizen is in fact indelibly stamped with heteronomy. In the second place, there is the perennial tension throughout Rousseau's work between the claims of duty enjoined by conscience (or, as we shall see, what claims to be conscience) and the drive to happiness. What the Kantian interpretation is unable to realize is that conscience for Rousseau is not a unitary force, given once and for all, but, like practically everything else concerning man, a product, a result of a complex and unfinished process unfolding over time. The Kantian interpretation of Rousseau is not unique in lumping him in his supposed ahistorical tendencies together with the rest of the Enlightenment. Most other interpretations suffer from the same shortcoming.[13] The reason this version is stressed here is that, in addition to its being the most influential, it is perhaps the most careful

[13] There are, however, a number that begin to go beyond the view of Rousseau as an ahistorical thinker. Ehrard has already been mentioned (see n 1); see also chap. 1, n 73. Muntéano, 'Les "Contradictions,"' 95-111, sees in Rousseau's efforts at self-examination the dawn of an awareness of personal identity as the temporal unfolding of contradiction: 'C'est dans le continuel bouleversement contradictoire que, selon Rousseau, l'homme est appelé à connaitre. Condamné à vivre son propre mouvement originel dans le mouvement de la temporalité, l'homme est tenu de recourir à l'unique solution que son triste sort lui concède, c'est à dire à la contradiction connaissante' (111). But for Muntéano this is a purely existential problem; it remains internally unrelated to the historical unfolding of social relations. More important is Lucio Colletti, *From Rousseau to Lenin*, who is correct in dismissing the view of the philosophy of history that stands behind the second *Discourse* as a rationalist echo of the Christian fall and redemption. But for Colletti what is of supreme importance is not Rousseau as a historical philosopher but his moralistic critique of civil society and the supposed answer to civil society in the political theory of the *Social Contract*. For Colletti Rousseau remains in fact an ahistorical pessimist who in his utopian thought anticipates the Marxian vision of the suppression of the division between civil society and the state. In opposition to the Christian myth of a transcendent heavenly community, Rousseau asserts the possibility of a truly egalitarian political community in history. This is definitely movement in the right direction, but in its eagerness to assimilate the real Rousseau to Marx it fails, paradoxically, to come to grips with an even deeper kinship between the two. Colletti himself relies heavily on Lionel Gossman's 'Time and History.' Gossman's article is perhaps the most sensitive to date in its treatment of Rousseau's 'acute awareness of *history* as the mode of being of all things.' But for Gossman the fact that Rousseau was himself trapped at a period in history when it was impossible to imagine any *practical* transcendence of the alienation of the individual in an atomized society, of the division of labour, and of the 'commercial' exploitation of man and nature, led his thought into an impasse: he despaired of historical 'salvation' but could not imagine any outside of history. For Rousseau, therefore, 'time appears as the absolute enemy. Time and all that is part of it ... appear as that which has to be transcended. The trumpet calls to virtue, the recurrent appeals to conscience ... are, in their way, attempts to achieve this transcendence' (344). Gossman, while achieving a beautiful sense of literary irony in this picture of Rousseau, fails to see that these efforts at transcendence are themselves the object of a theoretical scrutiny based upon their historicity. The *practical* impasse that Rousseau faced as a critic of both the *ancien regime* and its bourgeois critique may have led to a *personal* impasse, but this does not warrant the assumption that a *theoretical* impasse must coincide precisely with the personal. A fuller understanding of Rousseau's view of history is in this case foreclosed by too great a fascination with his realization that a certain amount of alienation and unhappiness are the 'inevitable consequences of the historical dialectic' (343). In other words, Rousseau's very real pessimism of the existential variety and his practical realism concerning contemporary possibilities of political transcendence are not in themselves sufficient to foreclose a further theoretical realization of the paths that a possible, though limited, practical transcendence of alienation in history must take.

to bring Rousseau into relation with the dominant philosophical movements of the Enlightenment.

It would be foolish to deny that the concept of nature was crucial to Rousseau's thought. Nevertheless, despite the rhetorical garb, there is a substantial case to be made that Rousseau's social theory is oriented not to the substitution of a different *content* for a static concept of nature. Rather, his thought as a whole can be seen as a fundamental challenge to any philosophy that would attempt to grasp the problems of society and politics by way of any abstract and static concept of nature. Far from sharing the Enlightenment concept of nature, Rousseau's work exemplifies the first turnings from nature to history. The following chapters will therefore attempt to demonstrate that, far from conceiving of the problems of society in terms of the fundamental goodness of human nature and the reversible evils of social institutions, Rousseau's work amounts to a profound transformation of the concept of human nature in the sense that the Enlightenment and its predecessors gave it. Part and parcel of this overthrow of the concept of human nature is the substitution of the idea of labour for that of receptive sense-experience as the primordial mode of interaction between nature and human subjectivity. For Rousseau the problems of politics must be grasped in the context of the contradictory unfolding of human nature as a historical process. Humanity's history is predicated and based upon the evolutionary necessity of social labour. The role of theory in this context is not the discovery of eternal laws of human nature. It will be oriented, rather, towards an understanding of the process itself as a prerequisite to the liberation of the social individual from its irrationality and the misery and injustice that its irrationality necessitates.

Nature and Method in the Second Discourse

Rousseau himself, in his adoption of the philosophical vocabulary of his age, has perhaps done more than anyone else to obscure the centrality of history in his thought. In fact, the one work that most strongly announces the inadequacy of nature as the central category of philosophical inquiry into politics seems to assert the reverse. In the *Discourse on the Origins of Inequality* Rousseau seems to be agreeing with the method adopted by the theorists of natural law in determining the central problems of politics: 'The very study of the original man, of his real wants, and the fundamental principles of his duty, is ... the only proper method we can adopt to obviate all the difficulties which the origin of moral inequality presents, on the true foundations of the body politic, on the reciprocal rights of its members and on many other similar topics' (*DOIC* 158). The key to political philosophy seems to be in the discovery of the true principles of the laws of nature and their real foundations. All the disagreements among the theorists of natural law indicate not the futility of their endeavour but seemingly only a mere ignorance of the truths of nature, which are in principle accessible to human reason: 'It is this ignorance of the nature of man which casts so much uncertainty and obscurity on the true definition of natural right; for, the idea of right, says Burlamaqui, and more particularly that of natural right, are ideas manifestly relative to the nature of man' (*DOIC* 156). Rousseau then seems to agree with the theorists of natural right in rejecting any political theory that attempts to dispense with the idea of a fundamentally static and transcendent human nature. To dispense with it would be to leave only an appeal to religious authority or to positive law. But it is precisely these that must be overcome, and this is precisely what natural law is fitted to accomplish.

The necessity of gaining a knowledge of human nature, however, does not obviate the difficulty of acquiring it. It is clear that Rousseau rejects natural law in the form of a system of deductions derived from axioms grasped by rational intuition. This procedure has evident faults in the age of Locke and Condillac. For Rousseau, as especially for the latter, the validity of any such axioms is fundamentally suspect: 'Nature has given us sensations and not knowledge.'[14] The senses, as the origins, instruments, and occasions of our knowledge, strictly circumscribe the limits of our penetration of nature: 'The human understanding, constrained and enclosed in its shell, cannot, so to speak, penetrate the body that contains it and only operates through sensations' (*LM* 1092-3). Newton has demonstrated that the essence of matter does not lie in extension and that the universal law of order in the physical cosmos does not follow deductively from an intuitive grasp of the substantial essence of phenomenal matter. Likewise, Locke has demonstrated that the essence of the soul is not pure thought and that, by reason of the empirical grounds of all knowlege, we have no intuitive grasp of substantial essences: 'Why is it we are unable to know what spirit and matter are? Because we know nothing except by our senses, and these are inadequate to learn that' (*LM* 1097-8). This being the case, we may no longer hope (as Locke

---

14 Rousseau, quoted by Pierre Burgelin, *La philosophie de l'existence de Jean-Jacques Rousseau*, 97

had still hoped) to have a purely rational insight into the laws of nature as they might obligate human beings in their social relations. In this matter as in most others, the operations of pure reason leave us 'surrounded by impenetrable mysteries. These mysteries are beyond the region of sense; we think we can penetrate them by the light of reason, but we fall on our imagination' (*E* 230).

According to Rousseau this has been one of the most serious of the mistakes of the philosophers of natural law. All of them, assuming the laws of nature to be immediately accessible to unaided rational intuition, 'have felt the necessity of going back to the state of nature; but not one of them has got there' (*DOIC* 161). Instead they are in the habit of abstracting the content of natural law from the behaviour of men in civil society, attributing the rationality they imagine they see there to an atemporal cognitive faculty and reconstructing the relations among men in such a way that nature turns out to correspond to those types of relations they would prefer to see in existence. The nature that they oppose to various forms of artifice thus turns out to be equally artificial and arbitrary: 'Modern writers begin by inquiring what rules it would be expedient for men to agree on for their common interest, and then give the name of natural law to a collection of these rules, without any other proof than the good that would result from their being universally practised. This is undoubtedly a simple way of making definitions and of explaining the nature of things by almost arbitrary conveniences' (*DOIC* 157). If artifice is to be brought down in the name of a nature that transcends both space and time, this cannot be accomplished by simply assigning to nature a different content, equally artificial.

One of the ways in which a supposed law of nature is revealed to be the product of a particular society or stage of development is through a broadened experience. If human nature is not revealed in the manner of a mathematical deduction from self-evident principles, then perhaps it can be approached through an inductive analysis of the phenomena. And in fact Rousseau places a high theoretical value on the empirical investigation of a wide variety of societies. Claude Lévi-Strauss goes so far as to claim that Rousseau is the founder of the modern science of ethnography.[15] Whether or not such a judgment overstates the case, there is little room for doubt that Rousseau predicated the self-knowledge of European society upon a systematic study of other cultures. In a note

---

15 Claude Lévi-Strauss, 'Jean-Jacques Rousseau, fondateur des sciences de l'homme,' 239; for a critique of Lévi-Strauss on Rousseau see M. Ryklin, 'Rousseau, Rousseauism and the Fundamental Concepts of Structural Anthropology.'

to the second *Discourse* he proposes such a study as a necessary step in acquiring a real knowledge of human nature:

Will one never see reborn those happy time when the multitude did not trouble themselves with philosophizing but when the Platos, the Thaleses, and the Pythagorases, taken with an ardent desire to know, undertook the greatest voyages solely to inform themselves and would go great distances in order to throw off the yoke of national prejudices, to learn to know men by their likenesses and differences, and to acquire that universal knowledge that is not at all that of one century or one country exclusively but, being from all times and all places, is, so to speak, the common knowledge of the wise ... the whole earth is covered with nations only whose names we know, and we bother to judge the human race! (*DI* 213)

The 'universal knowledge' that might be the outcome of an empirical and comparative ethnography would not, however, in itself be sufficient to establish a knowledge of human nature adequate to the purposes of political philosophy. The scientific study of human variability has for Rousseau a primarily critical and negative value. Such knowledge is useful for the task of ridding philosophy of the notion of a uniform human nature, 'that fine moral adage made so hackneyed by the philosophizing mob, that men are everywhere the same, that men having everywhere the same passions and the same vices, it is rather useless to attempt to describe the different peoples' (*DI* 212-13). But inductive generalization can only yield a knowledge of the product and not of the process underlying it. Therefore Rousseau would undertake in the second *Discourse* a different sort of inquiry, one that requires 'throwing aside, therefore, all those scientific books which teach us only to see men as they have made themselves' (*DOI* 157). The route that Rousseau chose to take is one that I will call his historical anthropology.

CHAPTER THREE

Rousseau's Historical Anthropology

> Whatever is, in the context of bourgeois delusion, called nature, is merely the scar of social mutilation.
> T.W. Adorno

From Analysis to Evolution

In the most general terms the *Discourse on the Origins of Inequality* is a critique of the European social order, an attempt to show that it is not the only one or the best, and that it is the product of history. Specifically, Rousseau sets himself the task of establishing 'in the progress of things, the moment at which right took the place of violence and nature became subject to law, and to explain by what sequence of miracles the strong came to submit to serve the weak, and the people to purchase imaginary repose at the expense of real felicity' (*DOIC* 157). In order to mark that moment the process must be reconstructed in the imagination; a thought experiment must be undertaken, a set of 'conditional and hypothetical reasonings ... just like the hypotheses which our physicists daily form respecting the formation of the world' (*DOIC* 160-1). Rousseau's positive conclusions regarding the illegitimacy of 'moral' or 'conventional' inequality, although certainly radically disturbing to the literate society of eighteenth-century France, are relatively minor results of the investigation. The rhetorical strength of these conclusions in based on adopting the device that informs a great deal of Enlightenment social criticism, that is, the contrast between nature and artifice as an abstract, static opposition. On this level it becomes crucial to reconstruct the independence and happiness of 'savage man' as a foil to the subjugation and misery of civilized man, 'l'homme policé' of European society. If nothing else, established literary convention and the ideology of nature demand it. Nevertheless, alongside this rhetorical theme and partially obscured by it there is a much more subversive theory also coming to the fore. Although the second *Discourse* purports to separate nature from artifice and condemn the latter in terms of the former, it actually accomplishes the collapse of the two concepts within a sophisticated concept of history. Artifice is essential to the nature of the historical being, yet artifice is never identified with nature, nor does it ever replace nature.

In opting, as he will in political theory, to pursue the resolutive-compositive method, Rousseau is certainly not breaking new ground. Many others, including Hobbes and Locke, had used this method of explanation, in which any given phenomenon is analysed into basic units and the whole is reconstructed from the essential properties of these units. Condillac, to whom Rousseau owes a great debt, uses it to great advantage in his psychology and epistemology. Nor in Rousseau's hands is such an inquiry free of presuppositions. They are not, however, the presuppositions of the natural-law school concerning both the existence of laws of reason in nature and the susceptibility of the human understanding to these laws.[1] For Rousseau as for the other sensationalist psychologists, 'to exist for us is to feel; and our sensibility is incontestably anterior even to our reason; whatever the cause of our existence may be, she has provided for our conservation in giving us sensations consonant with our nature; and no one could deny that these at least are innate. These sentiments with regard to the individual are the love of self [l'amour de soi-même], the fear of suffering and of death, and the desire for well-being' (*LM* 1109). If we may speak at all, therefore, of natural law, it is only in the sense of drives that are biologically grounded. In the second *Discourse* Rousseau calls these 'principles' 'the most simple operations of the human soul.' It is to these that the will is 'sensible,' not to reason, and it is these that constitute the 'voice of nature.' These biologically rooted drives are the grounds upon which reason later erects the rules of natural right 'when by its successive developments it has been led to suppress nature itself' (*DOI* 157). These principles also remain the source of reason's efficacy. Without them the rational injunction would remain powerless. Thus the result of the resolutive step in this inquiry

---

1 See Cameron, *Social Thought*, 43–61; but contrast with Lemos, *Political Philosophy*, esp. 246–52, who sees him as the culmination of the natural-law–social-contract tradition; similarly, Derathé, *Science*.

consists in stripping civilized man, the outcome of the process, 'of all the supernatural gifts he may have received, and all the artificial faculties he can have acquired only by a long process' (*DOI* 163). What we are left with is an animal, although, as we shall see, one of a peculiar sort.

The first problem, then, is not the derivation of the rules of natural right from the nature of an individual simply removed from society. It is rather the scientific reconstruction of the process of evolution or transformation of 'infant man,' 'an animal limited at first to mere sensation,' into what is recognizably human. Rousseau hopes that this starting point will allow him to avoid the pitfalls of, on the one hand, Locke and the school of natural law, who, in merely abstracting from the political state, held to be 'natural' merely the idealized actor of bourgeois society; and on the other hand Hobbes, who, although he pressed the resolutive step at least as far back as the level of physiology, read 'civilized' social relations back into a psychology that in fact did not follow from its ostensible grounds in physiology.[2]

Rousseau's critique of the theorists of natural law rests upon a radical rejection of their theory of human nature. It is a rejection not only of the content of human nature placed there by the school of natural law but also of the form of the concept. Human nature in Rousseau's hands becomes something that not only includes 'a principle of development'[3] but that develops itself in and through its interactions with and transformations of the external world: it is no longer a-temporal and inclusive of a faculty of pure rationality. In the second *Discourse* the resolutive-compositive method is taken to its extreme term and transcended in a theory of human nature as a twofold evolution of both biology and culture. Man in his inception and his essence is conceived to be a self-transforming creature. Human nature for Rousseau *is* history, is itself created within the historical process. And Rousseau's theory of human nature cannot be understood in isolation from the first, tentative steps of contemporary natural science towards becoming historical and dynamic. An understanding of Rousseau as an evolutionist is also necessary in order to arrive at a reappraisal of the ontological status granted to reason and the individual in his writings.

---

2 On Hobbes and Locke reading the substance of the social relations of market society into human nature and natural law, see C.B. Macpherson, *The Political Theory of Possessive Individualism*, and his introduction to *Hobbes: Leviathan* (Harmondsworth: Penguin 1968), 9–63.

3 Cf Cameron, *Social Thought*, 88–94; E.H. Wright, *Meaning*, 164.

Rousseau and Eighteenth-Century Evolutionism

The first problem that Rousseau faces in transforming the concepts of nature and artifice is the emergence of history from nature. If historical process begins from a condition of pure animality, natural causes alone must suffice to explain the transition to humanity. Rousseau was not alone in the eighteenth century in turning towards a dynamic and non-providential concept of nature. In many respects the way had been prepared for him by Maupertuis, Buffon, Diderot, and others.[4] By mid-century some geologists and biologists had formulated or accepted several important elements of what was to be the later Darwinian synthesis. The great antiquity of the earth was accepted on a time-scale far surpassing that of the Old Testament. Linked to the acceptance of that enormously expanded time-scale were geological theories that recognized vast changes in the earth's surface, not induced by a series of divinely inspired catastrophes but produced by the continuous operation of purely natural forces over many ages. In its advance comparative anatomy had compiled new evidence concerning similarities and differences among existing and vanished species. Even the idea of natural selection was widely accepted among the enlightened, although it was often conceived of as having been limited to only a relatively short time-span after the emergence of life on earth. In 1751 Maupertuis, in his *Système de la Nature*, after having worked out a remarkable anticipation of Mendelian genetics, announced that one could 'explain in this way' – that is, from mutation –

how from two individuals alone the mutiplication of the most dissimilar species could have followed ... They could have owed their first origination only to certain fortuitous productions, in which the elementary particles failed to retain the order they possessed in the father and mother animals; each degree of error would have produced a new species; and by reason of repeated deviations would have arrived at the infinite diversity of animals that we see today; which will perhaps still increase with time, but to which perhaps the passage of centuries will bring only imperceptible increases [5]

---

4 For more detailed treatments of evolutionism in the eighteenth century and before see Hampson, *Enlightenment*; Green, *Death of Adam*; Toulmin and Goodfield, *Discovery of Time*; Peter J. Bowler, 'Evolutionism in the Enlightenment,' and *Evolution: The History of an Idea*; Robert Wokler, 'Perfectible Apes in Decadent Cultures: Rousseau's Anthropology Revisited'; Jean Starobinski, 'Rousseau et Buffon'; and B. Glas et al, eds., *Forerunners of Darwin: 1745-1859*.
5 Maupertuis, quoted in Glas et al, *Forerunners*, 77

And in 1753 Buffon, in the fourth volume of his *Natural History*, having been suitably impressed with the evidence of comparative anatomy concerning the structural homologies among the vertebrates, put forth the hypothesis of a unitary evolution from a single simple source:

For if it were once shown ... that among animals and plants there has been (I do not say several species) but even a single one, which has been produced in the course of direct descent from another species ... then there would no longer be any limit to the power of nature, and we should not be wrong in supposing that, with sufficient time, she has been able from a single being to derive all the other organized beings.[6]

Rousseau's relation to the development of a naturalistic theory of organic evolution is complicated and vexed in the extreme. A.O. Lovejoy held the second *Discourse* to be 'chiefly notable in the history of ideas as an early contribution to the formulation and diffusion of an evolutionary conception of human history ... a manifestation of a new tendency which was to revolutionize modern thought.'[7] J.C. Greene, although he concedes that Rousseau abandoned the assumption of intelligent design and that in his theory of cultural evolution he lent an important impetus to the theory of organic evolution, nevertheless maintains that by his differentiation of men and animals on the basis of the perfectibility of the former only, Rousseau in effect denied the possibility of organic evolution in the rest of the animal kingdom as well.[8] Others, such as Norman Hampson, perhaps overly impressed by Rousseau's deism, grant that Rousseau treated organic evolution seriously but claim that in the end he rejected it in favour of a static providential order, and cite Buffon's scientific grounds for such a rejection: the sterility of hybrids.[9] Certain passages indeed seem to suggest that Rousseau could not accept the vision of extreme mutability suggested by a unitary theory of evolution. Particularly in the *Profession de foi du vicaire savoyard*, as he advances arguments against the materialism of La Mettrie, Diderot, and d'Holbach, Rousseau's deism appears to contradict the notion of development in nature: 'If organized bodies had come together fortuitously in all sorts of ways before assuming settled forms, if stomachs were made without mouths, feet without heads ... imperfect organs of every kind which died because they could not preserve their life, why do none of

6 Buffon, quoted in ibid., 97
7 A.O. Lovejoy, 'The Supposed Primitivism of Rousseau's *Discourse on Inequality*,' 25
8 Greene, *Adam*, 207; see also 210-11.
9 Hampson, *Enlightenment*, 226

these imperfect attempts now meet our eyes; why has nature at length prescribed laws to herself which she did not at first recognize?' (*E* 238) And a little further on an even stronger assertion of a fixed and static order in the biological realm appears: 'The mere generation of living organic bodies is the despair of the human mind; the insurmountable barrier raised by nature between the various species, so that they should not mix with one another is the clearest proof of her intention. She is not content to have established order, she has taken adequate measure to prevent the disturbance of that order' (*E* 238).

Aside from the difficulty of accepting at face value what Rousseau puts in the mouth of the Savoyard vicar, there are further difficulties in making of these passages an unqualified rejection of biological transformism. Peter Bowler points out that although the eighteenth-century materialists were able to make some advances towards a dynamic concept of nature, they were in effect limited by their very thoroughgoing materialism in conceiving of a pattern in the evolution of life.[10] In order to counter the argument from design they were forced, as it were, to develop a naturalistic and dynamic account of the origins of life. La Mettrie, for example, in his *Système d'Epicure* (1750), borrowed de Maillet's earlier hypothesis of the pre-existence of 'germs' of life distributed from eternity throughout the universe. Later materialists, Diderot among them, realizing that such a hypothesis merely begged the question of organic structure (in two senses: that of the structural differentiation of particular organs and that of the boundary between organic and inorganic matter), postulated a process of complete, continuous, and random spontaneous generation. The spontaneously arising, living products of inorganic matter would then be filtered through the sieve of selective adaptation to a pre-existing and static physical environment, the 'fit' organisms surviving. But as Rousseau himself is quick to point out in the first of the passages quoted above, random spontaneous generation excludes the possibility of a coherent pattern in the organic world, a fact that Diderot himself recognized in the structural similarity of the vertebrates and took as empirical evidence of their community of descent (in *On the Interpretation of Nature*, 1753).

It has therefore been said of the materialists that

their vision of nature as a totally dynamic chaos denied not only the existence of a pattern of organic development but also the whole concept of a meaningful direction in the history of life. Living forms are generated, change and may

10 Bowler, 'Evolutionism,' 163–5

ultimately die off, but there is little in Diderot's later work, or in that of d'Holbach, to suggest that the general picture of life on earth has changed very much with time ... their world remained the same because all changes occur at random and ultimately cancel out ... their final conception of nature was so dynamic that it became a perpetual chaos rather than a developing system.[11]

On the other hand, a number of deists, precisely *because* of their belief that nature operates within basic limits divinely imposed, were able to develop a more flexible and developmental outlook. If God's activity were understood to be restricted to the establishment of certain fundamental patterns, then the world would be free to develop according to the configuration of particular circumstances. This is ultimately the position of Rousseau and of his chief mentor in biology or 'natural history,' Buffon.

In his *Lettre á Voltaire* defending the goodness of God, Rousseau distinguishes between a universal and a particular divine providence. God's intervention does not extend to particular events or developments in the material world but only so far as to uphold the basic laws of nature underlying the pattern of the whole; in the biological realm providence is confined in its intervention to 'preserving the genera and the species' (*LV* 116).[12] Nature's God stands behind nature, which is 'the system of this universe, which *produces*, preserves and perpetuates all feeling and thinking beings' (*LV* 115; emphasis added). What is noteworthy is that in addition to conserving beings the natural order is also responsible for producing them, the implication being clear that there is a virtually indefinite amount of room open for its operations. The actual system of nature does not follow at all from our knowledge of God's existence; in fact our knowledge of God is, in essence, not at all an intellectual knowledge:

I believe ... that the world is governed by a wise and powerful will; I see it or *rather I feel it*, and it is a great thing to know this. But has this same world always existed, or has it been created? is there one source of all things? are there two or many? I know not; and what concern is it of mine? ... He hides himself alike from my senses and my understanding ... I behold him all around me; but if I try to ponder him himself ... he escapes me and my troubled spirit finds nothing. (*E* 239; emphasis added)

11 Ibid., 164-5
12 See also *Lettre à Voltaire*, in *Oeuvres complètes* 4. 1068: 'Les premiers qui ont gâte la cause de Dieu sont les Prêtres et les Dévots, qui ne souffrent pas que rien se fasse selon l'ordre etabli, mais font toujours intervenir la justice Divine à des évenements purement naturels.'

In the end God is for Rousseau, if indeed the Savoyard vicar can be identified with him, 'nothing' but a plausible inference. Natural religion in his hands turns out to be as much a matter of faith as it is with Hume. Rousseau even goes some distance to forming an anthropological theory of the inception of religion.[13]

In response to the attack of the Christian naturalist Charles Bonnet on the second *Discourse*, Rousseau in the 'Lettre à Philopolis' criticizes Bonnet for his excessive reliance on providence, Rousseau contending both that providence is an unacceptable principle of explanation and that belief in providence leads to intractable difficulties in dealing with the problem of evil:

If everything is the best that it can be, you ought to censure all action whatsoever; because each and every action necessarily produces some change in the condition of things at the moment at which it is done; one cannot then touch anything without doing evil, and the most perfect quietism is the only virtue remaining to man ... Nothing but an error in geography is necessary to overturn this entire sham of a doctrine that deduces what ought to be from what one sees. (*LP* 234)

Providence turns out to be merely an excuse for identifying the actual with the universal, what is with what ought to be, and a recommendation to the most extreme quietism. For Rousseau it is not any preconceived notion of the intent of a providential order that will decide, for example, whether the 'Orang-outang' is a beast or a man, but only careful observation and experiment.[14]

It does not therefore appear unwarranted to conclude that Rousseau's

---

13 Rousseau, *E* 218ff: 'The perception of our action upon other bodies must have first induced us to suppose that their action upon us was effected in like manner. Thus man began by thinking that all things whose action affected him were alive. He did not recognize the limits of their powers, and he therefore supposed that they were boundless; as soon as he had supplied them with bodies they became his gods. In the earliest times men went in terror of everything and everything in nature seemed alive ... Thus the universe was peopled with gods like themselves. The stars, the wind and the mountains, rivers, trees and towns, their very dwellings, each had its soul, its god, its life ... polytheism was their very first religion and idolatry their earliest form of worship. The idea of one god was beyond their grasp, till little by little they formed general ideas, and they rose to the idea of a first cause.'
14 See Rousseau, *LP* 234-5; Bonnet had attacked Rousseau for raising the question in the first place, while in Rousseau's eyes Bonnet had wrongly presumed to answer it in advance of all reliable empirical evidence. On Bonnet's position in contemporary debates, see Bowler, *History*, 55-8.

deism allowed of a large amount of transformation in the system of living beings. Although as a theological device he may not have dispensed with the argument from design, he took sufficient pains to exclude it from the realm of natural history, where no question can be decided on *a priori* grounds and where empirical methods and discoveries must remain unchecked and unencumbered by theological considerations. Nevertheless, old habits of mind die extremely hard.[15] And what is one to make of assertions concerning the 'insurmountable barriers raised by nature between the various species' and the operations of providence to 'conserver les genres et les espèces'? This question cannot be given an adequate answer without our at first characterizing, at least briefly, Buffon's thought concerning species and their transformations. Buffon was Rousseau's chief authority in matters of natural history and is referred to often by him, especially in the notes to the second *Discourse*.

Although Buffon speculated about a unitary evolution of all life from a single simple source, he was quick to deny its ultimate plausibility. In doing so he offered two reasons. One was the testimony of revelation, but most of those who have examined his work agree that such an appeal was intended merely for the eyes of censors. The second was the then experimentally established fact of the sterility of hybrids, and hybridization was the principal form in which Buffon could conceive of significant structural variation. This, together with a number of other empirical considerations, led Buffon to reject unitary evolution, as a highly improbable hypothesis. Although Buffon continued to experience doubts concerning the existence of true species in nature (which was what the sterility of hybrids was supposed to have established), he stuck to this view throughout his life. In the fourteenth volume of his *Natural History* (1766) he again raised the question he had posed fifteen years earlier, of whether modification and descent might apply to species, and in his essay on 'Mules' (1776) he reconsidered the possibility that hybrids may in fact be only relatively infertile. Relative infertility would in Buffon's terms enormously increase the possibility of the descent of one species from another. Throughout his career the question remained open, and Buffon did not abandon his commitment to a purely naturalistic resolution of the issue.

However, even within his scheme of species as fundamental constants of organic life there was room for a tremendous amount of transformation.

15 Greene's book *Death of Adam*, in which the demise over the course of two centures of the Christian idea of a divine order in the biological realm is painstakingly described, is ample confirmation of the old adage.

For Buffon continued to explain the diversity of organic forms by modification in the course of descent:

> Though Nature appears always the same, she passes nevertheless through a constant movement of successive variations, of sensible alterations; she lends herself to new combinations, to mutations of matter and form, so that today she is quite different from what she was at the beginning or even at later periods.
>
> Nature's great workman is time. He marches ever with an even pace, and does nothing by leaps and bounds, but by degrees, gradations and successions he does all things; and the changes which he works – at first imperceptible – become little by little perceptible, and show themselves eventually in results about which there can be no mistake.[16]

Among the causes of modification he did include random mutation, the inheritance of acquired characteristics, and even the struggle for existence among species as a result of overpopulation.[17] The way in which Buffon accounted for this apparent contradiction between the mutability of organic life and the Linnaean view of species (acceptable to Christians and deists alike) as immutable constants, lay in the distinction he drew between species and varieties. Buffon in fact distinguished only a comparatively tiny number of true species – he reduced the entire order of vertebrates to only thirty-eight such classes – which were constant and invariable. Within each of these species, modification by descent could account for a tremendous number of varieties: 'It was characteristic of his biological system that he set up an absolute distinction between species and varieties, gave an extreme extension to the notion of a variety, and sought to reduce the number of separate species as much as possible by assuming – until the establishment of the sterility of hybrids should prove the contrary – that most of the Linnaean species were mere varieties descended from a relatively small number of original specific types.'[18] This being the case, it now becomes possible to reconcile Rousseau's deistic assumption that species are preserved with his evident belief in some form of transformism.

Rousseau shared Buffon's belief in micro-evolution in the organic realm. His differentiation of men and animals on the basis of the exclusive perfectibility of the former is therefore not, as Greene suggests (see note

16 Buffon, quoted in Glas et al, *Forerunners*, 104
17 Buffon did not, however, see the struggle for existence as being an important factor in a process of natural selection but as resulting in a more or less stable equilibrium; see ibid., 107.
18 Ibid., 105

8 above), a flat rejection of the theory of organic evolution. What Rousseau is pointing to in this distinction, among other things, is a different mode of evolution in men as opposed to other animals. When he says that perfectibility with the help of circumstances develops human powers, 'whereas a brute is at the end of a few months all he will ever be during his whole life, and his species, at the end of a thousand years, exactly what it was the first year of that thousand' (*DOI* 170), this need not necessarily be taken as a statement that only humans evolve and humans only evolve 'culturally,' whereas animals do not evolve at all. To the reader aware of the Buffonian background it points merely (but crucially) to a distinction in the mode and rate of evolution. Humanity develops and undergoes transformations at a faster and accelerating rate because of its perfectibility – which is not to be taken as a simple quality inhering in a substance but is itself a result, is itself analysable. Animals may still evolve; Rousseau is silent on the subject. There is no need to give more offence to the censor than is absolutely necessary. And humans, as opposed to other animals, evolve *biologically* through the development of a cultural existence. At the same time, the evolution of culture presupposes certain biological, or less than metaphysical, peculiarities.

Rousseau ought therefore to be counted among the eighteenth-century evolutionists, even though in imaginatively reconstructing the process of human bio-cultural evolution he abstracts from physiological and anatomical changes. This abstraction is performed consciously on his part and is not meant to exclude the existence or the importance of such changes from any eventually complete account. It is worth reproducing here the lengthy passage in which he excuses himself for not examining the question of human physical transformation, for it helps lay to rest the notion that there is in his thoughts a metaphysical gap between the biological and the cultural-social realms (or between the material and the spiritual):

Important as it may be, in order to judge rightly of the natural state of man, to consider him from his origin, and to examine him ... in the embryo of his species, I shall not follow his organization through its successive developments, nor shall I stay to inquire *what his animal system may have been at the beginning in order to become at length what it actually is.* I shall not ask whether his long nails were at first, as Aristotle supposes, only crooked talons; whether his whole body, like that of a bear, was not covered with hair; or whether the fact that he walked upon all fours, with his looks directed towards the earth, confined to the horizon of a few paces, did not at once point out the nature and limits of his ideas. On this subject I could form none but vague and almost imaginary conjectures. Comparative anatomy has as yet made too little progress, and the observations of the naturalists are too uncertain, to afford an adequate basis for solid reasoning. So that, without having recourse to supernatural information on this head, or paying any regard to the *changes which must have taken place in the internal as well as external conformation of man, as he applied his limbs to new uses*, and fed himself on new kinds of food, I shall suppose his conformation to have been at all times what it appears to us at this day; that he walked on two legs, made use of his hands as we do, directed his looks over all nature, and measured with his eyes the vast expanse of heaven. (*DOI* 163; emphasis added)[19]

Therefore, far from splitting off biological and cultural evolution or, by only a slight extension, nature from history, Rousseau is quite clearly indicating that the two are wrapped up in a dialectical process. History emerges from nature, from the activity of sensuously real animal life-forms rather than from the mind of God (as with Christians such as Bossuet) or some arbitrarily posited world-spirit (as with Fichte and Hegel). At the same time human history *is* the history of nature both as it is transformed within and outside men. With this conception Rousseau's thought begins to establish links with modern anthropological theory concerning human evolution. The modern anthropological theory of human evolution places at its centre a notion of the reciprocal interdependence of cultural and biological factors in the evolution of *homo sapiens*: 'It is probably more correct to think of much of our structure

19 A number of other scholars agree that Rousseau is proposing a theory of organic evolution. See Lemos, *Political Philosophy*, 15, as well as Lovejoy, 'Supposed Primitivism,' and chap. 3, n 8 above. For Plattner, *Rousseau's State of Nature*, esp. 35-51, Rousseau's theory of organic evolution is 'transformism' in the manner of Diderot and Buffon (37) and an essential part of his 'mechanistic metaphysics': 'Rousseau in the second *Discourse* gives the appearance of upholding a kind of dualist metaphysics by suggesting that human liberty proves the spirituality of the human soul' (44). But since Rousseau believes that 'perfectibility' is not inexplicable by the laws of mechanics (46), his 'concept of perfectibility, with its dependence on the chance workings of external causes, makes sense only in terms of the mechanistic understanding of nature supplied by modern science' (50). Thus Rousseau abandons teleological explanation once and for all (50), 'spurns the entire classical tradition of moral and political philosophy,' and aligns himself not only with Cartesian mechanism (although he only appears to be a dualist) but with the infamous Hobbes and Machiavelli (64). Goldschmidt, *Anthropologie*, who also, like Plattner, follows Strauss closely, asserts that like Buffon, Rousseau was *not* a transformist (242-3) and remained a dualist of a certain sort (281-3), thus, even though he attempted wrongly to base a defence on the naturalistic and scientific outlook, remaining still a defender of natural law (151).

as the result of culture than it is to think of men anatomically like ourselves slowly discovering culture.'[20] And it is precisely this sort of process that Rousseau, even if he is unable to reconstruct it, thinks 'must have taken place.'

Animals, Men, and Metaphysical Lacunae

If, therefore, Rousseau's deism is not to be taken as an objection to his being truly an evolutionist (even in a limited, micro-evolutionist sense) and if his differentiation of men and animals according to presence or absence of perfectibility is rather a positive theoretical virtue than a drawback, there nevertheless remains the possibility that an objection might be raised on the basis of Rousseau's supposed spiritualism or idealism.

In this view, which is superbly represented by Starobinski in an article entitled 'Rousseau et Buffon,'[21] Rousseau conceives of men and animals as separated by a metaphysical frontier. Like Descartes, Rousseau (along with Buffon) recognizes, according to Starobinski, no ontological gap between organic and inorganic matter. Life is in principle explicable through the motion of bodies according to the laws of mechanics. Rousseau, however, exactly like Descartes, does recognize a gap between matter and spirit. Thus men are distinguished in the biological realm by their spirit, which is identified with free will. Rousseau supposedly bases his ideas on a 'Cartesianism modified by Locke.' The distinction between men and animals is absolute and the history that Rousseau introduces to mediate between 'l'homme sauvage' and 'l'homme policé' does not involve a transformation of nature but merely the development of latent powers already in existence.[22] 'Le sauvage de Rousseau sera

---

20 S.L. Washburn, 'Speculations on the interrelations of the History of Tools and Biological Evolution,' in J.N. Spuhler et al, *The Evolution of Man's Capacity for Culture*, 21; see also 28-9: 'Our brains, then, are not just enlarged, but the increase in size is directly related to tool use, speech, and to increased memory and planning. The general pattern of the human brain is very similar to that of the ape and monkey. Its uniqueness lies in its large size and in the particular areas which are enlarged. From the immediate point of view, this human brain makes culture possible. But from the long term evolutionary point of view, it is culture which creates the human brain.' See also other articles in the same collection and in M.F. Ashley Montagu, ed., *Culture: Man's Adaptive Dimension*, and Weston LaBarre, *The Human Animal*, espec. chaps. 1-7.
21 Starobinski, 'Rousseau et Buffon,' 138-40
22 Starobinski manages to obscure the issue by making what appears to be a meaningless distinction between a transformation in the 'constitution' of human nature and a transformation of human nature itself (ibid., 140).

completement homme en l'absence de tout activité intellectuelle ou technique. Le seul caractère qui le distingue de l'animal est sa liberté: encore reste-t-il sans emploi puisque l'homme n'est engagé dans aucune activité pratique.'[23] For Starobinski the existence of a metaphysical gap between man and animal is based on the reading of human development as the unfolding of *latent* powers. But Starobinski's assimilation of *l'homme sauvage* to the human *species* ignores the implications of the Buffonian distinction between species and varieties. Thus *l'homme sauvage*, although he belongs to the same species, is of a distinctly different variety, and it makes little sense to say of him that he is 'completely a man.' For these latent powers are nothing but postulates necessary to explain the development of the powers produced in human historical and social activities. Starobinski also ignores the anatomical and physiological changes that Rousseau thinks must have taken place in the course of human development. Yet at the same time the divergence, for Starobinski, between the savage and the civilized man is almost as great as that between man and animal.

Although it would be difficult to include Starobinski among the Kantian interpreters of Rousseau, his version of Rousseauan cultural evolution would seem to lend itself to their notion of Rousseau's anticipation of Kant's distinction between the phenomenal and the transcendental ego. Rousseau's supposed modified Cartesianism in anthropology thus guarantees the autonomy of the ego in its moral *intent* from the sensitive-passionate pressure suffered by the phenomenal ego. Starobinski thus supplies a missing link to the Kantian interpretation of Rousseau. And conscience, or the autonomy of the moral will, is now grounded in his thought in a metaphysical dualism of substance. For Descartes the dualism is of *res extensa* and *res cogitans*; for Kant it is no longer one of substance in the classical sense but can be seen as the reinstatement of a substantial dualism in different terms, in terms of phenomena and noumena. Conscience remains suprahistorical and pure, the highest expression of a spiritual nature.

Convenient as this view may be for assimilating Rousseau to a Kantian theory of morality, it simply over-reaches in reading spiritualism into Rousseau's opposition to mechanical materialism. However much he may at times protest about the 'spirituality' of the human soul, Rousseau is not reaffirming a Cartesian dualism of *res extensa* and *res cogitans*. In the first place Rousseau does not, like Descartes, collapse organic and inorganic matter into one ontological level. Utterly unlike Descartes,

23 Ibid., 141

Rousseau cannot conceive of understanding the biological realm in terms of the mechanics of purely extended bodies in motion: 'chance combinations yield nothing but products of the same nature as the elements combined, so that life and organization will not be produced by a flow of atoms ... It is not in my power to believe that passive and dead matter can have brought forth living and feeling beings' (*E* 238-9). It is not merely thought that is inexplicable for Rousseau in terms of materialist mechanics, but 'living and feeling beings.' Thus the distinction between men and animals cannot be put in the Cartesian terms of machines and free spirits linked mysteriously to mechanical bodies. The system of organic nature, if it is to be understood, must be grasped according to different principles. This may mean that the gap between life and intelligent, self-conscious life is not absolute, even though the differences amount to qualitative ones.

If Rousseau does assert that what separates human life from other animal life is 'free agency,' this distinction is not elevated to the status of an ontological dualism. Knowledge of freedom is not deducible, as it is for Descartes, from the intuited essence of a non-material substance. 'The will is known to me in its action, not in its nature' (*E* 236). In fact Rousseau, far from basing himself on a Cartesianism modified by Locke, uses Locke as a lever to overthrow the Cartesian dualism of substances. Rousseau is not interested in substances and their qualities but in a scientifically viable theory of the development of human intellectual and moral powers. If anything, he is searching for an explanation of human intelligence and reason that could dispense with Mind. In his discussions of the role of sense-experience in the process of knowledge, Rousseau is adamant that we have no knowledge of substance at all. And in this respect Rousseau is incomparably closer to Hume and to the phenomenalism of the Enlightenment in general[24] than he is to Descartes. According to Rousseau, Descartes's definitions of the two substances, 'which seemed incontestable, were destroyed in less than a generation. Newton demonstrated that the essence of matter does not at all consist in extension; Locke demonstrated that the essence of the soul does not at all consist in thought. Goodbye to all the philosophy of the wise and methodical Descartes' (*LM* 1096). Even the very category of substance is profoundly suspect, whether the substance in question be matter or spirit: 'The idea of matter was developed as slowly as that of spirit, for the former is itself an abstraction' (*E* 218), while 'the word "substance" ... is at bottom the greatest of abstractions' (*E* 219). To reason concerning

---

24 On the phenomenalism of the Enlightenment see Cassirer, *Enlightenment*, esp. 54-64.

human nature and natural law by deducing one quality after another from the essence of a given substance is precisely to err after the fashion of those theorists whom Rousseau accused of merely fashioning convenient rules of behaviour and then giving them the name of natural law.

Rousseau does assert that the human or proto-human animal is distinguished from the remainder of the animal kingdom by free agency. But free agency is not a quality inhering in an autonomous susbtance; nor does Rousseau use the concept as something that can subsist, in Hegelian terms, 'independently of its concrete determinations.'[25] In the second *Discourse* free agency is a logical presupposition of the emergence of history from nature. It is both a condition of the process of historical development and at the same time a result, inseparable from the conditions of its own development in history. It would be better to think of free agency as being for Rousseau primarily a biological category rather than an ontological one predicated of an independent substance.[26] This does not mean, however, that it is without ontological significance. Human nature for him, in both its passive, sensual side of drive, desire, and passion and its active side of labour and nature transforming activity, is conceived of as a historical process. As a process constituted in historical activity human nature is not to be thought of as the sum of a constant and a variable component but as the product of the human interaction with external nature, as that interaction is molded by specific sets of social relations. History is a process of self-creation (even if consciousness of this process has hitherto been submerged or expressed in distorted form), while 'nature has, so to speak, abandoned its functions as soon as we usurped them.'[27] Rousseau's pronouncements concerning free agency

---

25 The phrase is used by Schmidt, *Nature*, 34, in discussing the relation between Marx's materialist philosophy of praxis and previous, ontological forms of materialism.
26 In the *Profession de foi du vicaire savoyard* Rousseau does have the vicar speak of 'two distinct principles' in human nature intuitively grasped, which lead to the 'doctrine' of two distinct substances. Yet the vicar's method, which is an inversion if not a parody of that of Descartes (cf Henri Gouhier, 'Ce que le Vicaire doit à Descartes,'),is belied by Rousseau's method throughout the rest of *Emile*. There he relies almost exclusively upon an extension of Locke's 'plain historical method' in building up thought and will out of the interaction of desire and nature. Even the vicar himself is extremely tentative about the results of his investigation, admitting that he 'prefers to be deceived rather than to believe nothing' (E 230). It is also worth noting that in the *Lettres morales* (LM 1079-1118), where much of the same ground traversed in the Profession de foi is covered again but without fear of the censor checking his words, Rousseau is much more frank concerning his scepticism concerning matters metaphysical.
27 Rousseau, *Lettres morales*, quoted by Burgelin, *Existence*, 327. Lévi-Strauss is essentially correct in pointing out that Rousseau is attempting a radical overthrow of the

cannot be thought of as answers to the central questions of traditional metaphysics, except in so far as Rousseau felt the need to undermine the metaphysical pretensions of philosophical materialism. Even the Savoyard vicar can, in the midst of seeming to develop a metaphysics, turn around with a statement such as the following: 'The chief source of human error is to be found in general and abstract ideas; the jargon of metaphysics has never led to the discovery of any single truth and it has filled philosophy with absurdities of which we are ashamed as soon as we strip them of their long words' (*E* 236).

Rousseau, then, does not take for granted a metaphysical gap between men and animals based on an ontological distinction between matter and spirit. He does, however, refuse to account for either the phenomenon of life or that of free agency in terms of the mechanical laws of the physical universe. An alternative metaphysics is not offered to account for either of these; they are taken rather as presuppositions of the process of human history. It therefore does not appear that, in the history of the transformation of savage man into civilized man, we are dealing with an affair restricted, as Starobinski would have it, to men as metaphysically distinct from animals. Savage man is not already 'completely human.' We are instead dealing with the transformation of a non-human animal into a human animal. When Rousseau makes a strict distinction between monkeys and those creatures, the 'Pongo' and the 'Orang-outang,' that he calls 'anthropoformes' (*DI* 211), on the basis of their possibly sharing

---

philosophical tradition and proclaiming an 'end to the Cogito': 'Descartes croit passer directement de l'intériorité d'un homme à l'extériorité du monde, sans voir qu'entre ses deux extrêmes se placent des sociétés, des civilizations, c'est à dire des mondes d'hommes. Rousseau qui, si éloquemment, parle de lui à la troisième personne ... s'affirme le grand inventeur de cette objectivation radicale, quand il definit son but qui est ... "de me rendre compte des modifications de mon âme et de leur succession" ... Ce que Rousseau exprime, par conséquent, c'est – vérité surprenant, bien que la psychologie et l'ethnologie nous l'ait rendue plus familière – qu'il existe un "il" qui se pense en moi, et qui me fait d'abord douter si c'est moi qui pense. Au "que sais-je" de Montaigne (d'ou tout est sorti), Descartes croyait pouvoir répondre que je sais que je suis, puisque je pense; à quoi Rousseau rétorque un "que suis-je?" sans issue certain, pour autant que la question suppose qu'un autre, plus essentielle, ait été résolue: "suis-je?"; et que l'expérience intime ne fournit que cet "il" que Rousseau a découvert et dont il a lucidement entrepris l'exploration' ('J.-J. Rousseau, fondateur,' 242–3). For Lévi-Strauss, however, Rousseau remains the founder of ethnology without being equally a philosopher of history. It is striking that in an article devoted to Rousseau as anthropologist he should make no mention of evolution and temporality. It seems to escape Lévi-Strauss's notice that the 'worlds of men' that Rousseau interposes between the interiority of man and the exteriority of nature is a world of historical, practical activity.

in the quality of perfectibility, he is not reaffirming the metaphysical frontier in spite of thus enlarging the human species. He is merely speculating that the Buffonian species man may still include living representatives of its original variety (or something resembling more closely its original variety). Both modern man and the anthropoformes would be varieties of the more inclusive Buffonian category of species. In the end the test for Rousseau as to whether they are men (same species, different variety) is not whether they demonstrate perfectibility but the Buffonian test of producing hybrids and seeing whether the hybrids would be able to continue reproducing (*DI* 211).

The Presuppositions of Historicity

The product of the resolutive stage of Rousseau's reconstruction of human history, his version of savage man, is, to be sure, an abstraction. It is, however, meant to be utterly unlike the abstractions performed by Hobbes, Locke, and the natural-law school. Their versions of nature stop with essentially civilized men existing outside political society but embedded in highly developed social relations patterned after the market. Rousseau's savage man is truly solitary and an animal. The device of abstracting from existing social relations has also in his hands a different aim. Rousseau's original man is an abstraction not from an essentially static social condition that can be opposed to an equally static nature but from a dynamic process of development. In order to be able to reconstruct the development process logically, Rousseau requires a starting-point that embodies several presuppositions. We have seen that these do not include the assumption of a metaphysical gap between man and animals. Savage man is therefore an animal of a peculiar sort. Like any other he is endowed with drives and desires for the physical necessities of life. He is also equipped with a particular anatomical structure and a sensorium compatible with his self-preservation. Yet in order to assure a human 'species' able to emerge from nature, Rousseau must make further presuppositions. The abstraction that he calls 'l'homme sauvage' is not simply an ideal of freedom and happiness[28] against which the misery and oppression of the social state can be measured. He is also the hypothetically real starting-point of a hypothetically real historical evolution. A further presupposition must follow if savage man, 'dull and stupid,' lazy and

---

28 Many scholars of varying opinions on other aspects of his work – eg, Starobinski, Colletti, Cassirer – in wishing to absolve Rousseau of all 'primitivist error,' see in 'l'homme sauvage' merely an ideal of freedom and happiness rather than also a scientific hypothesis capable of further testing and refinement.

self-sufficient, is to be capable of both accomplishing the transition to a historical existence and undergoing the transformation associated with it.

The further presuppositions required are concerned with the biopsychological structure of the human animal. these peculiarities, which are presuppositions of proto-human and human openness to historical development, also constitute a fateful dimension of the process of real historical development. As we shall see, it is the unique malleability of the human drive that both permits the emergence of a historical existence and constitutes the chief source of the human capacity for psychic misery.

Savage man in *his* mode of existence is, to begin with, virtually indistinguishable from other animals, a variety in whom Rousseau tends to see nothing more than an 'ingenious machine' (*DOI* 169). Animal existence in general is governed by a homeostatic principle. And the equilibrium this principle demands is established through an inherited repertoire of instinctual behaviours. In thus championing the role of instinct in animal behaviour, Rousseau was going against the tendency of sensationalist psychology to make even animals into blank slates, their behaviour governed by the patterned associations of sensory experience.[29] Animals are endowed with a complex of instincts responsible for the preservation of the individual in the species; this is one of the meanings of *amour-de-soi*. And, to the degree to which they are social, animals are endowed with mechanisms for checking the expression of aggression and facilitating identification with their fellows. Savage man shares this

29 Rousseau, *E* 249, n 1: 'Modern philosophy, which only admits what it can understand, is careful not to admit this obscure power called instinct which seems to guide the animals to some end without any acquired experience. Instinct, according to some of our wise philosophers, is only a secret habit of reflection; and from the way in which they explain this development one ought to suppose that children reflect more than grown-up people, a paradox strange enough to be worth examining. Without entering upon this discussion I must ask what name I shall give to the eagerness with which my dog makes war on the moles he does not eat ... no one has trained him to this sport ... Again I ask, and this is a more important question, why, when I threatened this same dog for the first time, why did he throw himself on the ground with his paws folded, in such a suppliant attitude ... a position which he would have maintained if ... I had continued to beat him in that position. By what acquired knowledge did he seek to appease my wrath by yielding to my discretion? Every dog in the world does almost the same thing in similar circumstances, and I am asserting nothing but what any one can verify for himself. Will the philosophers who so scornfully reject instinct, kindly explain this fact by the mere play of sensations and experience, which they assume we have acquired?'

endowment (*DOI* 169). There is thus in every animal, and in the proto-human to begin with, a kind of pre-adaptation of the organism to its environment, a unity of instinct and instinctual aim that underlies the psychological unity of the organism. The proto-human, since he has not dispensed with instinctual forms of self-regulation, can therefore be essentially independent of the other members of his species. At this stage and only at this stage is he truly an atom, and moreover an atom that is fundamentally contented, since the environment offers him immediately (that is, without reflection, labour, co-operation, communication, or the postponement of drive-gratifying behaviour) whatever he is capable of wanting. What he might want is identical to what he is programmed and adapted to pursue. Like all other animals he lives entirely in the here and now: 'His soul, which nothing disturbs, is wholly wrapped up in the feeling of its present existence, without any idea of the future, however near at hand' (*DOI* 172). There is, as it were, no difference between satisfying the demands of reality and pursuing his immediate desires, no distinction between reality principle and pleasure principle, a perfect identity of subject and object, because subject and object do not yet exist.

These qualities, this mode of existence, the proto-human shares with animal life in general. At this stage what separates him from the rest is the degree to which his instincts are 'open' rather than 'closed.'[30] Closed instincts are patterns of behaviour fixed in every detail by genetic programming, so that even an animal reared in total isolation from other members of its species will, in appropriate circumstances, reproduce the complicated behaviours characteristic of that species. Closed instincts are at that end of the continuum of instincts where learning plays no part in development. Learning, for the closed-instinctual structure, is identical with physical maturation. Open instincts, on the other hand, are incompletely determined patterns of behaviour. What is given biologically is a general tendency to certain kinds of behaviour, but a tendency that remains open to various forms of learning dependent on experience. Thus the other animals, which tend to be governed more by closed instinctual patterns, also tend to be fitted more narrowly into a specific ecological niche. In Rousseau's terms:

hence the brute cannot deviate from the rules prescribed to it, even when it would be advantageous for it to do so; and, on the contrary, man frequently deviates from such rules to his own prejudice. Thus a pigeon would be starved to death

30 See Mary Midgley, *Beast and Man: The Roots of Human Nature*, 51ff.

by the side of a dish of the choicest meats, and a cat on a heap of fruit or grain, though it is certain that either might find nourishment ... did it think of trying them. (*DOI* 169-70)

Yet even Rousseau, who, in over-reaction to the sensationalist idea of the blank slate, tends to overplay the role that closed instincts play in animal life, leaves a certain amount of room for animal learning: 'Every animal has ideas since it has senses; it even combines those ideas in a certain degree; and it is only in degree that man differs, in this respect, from the brute' (*DOI* 170).

In the proto-human stage, human free agency is thus severely restricted. It consists, that is, in a greater openness to experience, a capacity to temporarily check the promptings of instinct. At this stage, however, there is little or no occasion or reason for the proto-human animal to rein in the pressure of the biological drives. Nor are the mechanisms that make this checking and transformation of the drives available to him. Thus, although at this stage (which is conceived as the minimal prerequisite to the development of a human and social historical mode of existence) man already 'has some share in his own operations, in his character as a free agent' (*DOI* 179). But freedom from the total rule of the instincts is manifested only in the degree to which proto-human activity is generalized activity. 'Savage man,' whose instinctual structure is relatively open, is restricted in his modes and opportunities of learning to the rudimentary form of mimesis or imitation; he 'would observe and imitate [the] industry [of the other animals] and thus attain even to the instinct of the beasts, whereas every species of brutes was confined to one particular instinct, man who perhaps has not any one peculiar to himself, would appropriate them all' (*DOI* 164).

As a form of learning, mimesis does not depend upon language and the abstract thought language makes possible. Nor is it linked with any high degree of autonomy from the drives themselves. A mimetically learned response to any situation is only the form into which, as it were, the untransformed instinct can freely flow.

Savage man, left by nature solely to the direction of instinct, or ather indemnified for what he may lack by faculties capable at first of supplying its place, and afterwards of raising him much above it, must accordingly begin with purely animal functions: thus seeing and feeling must be his first condition, which would be common to him and all other animals. To will and not to will, to desire and to fear, must be the first, almost the only operations of his soul, til new circumstances occasion new developments of his faculties. (*DOI* 171)

Free agency, in its human rather than its proto-human form, can therefore be seen to be as much a result of socio-historical development as is the rest of the complex of processes that constitute 'human nature.' What is confusing, and has also led to a great deal of confusion in treating Rousseau as a spiritualist, is that free agency is both a condition and a result of the historical process. Yet in its beginning there is nothing supranatural about it. It is used in the second *Discourse* as a concept proper to a philosophical biology[31] and not as a partial or total or final determination of an ahistorical human essence. When Rousseau asserts that this 'power of willing or rather of choosing' is 'inexplicable by the laws of mechanism' (*DOI* 170), he is not asserting the co-existence in human beings of two distinct substances that persist unchanged in the midst of differences in their formation and development. He is simply indicating that biological thought cannot be reduced to the same categories as underlie the physical laws of matter and motion. There are also the important implications that historical and cultural existence has a definite biological ground and that biology therefore cannot be totally neglected in the analysis of particular cultures or phases of historical development, or in the transition from one to another: 'Nature lays her command on every animal, and the brute obeys her voice. Man receives the same impulsion, but at the same time knows himself at liberty to acquiesce or resist, and it is particularly in his *consciousness* of this liberty that the spirituality of his soul is displayed' (*DOI* 170; emphasis added). In its *origins*, however, there is no spirituality since there is no self-consciousness. And self-consciousness is in turn the product of social relations and linguistic communication – it is predicated upon the existence of a symbolic order. It is not spirituality that is the metaphysical ground and origin of conscience and virtue. Rather, spirituality, as the ability and need to delay and modify or negate the 'voice of nature,' is first of all the result of a bio-cultural evolution that, secondly, creates the pre-conditions for the socialization of individuals in such a way as to internalize the laws of the community as conscience. (See especially chapter 6 below.)

Both self-consciousness and conscience presuppose a considerable distance from raw biological need. But *l'homme sauvage* is as yet entirely identified with his desire. He is totally at one with his environment; in every sense he is part of nature. If he engages in any action such

---

31 See the discussion of Helmuth Plessner's use of 'open and closed positionality' as philosophico-biological categories in Marjorie Grene, *Approaches to a Philosophical Biology*, 55–117.

action expresses no distance from either his environment or his desire. 'Action' is merely an automatic device for the restoration of the state of static equilibrium in which nothing is transformed, neither without nor within him. None of his acts leaves any traces; there is no object (neither thing nor person) in which he can recognize himself. If desire for the satisfaction of some simple physical need should rouse him to some activity, the activity performed is a simple, unitary response, unarticulated into means and end and out of which he immediately falls back into the eternal present, a present in which there is no consciousness of the passage of time or of death. Under these circumstances the I cannot arise out of opposition to the It: 'in the true state of nature, egoism [amour-propre] did not exist; for as each man regarded himself as the only observer of his actions, the only being in the universe who took any interest in him, and the sole judge of his deserts, no feeling arising from comparisons he could not be led to make could take root in his soul' (*DOI* 182). Strauss is therefore correct in asserting that it is freedom rather than reason that, at least in his origins, distinguishes man from the other animals. Freedom consists in the biological endowment of a creature with relatively open instincts and therefore possessed of a rudimentary negativity, a rudimentary capacity to oppose himself to things, other 'persons,' to his own drives, to his own past, and to the objectified image of himself he constructs from his interactions with others.

Negativity is the *sine qua non* of both human evolution and the later historical and cultural development with which the former insensibly merges. But in no sense does the free agency that contains negativity constitute an entelechy driving human development forward. Rousseau's theory of human evolution through the development of culture is not a restatement of the problem of teleology in different terms. Evolution and history are not to be understood as the realization of an immanent teleology. Rousseau throughout restricts himself to what Hegel would call the finite-teleological viewpoint.[32] The sole ends and goals recognized are those that belong to finite, sensuous, needy men (or proto-men) acting in definite situations. Because there is no overarching structure of meaning prior to existing men, history, including the history of human evolution,

---

32 See Schmidt, *Nature*, 35–6: 'All goals and purposes arising in reality can be traced to men, acting in accordance with their changing situations. There is no meaning in isolation from these situations. Only where, as in the case of the Hegelian Spirit, the subject is given an infinite, universal extension, can its purposes be simultaneously those of the world itself. For Hegel the "finite-teleological standpoint" was something restricted, to be superseded in the theory of Absolute Spirit.'

cannot be grasped by referring back to a prior principle but must be understood through the analysis of the delimited and particular processes[33] of human interaction with nature in definite social settings. In the beginning, of course, society is absent; but then so is interaction with nature in any meaningful sense. Although the biological prerequisites of historical evolution are present, the impetus for development is not present in them.

Perfectibility and Labour

At the proto-human stage nature is still an undifferentiated whole, a simple unity in which neither subject nor object can be said to have yet appeared. Any transformations that appear within nature at this stage do not constitute an essential rupture in its fabric. Transformations in the biological realm, when they do appear, appear as the result of organic adaptation and do not constitute a qualitative change in the order of beings, only minor modifications and adjustments. The proto-human, however, is biologically predisposed to be able to acquire a different mode of adaptation than the animal. The rudiments of free agency are the grounds of human perfectibility. But perfectibility *per se* is meaningless in a state of static equilibrium. Perfectibility itself is not an abstract quality, although Rousseau refers to it as a 'specific quality' and a 'faculty' (*DOI* 170). Perfectibility does not mean the capacity to achieve an ideal state but refers to the process of self-transformation that occurs when men at first unconsciously and later consciously set out to transform nature. It encompasses broadly speaking two stages: a first stage during which the biological and psychological foundations of culture are laid (a stage of pre-history, as it were) and a second stage during which adaptation

---

33 The fact, therefore, that Rousseau treats evolution and history after such a fashion should be sufficient indication that his deism has a primarily social and pragmatic value. As Marx knew very well, 'the whole of what is called world history is nothing but the creation of man by human labour, and the emergence of nature for man. He therefore has the evident and irrefutable proof of his self-creation, of his own process of origination. Once the essentiality of man and of nature, man as a natural being and nature as a human reality, has become evident in practice, and sensuously, the quest for an alien being, a being above nature and man (a quest which is an avowal of the inessentiality of nature and man) becomes impossible in practice' (*Economic and Philosophic Manuscripts of 1844*, in *Early Writings*, 357). God, for Rousseau, despite his occasional, passing obeisances to the activity of providence (eg, *DOI* 159), plays no part in 'world history'; neither is providence the realization of any transcendent purpose. Belief in God is meaningful as a guarantee of virtue, as a restraint on the rapacity of 'les grands,' and as a personal consolation in the face of misery and death (see eg, *RPS*, 3^e promenade, 1011-23).

is primarily cultural. In this section we are concerned primarily with the first. The second, which merges with it, belongs more appropriately to the discussion of history in later chapters.

In the state of equilibrium that characterizes savage man, perfectibility along with free agency means little more than that man has a slight advantage over the other animals in a greater capacity for learning. Yet even the mimetic form of learning is, like the rest of proto-human activity, essentially a passive relation to the environment. Although proto-men, in the activity of satisfying their desires, take up a position of opposition to their environment, as soon as the pressure of whatever drive they are obeying is reduced, they immediately fall back into a state of rest. Their activity is in essence identical to that of the rest of organic nature. There is no essential opposition to either themselves, external nature, or other 'men.'[34] In keeping with the attempt at a purely naturalistic explanation of human development, Rousseau can only envision the process as in its inception caused by an external interruption of the condition of static equilibrium. The bio-cultural evolution that follows is therefore essentially fortuitous, ungoverned by providence or by the logic inherent in any world-spirit: 'Barren years, long and sharp winters, scorching summers must have demanded *a new industry*' (*DOI* 193; emphasis added). It is worth noting that among the environmental pressures responsible for the process, Rousseau counts relative over-population, a factor of great importance in the Darwinian theory as part of the account of the struggle for existence: 'In proportion as the human race grew more numerous, men's cares increased ... he learnt to surmount the obstacles of nature, to contend in case of necessity with other animals, and to dispute for the means of subsistence even with other men' (*DOI* 193). At the same time Rousseau recognizes the activity of natural selection as an agency of organic transformation: 'Nature in this case treats them exactly as Sparta treated the children of her citizens: those who come well formed into the world she renders strong and robust, and all the rest she destroys' (*DOI* 164). But all the while that organic evolution continues, it is being supplanted by the inception of a new mode of adaptation – culture. In a sense the physical changes that take place

34 Rousseau hints that at an early stage men compared themselves with other animals and acquired pride as the first glimmerings of self-consciousness. It seems that this might even constitute the origins of political domination, since 'by looking upon his species as of the highest order, he prepared the way for assuring preeminence as an individual' (*DOI* 194). But this idealistic version of the grounds of domination is belied by the fact that men already laboured according to definite social relations (193-4).

are those necessary for the emergence of culture. Rousseau has already mentioned erect stature, bipedal locomotion, and implicitly at least the prehensile thumb ('he ... made use of his hands as we do').

The essential distinction, however, between organic evolution and incipient human-cultural evolution is based on the emergence of labour as a distinct forming and transforming force. When Rousseau alludes to a 'new industry' as being called forth by the physical necessity that ruptures the static equilibrium, this is not meant to indicate a quantitative change in energy expended but the birth of a new mode of existence, qualitatively different from the rest of the animal realm.[35] At this stage, however, the social relations in which men labour and oppose themselves to nature are not as important as the fact of production as such. For it is labour or, more properly, social labour that in Rousseau's eyes constitutes the core of the process of humanization. Human phylogenesis is conceived of as impossible without social labour. Society and the *human* being emerge together in a *single* process. The abstract man of the theorists of natural law and the rational subject whose essential expression is the maximization of utilities are therefore concretely demonstrated not to belong to nature but to be the result of a concatenation of social forces in process.

The precise order and logic of the stages of bio-cultural evolution remain 'conditional and hypothetical reasonings.' All we know is that by the time of the 'Golden Age,' the earliest stages of primitive society, 'men' were fully human. The process of bio-cultural evolution is pictured as a long and complex course of interaction among various factors, issuing in a new mode of species existence that can be characterized as historical or cultural evolution. In a real sense perfectibility, which is 'inherent in the species as in the individual' (*DOI* 170), just as much as free agency, is a result more than it is an origin, substantial essence, or end. Human cultural existence, and therefore the possibility of historical development, rest on a number of biological acquisitions, which in turn make possible further biological transformation, and so on. The process in its concrete specificity is not even known to modern anthropology and will certainly

---

35 Ninety years later Marx would adopt a similar point of view in his own historical anthropology. See *The German Ideology*, in *The Marx-Engels Reader*, 114: 'Men can be distinguished from animals by consciousness, by religion or anything else you like. They themselves begin to distinguish themselves from animals as soon as they begin to produce their means of subsistence, a step which is condition by their physical organization. By producing their means of subsistence men are indirectly producing their actual material life.'

always remain largely a matter of informed conjecture. We can only indicate some of the most important factors Rousseau recognizes and some of the relations among them.

One of the most important, if not one of the first of the transformations, is the creation of human language. What is most noteworthy in this connection is that Rousseau establishes a substantial gulf between what he calls 'the first language of mankind' (*DOI* 176) – a combination of auditory signal, 'excited only by a sort of instinct,' gesture, and onomatopoiea – and human language properly so called. Human language is based on the 'articulate sounds of the voice, which, without bearing the same [iconic] relation to any particular ideas, are better calculated to express them all, as conventional signs' (*DOI* 176). The gulf between a naturally given system of signals that recognizes only particular things, events, and states and a system of conventional signs is the gulf between sense-perception and conceptual thought. It is the process of social labour that leads from one to the other. Tool making and co-operative labour, the necessity of an active technical mastery of nature together with others, established both a stable context for meaning and the practice of bringing things into relation. The relation is itself what 'occasions' the concept. Concepts, which in Rousseau's eyes express relations, cannot arise except in the activity of bringing things into relation: 'This repeated relevance of various beings to himself [as a result of the "new industry"], and, one to another, would naturally give rise in the human mind to the perception of certain relations between them. Thus the relations which we denote by the terms great, small, strong, weak, swift, slow ... and the like, almost insensibly compared at need must have at length produced in him a kind of reflection' (*DOI* 193). Human consciousness that takes the unique form of conceptual thought is therefore from the start a product of social labour.[36] Rousseau even goes on in the *Essay on the Origin of Languages* to suggest that particular historical forms of social existence are 'mirrored' in different forms of language, psychology, and cognition.[34]

One of the ways in which the essential connection of labour with perfectibility can be expressed is as an equation of 'enlightenment' (meaning here the ability for conceptual thought) and industry: 'In proportion as they grew enlightened, they grew industrious' (*DOI* 198). Although Rousseau puts his words to indicate the possible priority of the first quality, the sentence can just as well be reversed. The connection between labour and language capable of embodying conceptual thought

---

36 See Schmidt, *Nature*, 109–11.
37 Rousseau, EOL 5–74

receives a further emphasis precisely from the lack of a role assigned to the family in its inception. Both Condillac and the theorists of natural law assumed that the family was natural. But Rousseau opposes the notion that 'language arose in the domestic intercourse between parents and their children' (*DOI* 174). In the first place the two sexes did not remain united long enough for the father even to see the child's birth; in the second place the type of activity relating mother and child could not have been of the proper kind to occasion the growth of any but a language of cries and gestures.

Rousseau goes to some lengths in note 12 to the second *Discourse* to criticize Locke's theory[38] that the naturalness of the family – that is, that men and women are obliged by nature to a longer period of conjugal society – is due to the prolonged dependence of the human infant as a result of neoteny in the human species. Rousseau does recognize the fact of neoteny and prolonged dependence. To a great extent the educational theory of *Emile* (see chapter 8 below) rests upon this foundation. Neoteny and prolonged dependence are, as it were, the obverse of educability and of cultural as opposed to biological adaptation.[39] But the fact of prolonged dependence does not follow, as it seems to for Locke, from nature (in this case from the nature of the carnivors). Neoteny too is a result: 'With respect to children, there are many reasons for believing that their forces and their organs develop later on among us than they did in the primitive condition of which I am speaking' (*DI* 217). Although in its functions the family may be beneficial to mankind, there is no reason to assume, as Locke does, that this means that it is natural (*DI* 215-16).

Locke not only believed that the family was natural but that it was instituted by a wise creator to stimulate human industry. In Rousseau's terms this providential reasoning is the most specious of arguments and means that 'Locke's argument therefore falls to the ground, and all the logic of this philosopher has not secured him from the mistake committed by Hobbes and others' (*DOIC* 255). The crucial question is rather why the male and female would remain together, not after the birth of the

---

38 Locke, *Second Treatise of Government*, in *Two Treatises of Government*, secs. 79-80, p 362-4
39 On the significance of neoteny and prolonged dependence see Grene's discussion of Portmann's work, *Biology*, 42ff; LaBarre, *Human Animal*, 160-1, 258-9. On the crucial importance that Freud attributed to both factors see G. Horowitz, *Repression*, 20-1: 'Freud often stated that the ultimate cause of neurosis is to be found in the extreme helplessness and protracted dependence of human children as compared with the young of animals.'

child but after it was conceived. It is much more likely that after the period of gestation they would not even recognize each other (*DI* 217). The conjugal bond therefore presupposes the development of a peculiarly human form of sexuality. Humans are unique in not having, like the other animals, 'their stated times of passion and indifference' (*DOI* 187).[40] But human sexuality is not a simple natural given, for *l'homme sauvage* did not suffer the 'moral ingredients in the feeling of love' (*DOI* 186). Human sexuality is open and malleable sexuality. It depends essentially on these 'moral ingredients' to lend it that 'glowing impetuosity' that arises with society.[41] The frequency of social contacts, which might arise from the necessity of co-operative labour, does not immediately give rise to a malleable sexuality. It rather finds itself the intermediate result of society by way of the moral ingredients that arise with language, conceptual thinking, and imagination. These are in turn dependent upon the emergence of labour, which presupposes and expresses the active, negative stance in relation to nature, the stance that relates all entities and in a very real sense constitutes them as instances of symbolic structures of meaning.

Society is not, then, the creature of the family. If anything, the reverse is true; the family is the creature of society. And the family is conceived of as the creature of society in much more than a juridical sense. The transition to a symbolic mode of existence issues in a gradual alteration of biological desire. In place of a seasonal urge that embodies no meaning for the 'savage,' human sexuality is extended in scope by virtue of its being affected, extended, and transformed by symbolization. Whereas savage man finds that 'every woman equally answers his purpose,' the human cannot choose without expressing ideas of 'beauty and merit.' Human sexuality emerges out of a process (and becomes part of that process) that establishes a decisive change in the human bio-psychological constitution. In place of the earlier identity of relatively open instinct and adaptive behaviour that characterizes savage man, human beings exhibit malleable drives organized and modified by cultural systems of meaning. The consequence of the acquisition of culture is that the biological drives no longer constitute a hermetically distinct sphere. Biological nature is itself now essentially modified by culture. Rousseau puts the distinction in terms of the differentiation in the human of what

---

40 Rousseau, *DOI* 187: 'in the human species ... love is thus not seasonal.'
41 On the role of non-seasonal sexuality in the emergence of the species see LaBarre, *Human Animal*, 44-6, 120-5.

was previously a purely 'instinctual' organization into a 'physical' (read biological) and a 'moral' (read cultural or symbolic) dimension, a differentiation that applies not only to sexual desire but to 'all the other passions' as well: 'The physical part of love is that *general desire* which urges the sexes to union with each other. The moral part is that which *determines and fixes this desire* exclusively upon one particular object; or at least *gives it a greater degree of energy toward the object* thus preferred' (DOI 186; emphasis added). Thus *human* aims and objects are no longer biologically given, although they do have the force of biological desire. What allows the energy of the general desire to be fixed and determined is the acquisition of the symbolic function, which is simultaneously the cause of the desire's generality.

For Rousseau the general energy of desire can be displaced from object to object and from aim to aim through the operation of the imagination, which 'never speaks to the heart of savages' (DOI 186). And the faculty of imagination is in turn conditional upon the acquisition of language, the articulation of the world into entities defined by the relations discovered or produced in the course of the social negation of nature. Henceforward the passions cannot be considered to be solely the work of nature but are suffused by the distinctively human form of cognition: 'The human understanding is greatly indebted to the passions, which ... are also much indebted to the understanding ... The passions ... originate in our wants and their progress depends on that of our knowledge; for we cannot desire or fear anything, except from the idea we have of it, or from the simple impulse of nature' (DOI 171). And it should be understood that when Rousseau refers to the understanding, he does not include only conceptual thought but also the work of the imagination. Imagination thus ensures both that the human drives are open to the moulding influences of culture and that the drives are in a continual process of transformation. 'Everything is in constant flux on this earth. Nothing keeps the same unchanging shape, and our affections, that are attached to things outside us, necessarily change and pass away as they do' (RW 88).[42] The malleability of the passions is therefore both a result of historical activity (social labour) and a precondition of history properly so called. History includes, in a sense, the course of the vicissitudes of desire under the various social forms of the organization of labour.

---

42 See also RPS 1085: 'Tout est sur la terre dans un flux continuel qui ne permet a rien d'y prendre une forme constante. Tout change autour de nous. Nous changeons nous-mêmes et nul ne peut assurer qu'il aimera demain ce qu'il aime aujourd'hui.'

From Anthropology to History

Perfectibility, which among other things refers to a biological openness to the acquisition of culture, is not, as it turns out, an abstract quality inhering in a substance by virtue of its essence. Nor does Rousseau use the concept to refer human history back to a supposed origin in a hypostatized abstraction. The concept of perfectibility comprises, in its anthropological sense, a number of interlocking factors describing an open-ended process. To recapitulate, these factors include labour, the acquisition of language, neoteny and its obverse of prolonged infantile dependence, non-seasonal sexuality and the family, and the substitution of culturally malleable drives for the instinctual structure of ecologically restricted animals. If any factor is of primary importance in the inception and continuation of this process it is the necessity that men face to undertake labour in co-operative relations. If there is any preconception, it is that of an animal capable of evolving to the point where cultural and historical development takes the place of organic evolution as the mode of response to environmental change. But human history, although it presupposes an emergence from nature, does not, as Rousseau envisions it, do away with the necessity embodied in nature. Human history as opposed to pre-history will reproduce a blind, quasi-natural necessity in its own sphere. Also, and in a different sense, nature is preserved as desire that cannot be integrated into the cultural order.

The general conception of nature among the thinkers of the Enlightenment and the theorists of classical liberalism was embodied in the idea of phenomena governed by abstract universal laws. This view of nature was also applied to human nature, which was therefore conceived of as static, fixed, sealed off from any essential transformation. This was supposed to be true of human nature whether what was referred to was the sensuous, bodily, affective, desirous dimension, a with the materialists and utilitarians, or the cognitive, rational, moral dimension, as with the theorists of natural law. Even for Locke and those who followed him, the discovery that reason had a history determined by experience did little to shake the belief in its ability to discover universal laws of nature in the ethical domain suited to the needs of a sensuous and desiring creature. Nature itself was taken to be immediately accessible to experience as long as it remained untainted by the inheritance of the artificial, 'metaphysical' contrivances of the old order. The problem of politics was thought to be in principle reducible to the same experientially based knowledge of human nature. The laws of nature when revealed would give the lie to the irrational artifice of the *ancien régime*. The problem of politics *was* the problem of liberating nature.

Rousseau's essential discovery was aimed at transforming the entire program of the Enlightenment. Agreeing that the central problems of politics require an understanding of human nature, he disagrees with all the rest: the identification on the one hand of human nature with reason, according to which men were endowed with social instincts; the equation on the other of human nature, with abstract and general laws arrived at inductively; and the opposition of nature and artifice. His attempt at 'reducing the question to its proper form' (*DOI* 155) rather collapses the distinction between nature and artifice, upon which the political thought of the epoch rests, into a conception of nature as the history of artifice. In this history man is his own artificer, even to the extent that he creates himself as a species. Human nature, which cannot be identified with the logic of abstract body or abstract thought, or with either biology or culture, is therefore not something fixed or static; nor does it appear whole, either at the origin of the historical process or as an abstract end transcending it. Human nature is, rather, constituted in historical activity, primarily in the social process of labour, as praxis. To understand human nature it is necessary to understand the variety of human social formations,[43] the forms in which men undertake to transform external nature. 'It is in fact easy to see that many of the differences which distinguish men are merely the effect of habit and *the different methods of life men adopt in society*' (*DOI* 188; emphasis added).

43 Goldschmidt, *Anthropologie*, 779-80, agrees with Lévi-Strauss (see chap. 3, n 30 above) in stressing the power and indepenence that social formations exercise and hold over human beings: 'Rousseau a découvert la contrainte social, le rapport (ou relation social), enfin la vie et le développement autonomes de ces structures ... c'est à dire leur indépendance à l'egard des individus et, correlativement, la totale dépendance de ces mêmes individus à l'égard de ces structures, auxquelles ils sont forcés de soumettre, contrairement à leur intention personelle.' Goldschmidt goes on to stress, though, that the centre of Rousseau's thought is not the functioning of systems of social relations but their impact on the conscience of individuals and the depravation they provoke (781). And he even recognizes that one of the ways Rousseau proposes to lift the contradiction between man and society is to continue to develop society's structures. But this implies that for Rousseau, at least, there is a potential independence of individuals from the social forces rooted in their activities. Although this would seemingly contradict his earlier insistence upon the total dependence of individuals on these structures, Goldschmidt draws attention to the 'rigorous analogy' that he believes exists between the efforts to join man and citizen and the effort to join existentialism and Marxism in Jean-Paul Sartre's later philosophy (782). Cf G. Lapassade, 'Sartre et Rousseau.'

It is also to understand the vicissitudes that human drives undergo as they are affected by various modes of the social labour process. The inquiry into human nature can therefore not stop with anthropology. Anthropology is the necessary foundation for and propaedeutic to a philosophical inquiry into history. But with the discovery that nature is constituted in historical activity, anthropology must pass over into an examination of the historical process itself.

It does not therefore seem unwarranted to assert that in grasping a historical anthropology as the self-constitution of human nature in the social process of labour, Rousseau surpasses not only the social philosophy of seventeenth- and eighteenth-century liberalism but even in some respects the historico-philosophical insights of German idealism. Unlike the natural-right thinkers Rousseau succeeds in not establishing society as an abstraction in opposition to the individual. This goes far beyond the views usually attributed to him – either that men are born good and corrupted only by false social institutions, or that there is an inescapable contradiction between individual and society. His aping of the social-contract versions of the inception of civil society has for too long obscured attention to his breakthrough. The genetic analysis of human nature is in reality an analytic description of a process of phylogenetic humanization predicated upon socialization. Society and the human being are constituted in a single process that is only remotely analogous to the association of atomized individuals. For Rousseau, individuals are already social beings.[44] Unlike the German idealists he understands history not as the activity of an absolute subject but as the product of men who are objective, sensuous, suffering beings. These men are not to be equated with the passivity of nature, but in confronting the necessity to labour, they emerge as an independent transforming force.

In order to understand the transformation that Rousseau effected in the status of the human subject, it is useful to compare his genetic analysis of human history in the second *Discourse* with Condillac's genetic analysis of cognition.[45] Between the two there is an important parallel and an even more important difference. Condillac had criticized Locke for not extending the 'plain historical method' to what the latter had termed 'ideas of reflection' – the operations of comparing, judging, willing, and

44 Rousseau might have asserted along with Marx that the 'individual is the social being. His vital expression – even when it does not appear in the distinct form of a *communal* expression, conceived in association with other men – is therefore an expression and confirmation of social life. Man's individual and species life are not two *distinct things*' (in *Economic and Philosophic Manuscripts, Early Writings*, 350).
45 On Condillac see esp. Cassirer, *Enlightenment*, 100–4, 117–18.

so on – and undertook to demonstrate that all ideas were explicable in terms of sensation. He did not reduce these operations to sensation, although by referring to reflection as 'transformed sensation' he might seem to have suggested as much. Condillac's real innovation lay, however, in turning away from analysis of the mind as a merely contemplative, theoretical organ. Instead, he sought to demonstrate that the mind develops its various forms and powers in an uninterrupted interaction with the external world. That which guides the mind in its development is not, as it was for Locke, simply the idea of a future good, but rather an 'uneasiness' that has all the power of biological need. For Condillac 'inquiétude' is not merely the occasion for the development of the higher mental faculties and the motive power behind the will, as it was with Locke; it actively guides both the formation and subsequent movement of even the highest and most abstract acts of reflection. Thus it is not the mechanical association of ideas that underlies the various faculties but the attractive power of desire: 'The logical order of our ideas ... is not a primary but a derived fact; it is only a sort of reflection of the biological order. What on a given occasion seems to be essential, depends not so much on the nature of things as on the direction of our interest; and our interest is determined by that which is advantageous for us and necessary for our self-preservation.'[46] Thus for Condillac the essence of mind can no longer be thought of simply as thought. Nor can the mind be conceived of as primarily a passive, theoretical organ. The mind develops out of its own practical relation with an external world that is experienced primarily as need and privation.

Obviously Rousseau's *Discourse on the Origins of Inequality* can be seen to be deeply indebted to Condillac's genetic analysis of cognition. Rousseau also emphasizes the emergence of reflection and abstract ideas out of a process of interaction with the external world. There is an attempt to do for the species what Condillac had undertaken for the abstract subject of cognition. But it is precisely in the substitution of the species for yet another variety of the abstraction Man that Rousseau paradoxically departs from the abstract idea of nature still expressed in Condillac's biological voluntarism. The key to this departure lies in Rousseau's idea that the emergence of the species can only be conceived of as a process of social labour. In Condillac's account of mental development the subject remains essentially both passive and isolated, ultimately determined by the given nature of biological desire in even his highest and most human capacities. But when the anthropogenetic process is analysed in terms

---

46 Ibid., 104

of human social labour, men can be seen to take an active part in the formation of internal and external nature, for labour presupposes a conscious opposition to and distance from both the object of activity and the activity itself. For Condillac the primary mode of practical interaction of the subject and the external world remains sensation. Reflective operations arise because the world does not immediately coincide with desire. In Rousseau's account, however, the introduction of labour as the primary mode of practical interaction is not abstracted away. Thus human cognition and the malleability of desire are both essentially dependent on the emergence of labour. The connection between cognition and labour is perhaps seen most directly in Rousseau's account of language. It will be recalled that for Rousseau language can only arise in the labour process since it is only labour that actively brings things into relations that cannot be expressed as signals. Labour transforms desire in two ways. In the first place, the necessity to labour requires that biological desire give way to foresight and reflection. Although for savage man there is a coincidence of pleasure principle and reality principle, the human must delay and arrest the drive for gratification and learn to substitute rationality for direct instinctual gratification. Secondly, the same process of cognitive transformation that produces language together with the necessity of delayed gratification accounts for the malleability of human drives. In learning, the drive is not abolished; its force is rather transferred more or less imperfectly to new aims and objects, aims and objects that can only arise as a result of transformed cognitive processes. It is important to emphasize that, while the force of desire is not abolished, desire may be substantially transformed. Cognitive development remains for Condillac essentially what it was for Locke, an instrument of the will; his innovation lay in reducing the will to 'inquiétude' and then assigning the direction of the mind via the will to this prior and primary level, which remains fixed and static. He was thus unable to go beyond the general conception of nature held by the Enlightenment as an abstract entity existing outside history.

By contrast, Rousseau with his conception of humanity as biologically formed to be the cultural animal (and, obversely, culturally formed to be biologically 'unfinished') transcends both the fundamental biologism of Condillac and the unqualified culturalism of some of the other empiricists. Rousseau's essential modification with respect to Condillac is thus not a reversion to Cartesian spiritualism but the demonstration that the human subject cannot be identified with biology. The drives are modified and transformed in human culture, in the necessity of labour, which drives an immovable wedge between biological need and its expression. With respect to the empiricists, however, Rousseau effectively denies that the human subject is a *tabula rasa*, to be wholly identified with the cultural order. In fact, this can be seen as the main significance of *l'homme sauvage* in the second *Discourse*. Savage man refers not only to the Buffonian species, of which civilized man is a descendant and a variety, but to a certain biological core in human nature 'which your education and habits may have deparved, but cannot have entirely destroyed' (*DOI* 162). Cultural transformation is therefore limited in the species and in the individual by the dependence of the mind on bodily desire. In the *human* being, the social being, there is an eternal tension between biology and culture, between bodily desire and its modes of expression and satisfaction. Nature is therefore something that lives on in history just as history is the dialectical unfolding of human nature.

CHAPTER FOUR

Anthropology as History: Pre-modern Social Forms

> Why should not the historic childhood of humanity,
> its most beautiful unfolding, as a stage never to return,
> exercise an eternal charm?
> Marx, *Grundrisse*

The Problem in Its Setting

In the preceding chapter I attempted to demonstrate that Rousseau developed a theory of human evolution as the creation of a cultural, superorganic realm in the social process of labour. This theory of human nature in terms of 'perfectibility' served, moreover, as the figurative elaboration of a historical anthropology. For Rousseau any adequate or correct account of political life would demand such a theory as an essential pre-condition. Yet this form of philosophical anthropology must necessarily remain incomplete. Since human nature is not an abstract, pre-existing datum of either experience or reason[1] but is constituted in proto-

---

[1] It is possible, however, that inner experience could render the active role of consciousness immediately present to consciousness itself. See R. Derathé, *Rationalisme*, 67–71; according to Derathé, Rousseau borrowed from Malebranche the theory that 'interior feeling' gives access to knowledge about the soul. The ideas gained in this way lack the clarity and distinctness of Cartesian ideas but still render a certain, though imperfect knowledge of areas inaccessible to Cartesian reason. For Derathé, however, Rousseau remains a 'spiritualist' after Descartes and even Plato. But the awareness of consciousness of its own freedom by means of this interior feeling would not, in my opinion, necessarily contradict either the rational hypothesis predicating freedom (or negativity)

human and human historical activity, philosophical anthropology cannot give rise immediately to a theory of the state and political life. These can be understood only as they are themselves constituted in history. Politics and theories of politics are now to be understood through their roles in the historical process itself. A historical anthropology that places at its centre an idea of history as self-constitutive practical activity would seem to invite a theory of historical development.

As is well known, there is no single work of Rousseau's that attempts the elaboration of such a theory. The one work that comes closest to this is, of course, the *Discourse on the Origins of Inequality*. In that essay there is a sketch of what seems to be a more or less orderly progression of social forms, from the primitive up to contemporary European civilization. Yet types are not clearly delineated and relative chronology is at best vague – as, for example, in the relation of the cycle of forms of government to the development of bourgeois society. More important, the entire description and analysis of world history is subordinated to the polemical purposes of contrasting unfavourably the life of civilized man with that of primitive man and savage man and to the negative task of invalidating the equation between nature and inequality. And nowhere outside the second *Discourse* does it seem important to Rousseau to offer an explicit theory of the development of human nature as the history of distinct social formations.

There is thus a paradox (or at least an obvious difficulty) at the heart of Rousseau's work, a paradox that surfaces when the second *Discourse* is brought into relation with his other writings. This paradox lies at the centre of nearly every important treatment of Rousseau's work as a whole. Rousseau is a historical thinker who seems to place a low priority on the empirical investigation of the substantial differences between specific historical forms of social organization.[2] Although his anthropology would help to make it impossible for later theorists to resort to the analytic fiction of a state of nature, what seems like the obvious next step to us, an attempt to construct a comprehensive theory of historical development, is absent. The general characterization of Rousseau's work

---

as a necessary postulate of the emergence of history from nature, or the notion that freedom is also a result of natural evolution.

2 Thus Judith Shklar, *Men and Citizens*, takes Rousseau to be a purely utopian thinker with no interest in historical investigations, while at the other pole David Cameron recognizes that Rousseau 'included as a constitutive element of human nature the operation of social relationships extended over time' (*Social Thought*, 82) and that what is important is his 'explanatory insight ... not [his] historical knowledge as such, nor ... images of the past' (83).

is dependent upon how the interpreter relates the notion of the indeterminacy of human nature to this relative absence of social typology and of a theory of historical development. The essential meaning of Rousseau's project will always be defined in the attempt to manage this paradox on the part of the interpreter. And there are in practice as many specific ways of managing this gap as there are interpretations of Rousseau's writings. Nevertheless, underlying the plethora of different interpretations there seems to be a basic choice.

Either Rousseau's theory of history is treated as a secular version of the Fall, or else his work is understood as a kind of neo-Aristotelianism in which politics is given primacy. Sometimes the two sides are presented as existing side by side in an uneasy tension. In the first case the management of the paradox generates an interpretation of Rousseau as a utopian thinker, as anti-historical (negating negativity, as it were). His thought is grasped as a more or less interesting, sophisticated, or damnable search after transcendence as unity, immediacy, authenticity, or innocence. Transparency, autarky, and intimacy could easily be added to the list. The contrast between successive historical forms pales in significance and tends to disappear beside the overwhelming contrast between society as such (the realm of artifice, appearance, dissimulation, guilt, or sin) and nature (the realm of truth, immediacy, innocence, transparency, happiness). Rousseau's political thought is understood (and most likely rejected) as a fundamentally chiliastic misapprehension of the nature of politics, social life, and human psychology. Rousseau's politics are seen as one form, or *the* form, of the secularized quest for divine absolution and grace.[3]

In the second case, the management of the paradox generates an interpretation that tends to deny the existence of the paradox in the first

---

[3] The most successful and interesting interpretation along these lines is by Jean Starobinski, *Transparence*; see also Judith Shklar, *Men and Citizens*, esp. 2. On Rousseau as a specific type of utopian, see Frank E. Manuel, 'A Dream of Eupsychia.' For Marshall Berman, Rousseau's quest is for the social form of personal authenticity (*Authenticity*); for Pierre Burgelin, Rousseau's opus is an existentialist philosophy outlining the experiential dialectic fulfilled in a religious sense of wholeness (*Existence*). Lionel Gossman, 'Time and History,' sees his fundamental project as the doomed transcendence of time, and in his 'Art of Confession,' esp. 73, the rejection of individuation. Even Leo Strauss, *Natural Right*, who sees in Rousseau the beginnings of the modern reliance on history as the vehicle of human emancipation, thinks Rousseau's final word is the transcendence of history in love and art (see esp. 290-3); in this, Strauss agrees with Hannah Arendt, for whom Rousseau is an anti-political thinker striving after 'intimacy' (*The Human Condition*, 38-9).

place. These sorts of interpretation also take up Rousseau's problem of history as the problem of evil. Rousseau's anthropology is here seen as recognition of the mere indeterminacy or plasticity of human nature. Human nature is not responsible for political and social evil, but specific social forms are. His solution to the problem of evil (which by the way constitutes a theodicy) therefore lies in a political transformation, for which the *Social Contract* provides the model. The *Social Contract* represents the realization of the ethical role of the state or perhaps the institution of pure democracy.[4] In any case the problem of social forms and historical development is rendered quite secondary, in so far as it seems that Rousseau has stumbled upon a more or less adequate solution to the problem of evil. Since history as such is not problematical, the need to elaborate a theory of historical development can be seen as a minor tributary to his thought.

The central thrust of interpretation in both cases tends to withdraw attention from the implicit models of the historical forms of society that underlie much of Rousseau's work.[5] The decision may have been made too quickly to consider Rousseau a merely transitional figure in our general understanding of the replacement of the Renaissance and post-Renaissance static view of human nature by a dynamic, historical, and social view. To be labelled a transitional figure is, of course, all too often to be relegated to the dustbin of history. Although it is true that Rousseau does not explicitly develop a formal theory of historical development through successive distinct stages, it is none the less possible to detect the presence of implicit models of dynamic social forms in Rousseau's writings. Once these are brought into view, his grasp of history begins to reveal a complex dialectical structure; it begins to form a pattern aimed at supplanting the philosophy of history of the Enlightenment without retreating from all the achievements of enlightenment. At this point, however, the full meaning of Rousseau's anti-Enlightenment philosophy of history cannot simply be stated formulaically. To attempt to reconstruct

---

4 Such interpretations represent a somewhat older orthodoxy than the one represented in n 3 above. See, eg, Barker, *Political Thought*; Colletti, *From Rousseau to Lenin*; Cobban, *Modern State*.

5 The only real but partial exceptions are Colletti, *From Rousseau to Lenin* (but the only form dealt with is bourgeois society, and Rousseau's purely political response to it); to a lesser extent Strauss, *Natural Right* (but in his eyes Rousseau's work follows a trajectory that eventually abandons historical solutions); and Gossman, 'Time and History' (who chooses not to deal with the history of society, perhaps as a result of a tendency to collapse temporality and historicity).

Rousseau's dialectic of social formations is one of the main tasks of the remainder of this essay.

Two caveats, however, are now in order. First, it should be stressed at the outset that this interpretation is not meant absolutely to deny validity to either of the two types of interpretation mentioned above. It seeks only to deny either of them exclusive validity and to grant to both a partial validity. In other words, it is my belief that Rousseau's thought arrives at a synthetic resolution of both themes – history as such is the irreducible source of human suffering and evil *and* there is the possibility in principle of a political, historical transcendence of at least the worst aspects of human historical degradation. It is too often the case that interpretations of Rousseau are constructed upon *a priori* critiques that are off target or that fail to notice his own self-corrections.[6]

Secondly, although it is my contention that Rousseau in the course of his writing implicitly develops a typology of social forms and that their temporal succession suggests a larger pattern in history, this does not mean that he ever arrives at a full-blown theory, in the scientific or philosophical senses, of historical development. The reasons for this remain indeterminable. The elements of a theory of historical development are present none the less in what he does achieve – that is, a shift in theoretical orientation.

Throughout practically all of Rousseau's non-'literary' writings there is an awareness of human history as articulated into distinct socioeconomic forms. Rousseau in fact recognized at least three such forms as successive, internally contradictory, and therefore unstable and incomplete realizations of human freedom and happiness. These can be termed primitive society, traditional or pre-capitalist society, and bourgeois or civil society properly so called. These are not for Rousseau necessary stages of historical development through which each society must pass, nor are they as ideal types necessarily to be equated with any concrete historical instances. Thus both Rome and Sparta are drawn upon as exemplars of qualities properly belonging to the second type, even though the Roman Republic already shows qualities belonging to the third. Each of these types represents a coherent whole in which the various social spheres such as law, politics, economics, culture, and psychology display logical relations internally and with respect to one another.

---

6 A useful illustration of this point would be a comparison of Talmon, *Origins*, and Crocker, *Rousseau's Social Contract*, with Cobban, *Modern State*. Such a comparison leads quickly to the conclusion that at least in the former cases Rousseau is being used primarily as the instantiation of some particular bogey.

Primitive Society

Both of the pre-modern social forms that Rousseau takes some pains to distinguish share an overriding negative similarity in not being structured as a 'system of needs' (see below, chapter 5). Likewise, in both the individual has not yet been separated from his natural basis in the community. They are therefore pre-contractual: their members do not conceive themselves in their immediate, 'natural' existence to be the points of origin of either society or the state. Yet both represent for Rousseau forms of individuality in many ways more genuine than that which is the inevitable product of civil society.

What immediately separates the primitive from all subsequent forms of society is the absence of a separation between social life and politics, between society and the state. The 'abuses' of the state are in Rousseau's opinion inherent in its institution: 'this is the consequence of an undue separation of two inseparable things, the body which governs and the body which is governed. In their primitive constitution, these two bodies are but one; they become separate only through the abuse of that constitution' (CAC 277).[7] Primitive society is *in this respect* a unity that has not yet undergone any differentiation; the tension between man and citizen has not yet been felt. None the less the unity of primitive society is not the simple unity of nature.

Primitive society already exhibits an internal differentiation, first of all in that it is a 'state of war.' The absence of the state is the absence of any specialized institution monopolizing the use of force and enforcing order. In its absence the appeal to force devolves upon individuals and less inclusive units of social organization.[8] There is a wide sphere for the expression of particular purposes and aims, and thus an inevitable clash of individual wills. At the same time social relations do not or only rarely degenerate into actual physical conflict. 'These barbaric times were a golden age, not because men were united, but because they were separated ... A state of war prevailed universally and the entire earth was at peace' (EOL 33). Although absolute separation and absolute peace belong to the pre-human savage (in so far as they can belong to any living being), primitive society is in actuality peaceful because of the nature of the conflicts generated and the means found for their resolution.

---

7 Modified trans., see also PC 901: 'Toutes choses ont leur abus souvent nécessaires et ceux des établissemens politiques sont si voisins de leur institution que ce n'est presque pas la peine de la faire pour la voir si vite degenerer.'
8 On the differentiation of the primitive from civilization on the basis of the presence or absence of the state, see Marshall Sahlins, *Tribesmen*, 5ff.

The bourgeois state is understood as a function of the conflicts of civil society. Its emergence, through contract, as an entity over and above, yet epitomizing, civil society, is predicated upon universal competition and the incipient struggle of opposing economic groups. This social struggle in turn follows from the structure of social relations as a universal network of instrumental reciprocity among putatively free and equal property owners, from social relations as a *system* of needs. The need generated by this economic system is inherently unlimited; and this is not an accidental property of the system but an essential one. At the psychological level the economic system of needs is reflected in the peculiar form of the *amour-propre* of its members – an egoism that is the dialectical obverse of the abstract equality of its members.

Primitive society, however, already includes the development of *amour-propre*, a wish for recognition that is coeval with a human and social existence and is therefore trans-historical.[9] At the same time need in primitive society is not frozen at the level of simple 'natural' necessity. The idea that Rousseau held that true needs are defined by physical necessity while social needs are artificial and therefore false is one of those oversimplifying misperceptions to which Rousseau is susceptible not simply through the fault of his readers. Hegel, for example, stated the case against the idea of Rousseauan 'natural need' in terms that Rousseau could have happily borrowed:

The idea has been advanced that in respect of his needs man lived in freedom in the so-called state of nature when his needs were supposed to be confined to what are known as the simple necessities of nature ... This view takes no account of the moment of liberation intrinsic to work. Apart from this, it is false because to be confined to mere physical needs as such and their direct satisfaction would simply be the condition in which the mental is plunged in the natural and so would be one of savagery and unfreedom, while freedom itself is to be found only in the reflection of mind into itself, in mind's distinction from nature, and in the reflex of mind in nature.[10]

Rousseau does indeed recognize the liberating moment in work; he in fact attributed to it the process of humanization itself. Hegel, taking Rousseau to be essentially a contract theorist, saw *l'homme sauvage* as being already a fully human being rather than a proto-human animal.

---

9 That *amour-propre* is trans-historical is clear from Rousseau's treatment of it in the *Discourse on Inequality*, (DOI 182, n 2); it also follows from the relation between society and the existence of conceptual thought.
10 Hegel, *Philosophy of Right*, sec. 194, p 128

What is more, Hegel fails to realize that the restriction of savage man to purely physical need is connected directly by Rousseau not with the *freedom* of the proto-human, since his freedom consists in his not being subjected to the will of another (or in fact sensitive to will at all), but to his *happiness*. The prototype of happiness (not the human or ideal form) is pure instinctual self-regulation, a form of existence in which the separation of subject and object has not yet taken place. Of course, indirectly, the giving way of physical need to culturally constituted need is a condition of unfreedom, but only in so far as particular cultural *forms* of both production and need require the subjection of the individual.

Primitive society, therefore, knows both needs not limited by nature and a certain form of 'competition.' Primitive man, as a fully human being (in the anthropological sense, if not the ontological), no longer lives a life that can be described in purely 'physical' terms. All his needs are expressions of desire symbolically displaced in and by cultural systems of meaning. What is conspicuous about primitive society is specifically its form of competition, its form of production, and its form of social solidarity. These combine to make the primitive condition 'the happiest and most stable of epochs ... the very best man could experience' (*DOI* 198-9). It is worth noting that primitive society, in so far as it represents an ideal, represents an ideal of happiness and not of freedom.

Competition in primitive society as in civil society is an outgrowth of the desire for recognition of *amour-propre*, the need for self-esteem found in the evaluation of oneself by others. Rousseau pictures this as coextensive with the intellectual faculty, and therefore with humanity as such: 'men began now to take the difference between objects into account, and to make comparisons; they acquired imperceptibly the ideas of beauty and merit, which soon gave rise to feelings of preference' (*DOI* 197). For Rousseau the concept is a relation, and a relation is always comparative. It seems to follow that self-consciousness, along with the concept of self, is likewise a comparative relation. In the psychological sphere this existential mode is experienced as a violent disruption of the primitive unity of self and other characteristic of a purely biological existence. In a way, therefore, *amour-propre* is a cultural substitute aimed fundamentally at *restoring* the condition of *amour-de-soi*, understood as the simple 'sentiment of existence'; it is an urgent attempt to draw from the other the conditions of unity. Yet it is impossible to restore the original unity, and *amour-propre* is forced to settle on appropriating the signs that represent recognition. These signs of recognition are conditions of self-esteem, which in turn is a fundamental condition of human happiness. At the same time the regulation of self-esteem is the crucial mechanism for forming and controlling social behaviour.

Competition in primitive society is a struggle for certain signs of recognition; but the way this struggle is carried out is simultaneously a form of social control and one that prevents the struggle for recognition from becoming a struggle for systematic domination:

> They accustomed themselves to assemble before their huts round a large tree; singing and dancing, the true offspring of love and leisure, became the amusement, or rather the occupation, of men and women thus assembled with nothing else to do. Each one began to consider the rest and to wish to be considered in turn; and thus a value came to be attached to public esteem. Whoever sang or danced best, whoever was the handsomest, the strongest, the most dexterous or the most eloquent, came to be of most consideration; and this was the first step towards inequality and at the same time towards vice ... these first distinctions ... ended by producing combinations fatal to innocence and happiness. (DOI 197)

Competition is, in primitive society, directly for public esteem, for the direct and personal recognition of qualities of personal excellence. This is what also makes for the limitation of the struggle. It is not yet the impersonal market that rewards and punishes, nor is the competitor driving in the economic struggle always to strive for pre-eminence. Since the prize is public esteem, the system of public esteem, embodying the code of common values, is clearly in a position to limit and socialize competition itself. Moreover, the avenues of esteem are open wide since, in the absence of economic struggle, values are not reduced to a single abstract common denominator but recognized as intrinsic to the full range of human expression; singing, dancing, beauty, strength, skill, eloquence are the qualities mentioned, but the list could be extended indefinitely.

In the *Constitutional Project for Corsica* Rousseau divides *amour-propre* as a form of social expression into two branches, 'pride' and 'vanity.'[11] Vanity is individual and attaches itself to objects of no intrinsic value. Money would be such a thing, because it is at two removes from nature – as a sign of a sign, a sign of a personal quality that is in turn a sign of personal worth. Thus vanity, or the striving for recognition inside a system of exchange relations, need not depend on the cultivation of personal qualities of direct services to the community. Production for exchange cultivates money-seeking accumulators rather than communal individuals; it develops skills for making money and is thus a

---

11 See Rousseau, PC 937-8, for the relation between 'pride' and 'vanity' as twin aspects of *amour-propre*.

one-sided limitation of the cultivation of the human powers of the individual. At the same time it instrumentalizes the relation between the individual and all the others (who can no longer be called a community, or in Rousseau's terms a 'nation') and separates communal life from individual activity. The shadow of communal life comes to rest in the state.

Pride, however, involves seeking recognition in the possession of qualities of intrinsic worth. It is therefore suitable to the creation of a nation or community, since these qualities are recognized only when put in the service of others. Communal life is a direct expression of individual powers, while the expression of individual powers would be meaningless outside of the community. Communal life and individual expression are therefore conditions of each other when a nation is ruled by the principle of pride.

If competition or the struggle for recognition can be integrated into the life of a primitive community, if in fact in this way competition can become a direct mode of social integration, this should not give the impression that primitive society is given up to competition. For one thing, peace is promoted in primitive society by the existence of a communal economy under which no individual can be deprived of the necessary means of life.[12] In primitive society 'the fruits of the earth belong to us all, and the earth itself to nobody' (*DOI* 192). The first part of the above citation is especially striking in recognizing the sphere of generalized reciprocity[13] that exists in primitive society.

Rousseau is here clearly not enunciating a Lockean view of property, since according to Locke it would be absurd to recognize not only the earth but its fruits as belonging 'to us all.'[14] In Locke's state of nature labour is strictly individual, and the product of labour, be that only a fruit picked up from the ground, is naturally individual property. For Locke individual property is therefore coterminous with human existence; it is only the just extent of property that varies. According to Rousseau's idea of primitive society, true property or the exclusive right to use, dispose, and alienate belongs only to a system of market exchanges:

12 On the essentially communal economies of ethnographically documented primitive societies, see Sahlins, *Tribesmen*; also Stanley Diamond, *In Search of the Primitive*; Paul Radin, *The World of Primitive Man*.
13 On the concept of generalized reciprocity and its normal functioning in primitive society, see E.R. Service, *The Hunters*, 14ff, and Sahlins, *Tribesmen*, 81-6.
14 See Locke, *Second Treatise* in *Two Treatises*, secs. 25-36, esp. sec. 35: 'And the condition of human life, which requires labour and materials to work on, necessarily introduces private possessions.'

Among the savages self-interest pleads as strongly as it does among us, but it does not inculcate the same maxims. The love of society, and their solicitude for the common defence, are the only ties, by which they are united. The word *property* [Rousseau's emphasis], which makes even respectable people with us guilty of so many crimes, is a term of hardly any meaning with them: they lie under no manner of temptation to impose on each other: the public esteem being the only thing to which every one aspires, and which they all deserve. It is very possible for a savage to commit a bad action, but it is impossible he should acquire a habit of doing ill, because it could serve no purpose to him. I conceive a very just estimation of the morals of men may be formed from the multiplicity of business subsisting among them: the more trade they carry on, the more industry and ingenuity are admired, the more do they deceive and decently impose on each other, while they become themselves more the object of contempt ... the man of probity is he only who hath no need to impose on any one, and such only is the savage. (*PN* 140n)

The communal economy thus frees all its members from the need and at least some of the temptation to impose on each other. In place of a system of needs, bound up with a highly differentiated division of labour, the communal economy is organized as a domestic system of production. The only institutionalized division of labour is that between the sexes (*DOI* 196), and production is guided simply by the goal of the reproduction of the familial unit.[15]

At times Rousseau's text seems to imply that any division of labour at all would undermine the peace of primitive society, simply through bringing individuals into objective dependence on one another. They would remain free 'so long as they undertook only what a single person could accomplish' (*DOI* 199). Yet it is obvious that tasks were undertaken co-operatively: 'the women ... were accustomed themselves to mind the hut and their children, while the men went abroad in search of their common subsistence' (*DOI* 196). This seems like rank confusion to the point of meaninglessness. Are we to believe that individuals were at once completely autarkic and social? In reality this 'autarkic sociability' is an example of that deliberate ambiguity in which Rousseau delighted.

In primitive society a collective undertakes what a single person may possibly still accomplish. The point is not that primitive society is conceived as a system of economic exchanges in which domination is avoided as a result of the self-sufficiency of each producer and a cor-

---

15 On the 'domestic mode of production' as a non-alienating form of the labour process, see Sahlins, *Tribesmen*, 75–81.

respondingly low level of need, an economic system in which production is individual and there is strict limitation of the sphere of exchange, grounded in the brutish, rustic, limited needs of the producers. What Rousseau is really pointing to is a limit beyond which primitive society cannot develop without beginning to change its fundamental structure and its nature. This limit is strictly technical. When production is based on techniques that domestic organization cannot duplicate, society comes to be divided along different, functional lines – which it is not in primitive society properly speaking.

Rousseau points to metallurgy and agriculture as the destroyers of primitive society. But there is nothing inherent in either of these activities, no mysterious quality of 'unnaturalness' that somehow begins to corrode primitive organization. Rousseau is clear in stating that *both* of them must be present (*DOI* 199). In other words, when techniques evolve to a certain point that demands permanent functional specialization in distinct social groups, the domestic mode of production is doomed and the way is open to the organization of society as a system of specialized institutions – market, priesthood, state, whatever.

The point in reference to primitive society is to emphasize that for Rousseau that form of society is not the market writ small and tempered by the family. According to him primitive society 'had no more social structure than the family, no laws but those of nature' (*EOL* 31). This is somewhat obscured in the text by his appearing to follow a contractarian route to the emergence of modern society – which appears as an association of families headed by paterfamiliae.[16] In the same way human evolution was obscured by the same rhetorical conceit. The family that Rousseau is referring to is not the biological, nuclear family but some version of the extended family as a generalized institution within which most of an individual's life activities take place. Thus the family is not exclusively grounded in biology and is not simply based on the union of husband and wife. Rousseau refers to it as being the product of a 'novel situation, which united husbands and wives, fathers and children, under one roof.

---

16 This contractarian, associative version of social relations corresponds to a much later stage of historical development, once private property has been established and is defended by the state. It is the way that the family appears in the *Discourse on Political Economy*, ie, already mediated by the relations of civil society. See, eg, *DOI* 209–10: 'instead of saying that civil society is derived from paternal authority, we ought to say rather that the latter derives its principal force from the former ... The goods of the father, of which he is really the master, are the ties which keep his children in dependence, and he may bestow on them, if he pleases, no share of his property, unless they merit it by constant deference to his will.'

The habit of living together soon gave rise to the finest feelings known to humanity, conjugal love and paternal affection' (*DOI* 195). Again the ambiguity should be looked upon as deliberate and significant. It is a union of plural husbands and plural wives, plural parents and plural children. The relation of kinship is not a biological given; it is established rather as a habit, a form of convention, which relates in one domestic space (not literally under one roof) persons whose biological connections are not essential.

The principle of kinship is thus the basis of primitive society. And it is a relation that can be extended symbolically, but effectively, far beyond immediate biological relations: 'Permanent neighborhoods could not fail to produce in time, some connection between different families. Among young people of opposite sex living in neighboring huts, the transient commerce required by nature soon led, through mutual intercourse, to another kind not less agreeable and more permanent' (*DOI* 197). What appears in the text as semi-distinct chronological stages should be seen rather as complementary moments of a single organization. Out of marriages between families the principle of kinship is extended. And in one brilliant passage Rousseau even recognizes the role of the incest taboo as a technique that links 'families' at the same time that it makes family life possible:

The first men would have had to marry their sisters. In the simplicity of primitive customs, this practice would easily perpetuate itself as long as families remained isolated ... But the law that prohibits it is no less sacred for its human ordination. Those who see it only in terms of the bond it forms among families, fail to see its most important aspect. Given the intimacy that domestic life is bound to establish between the two sexes, from the moment such a sacred law ceased to appeal to the heart and mind there would be no more integrity among men and the most terrifying practices would soon bring about the destruction of mankind. (*EOL* 45-6 n 9)

Thus rules of exogamy make possible the social life of the human family and simultaneously create a larger structure of kinship within which social life is carried on.

Rousseau had neither the information nor the carefully developed analytic tools available to the modern anthropologist. He cannot and does not display an understanding of how prescriptions regarding exogamy and endogamy systematically relate groups in primitive society. Yet he has clearly begun to grasp the role and importance of the kinship principle. He can see, for example, that society based on kinship provides poor soil for universalist morality: 'They had the concept of a father, a son, a brother, but not that of a man. Their hut contained all of their fellow men. Stranger, beast, monster: these were all one to them ... Everyone they knew would be dear to them; enemies the rest of the world, whom they did not see at all, of whom they were ignorant. They hated only those with whom they could not be acquainted' (*EOL* 33). What cannot be classified as kin is alien and dangerous. To be akin is to be acquainted and therefore on peaceful terms.

Primitive society, therefore, however sketchily grasped, is understood not as a loose association of biologically given families but as a 'distinct nation, united in character and manners, not by regulations or laws' (*DOI* 197). In this 'epoch' of its existence society is not dependent upon the existence of a specialized institution, monopolizing force and pacifying through terror social relations. Conflicts that arise within society are resolved or contained within the generalized institution of the family. As Marshall Sahlins puts it, 'peacemaking ... becomes a continuous process, going on within society itself ... Kinship is a fundamental ground of peaceful human discourse. The wide extension of kinship idioms, relations and groups in tribal societies represents another way they seek peace.'[17]

Amour-propre, not terribly intense in such a society to begin with, does not have to become the negation of individuality but can rather be integrated into the communal life. Conflict is not contained by the police but is discharged in ritual, in 'singing and dancing.' The very absence of the state means that a market organization of society is ruled out. Economic life is a function of other relations; exchange is governed by a principle other than that of instrumental reciprocity. Property in the means of production is unknown, while sharing is the rule rather than the exception.

This form of social organization, although it is 'the very best man could experience' (*DOI* 199), is inherently fragile. Although it does not know either the domination or the generalized conflict of civil society, the war of each against all, it cannot always contains the forces it generates. The principle of pride together with the absence of a universalist morality can make 'revenge ... terrible, and men bloody and cruel' (*DOI* 198). Cruelty is a function of weakness, ignorance, and fear (*EOL* 32). And technical development beyond the capacity of the mode of domestic production eventually destroys, as we have seen above, this whole form of social organization. It is not a question of a transcendent historical

17 Sahlins, *Tribesmen*, 8, 10

necessity propelling primitive society towards its own transformation, and many savage nations have remained in this state. But the balance that maintains it is a matter of contingency, and many peoples have in fact evolved beyond it. For these it would be difficult if not impossible to imagine how they might devolve, even should they wish to. The growth of technique, the process of enlightenment, represents an impassable barrier on the road back. And when primitive society is brought into relation to civil society, history emerges even more clearly as a process of self-constitutive practical activity: 'When one investigates the origin of the arts and considers primitive customs, one sees that everything corresponds in its origins to the means of providing subsistence' (*EOL* 38).

The Reign of Virtue

Before setting forth upon the philosophical anthropology developed in the second *Discourse*, Rousseau had already begun to develop a critique of bourgeois society in the guise of a critique of the arts and sciences. An idea of the reign of virtue as the organic, substantial unity of the community had taken shape in his mind before he came to reconstruct its pre-conditions or pre-history. In the first *Discourse* virtue appears to be a unified thing, abstractly opposed to the self-interest of modern society and the *bonté* of the primitive.[18] Discussions of Rousseau's various ideals or utopian constructs, whether they are seen as complementary or irreconcilably opposed, usually assume that virtue and the reign of virtue are historically undifferentiated.[19] In fact, virtue is not precisely the same thing over historical time. The earlier version of the reign of virtue, in the first *Discourse*, operates primarily with the ancient polis as model. The later versions of the reign of virtue departs significantly from that model in an attempt to incorporate bourgeois social relations and historically subsequent ideals of individuality in their structure. Between the first *Discourse*, with its doctrinaire contrast between ancient and modern, and the development of the idea of the general will in the

---

18 The contrast between ancient and primitive virtue already begins to appear in the *Discourse on the Arts and Sciences* (DAS 125, n 1), but is as yet undeveloped.

19 For an interpretation of Rousseau that sees his ideals as complementary, see Featherstone, 'Rousseau and Modernity,'; Shklar, not only in *Men and Citizens* but also in 'Equality,' tends to reduce his thought to the oscillations of a utopian but authoritarian personality between the twin but opposed ideals of Sparta and the Golden Age; a very similar theme dominates Starobinski, *Transparence*.

third *Discourse* and the *Social Contract* lies the second *Discourse* and the philosophical foundations for the historicity of virtue.[20]

Rousseau proceeded at first, in the *Discourse on the Arts and Sciences*, via a nostalgic contrast of ancient virtue and modern corruption. But the critique of enlightenment was actually a critique of its ideological function and not the defence of a position that saw an *a priori* relation between enlightenment and corruption. As was often the case, however, his use of extravagant and paradoxical language afforded critics the opportunity of trying to force him to defend positions he never held. Hence the frequent reiterations of his esteem for science. Already in the first *Discourse* he claims that 'it is not science ... that I am attacking; it is virtue that I am defending' (*DAS* 119). This position is repeated later in, for example, the *Preface to Narcissus*, where science becomes something intrinsically positive: 'science considered abstractly, deserves our admiration' (*PN* 133); and in *The Government of Poland*: 'Science in itself is very good; this is evident; and one would have to have renounced his good sense in order to state the contrary' (*SGP* 31).

Rousseau's central criticism is directed at the equation of progress in instrumental rationality with progress in social well-being. The scientific reconstruction of society as the conventional harmonization of competing self-interests, which had begun with Hobbes and was to proceed shortly with a vengeance in Helvétius and Bentham, had repressed and forgotten the meaning of community, common interest, and political liberty. By presenting the nature of individuality as formal equality within a system of needs, the new moral sciences legitimized the negation of individuality inherent in civil society. Science had identified itself with a social order based on abstract, egoistic individualism, to the exclusion of an older concept that had come to be dismissed as metaphysics, superstition, or prejudice. This older concept grasped the social order as the reproduction of the reign of virtue. Science in the first *Discourse*

---

20 Strauss, *Natural Right*, 264ff, recognizes that there is a fundamental shift of grounds in the *Discourse on Inequality*. He simultaneously labels it a regression to the primitive and Rousseau's turn to modern, theoretical natural science, the science of Hobbes and Descartes. He thus sees in it an abandonment of the reliance upon the ancients and upon Socratic wisdom. On the latter point I believe he is correct. He does not, however, see that despite real points of agreement with Hobbes and an uncertain use of Cartesian phraseology, the science that Rousseau begins to develop is fundamentally different, as was pointed out in chap. 3 above. It is perhaps Strauss's most characteristic flaw to lose significant distinctions among the moderns in pursuit of the overarching contrast between ancients and moderns.

is therefore a part of that veil that civil society throws over its corruption: 'So long as government and law provide for the security and well-being of men in their common life, the arts, literature and the sciences, less despotic though perhaps more powerful, fling garlands of flowers over the chains which weigh them down' (*DAS* 120).[21] The reign of virtue is accessible only in the memory of its evanescent glory and utterly inexplicable on the basis of the principles of new moral sciences, except as the irrational products of prejudice and superstition. Rousseau recognized modernity as a society structured as a means for self-preservation and commodious living but refused to grant credence to the science that discovered in this pattern the eternal law of nature. On the other side lay the memory of ancient virtue, of the glory of Sparta and the Roman Republic.

The primitive community based on conventions of kinship begins to break down as soon as the logic of the division of labour undermines the autarky of the domestic mode of production. With this development comes the division of society into separate classes and the differentiation and institutionalization of separate spheres of social activity. In general the ancient civilizations are structured organically and hierarchically. But Rousseau is most interested only in a phase of the development of one of them, classical Mediterranean civilization as expressed in the polis. The ancient empires – Egypt, Persia, China, not to mention feudal Europe – might have embodied virtue, but that virtue was not political. In focusing on Sparta and Rome Rousseau was choosing to extol political virtue only when consciously and systematically abstracting from its basis in social hierarchy. 'In Greece all that the people had to do it did for itself; it was constantly assembled in the public square. The Greeks lived in a mild climate; they had no natural greed; slaves did their work for them; their great concern was with liberty' (*SC* 79). In spite of the omission from the frequent panegyrics to ancient virtue in the first *Discourse* and elsewhere of any mention of slaves, helots, or serfs, that form of virtue is, for Rousseau, probably inconceivable without them.

The classical world is then, if only for a time, a world in which a few, the citizens, are free. But political liberty here is not based on the prior separation of the individual citizen from the community, as it will be in bourgeois society. It would be more proper to speak of the freedom of the politically organized citizen body. The citizen body, constituted in the established network of customary relations and not by the private wills of individual men, is both the basis and the expression of the reign

---

21 Cf *PN* 132, 143–4.

of virtue: 'It is neither walls nor men who make the fatherland; it is the laws, the manners, and the customs, the government, the constitution, the manner of being that results from all this. The nation is in the relation of the state to its members: when those relations change or are annihilated, the fatherland disappears' (*CG* 10.337-8). The ancient reign of virtue Rousseau conceived of as a rule of law, but not in the modern sense of the positive decree of a legitimate sovereign, rather as the complete identification of social life with the customary, traditional law of the community. These laws were aimed at 'keeping within bounds that personal interest which so isolates the individual that the state is enfeebled by his power, and has nothing to hope from his goodwill' (*PE* 253).

This is accomplished, in the first place, through a system of property according to which productive resources are privately held only by virtue of membership in the political community with its attendant obligations. In the case of the Roman Republic, for example, this feature is fundamental: 'It was Numa who bound Romulus' robbers together into citizens, not so much by means of laws, however . . . as by mildly restrictive institutions that bound each of them to the rest and all of them to the soil' (*GP* 7). The aim of production is not exchange in the market and the extraction of a profit but the reproduction of the individual in a specific relation to the community. The polis is in a sense midway between the primitive community and civil society properly so called. In it a separate sphere of egoistic activity is continuously incipient, but it is not yet fully distinct, nor is it accepted as the basis and the principle of the political entity. At the same time the laws develop in part as a defensive mechanism inhibiting its emergence, while the labour of an underlying subject population pre-empts the need of the citizen-body to become absorbed in a process of unlimited accumulation.

In the ancient world the health of the body politic therefore depends on establishing an identity between the individual and his customary role. This fissureless identification is the basis and the expression of his virtue, while virtue is the basis of the freedom of the community. The permanent and lifelong process of molding citizens was thus 'the great art of ancient governments' (*PE* 243), an art that, by insinuating the public will 'into a man's inmost being,' was able to establish the most 'absolute authority' (*PE* 243). When the ancient model of legislation is followed, one 'will cause them to do by inclination and passionate choice the things that men motivated by duty or interest never do quite well enough. Upon souls like that, a wisely conceived legislation will take firm hold. They will obey, not elude the laws, because the laws will suit them, and will enjoy the inward assent of their own wills' (*GP* 12).

Public education was perhaps the fundamental role of the state, a function absolutely essential to its self-preservation and its freedom. In Sparta the laws of Lycurgus 'were mainly concerned with the education of children' (*DOI* 215), and in Rome, although public education was not directly the collective concern, the need was met by fathers who enjoyed unlimited authority over their children and whose households were 'schools of citizenship' (*PE* 253). The modern family by contrast has as its purpose to 'preserve and increase the patrimony of the father' (*PE* 234). Ancient public education produced citizens who were so much the creatures of custom that they felt themselves to be nothing outside the civic apparatus.[22] Obversely, each was protected by the strength of all, while 'nothing was so sacred among them as the life of a citizen; and nothing less than an assembly of the whole people was necessary to condemn one' (*PE* 249).

This vision of organic unity of individual and community was based neither on rational self-interest nor on the control of acts through rewards and punishments; it was based rather on the fusion of will with love of country. Love for the living social whole, expressed through love of a duty identified with customary law,[23] was the affective bond of society and the basis of virtue. Social solidarity was rooted in 'this fine and lively feeling, which gives to the force of self-love all the beauty of virtue' (*PE* 246). Citizenship was based upon a metamorphosis of *amour-propre*, itself already a transformation of *amour-de-soi*. The virtue of the ancient citizen was thus the sublimation of *amour-propre*:

> If ... they were early accustomed to regard their individuality only in its relation to the body of the state, and to be aware, so to speak, of their own existence merely as a part of that state, they might at length come to identify themselves in some degree with this greater whole, to feel themselves members of their country, and to love it with that exquisite feeling, which no isolated person has for himself; to lift up their spirits perpetually to this great object, and thus to transform into a sublime virtue that dangerous disposition which gives rise to all our vices. (*PE* 251)

Amour-propre is made sublime by changing its aim and its object. *Amour-propre* when sublimated in the classical form of virtue, is not self-

---

22 See *GP* 19: 'Your true republican is a man who imbibed love of the fatherland, which is to say love of the laws and of liberty, with his mother's milk. That love makes up his entire existence: he has eyes only for the fatherland; the moment he is alone, he is a mere cipher; the moment he has no fatherland, he is no more; if not dead, he is worse off than if he were dead.'

33 Rousseau, *PE* 236-7; also *PN* 142; *LA* 67

aggrandizement at the direct expense of the other; it rather becomes the pursuit of glory and public esteem in directly social endeavours, in the hope of winning the laurels that can only be awarded by the community as a quasi-personal, unitary entity.

The primary individual need is here the cultivation of personal qualities, so that communal virtue becomes the condition and occasion of personal virtue. This form of the establishment of the body politic points

> from afar to the paths – unknown to us moderns – along which the ancients led men up to that level of spiritual vigor, of patriotic zeal, of high esteem for the qualities that are truly personal and not foreign to the nature of man, of which we have no contemporary examples. Even now, however, the leaven they used is present in the hearts of all men, and awaits in order to produce its fermentation, only activation by appropriate institutions. (GP 23)

Individuality is thus not totally eclipsed in the polis. It is only not absolute. It is a dependent condition of a complex oroganism. And it only belongs to those who do not labour.

If science is in any way directly opposed to the reign of virtue, it is because it undermines the traditional authority of custom, patriotism, and religion while supplying at first only the rule of self-interest. It is thus in the first *Discourse* that Rousseau does truly tend to see society and the individual in essential opposition to each other. The real choice seems to be that between egoism and citizenship (which is pictured as merely the submersion of the self in the universal). But complete egoism is impossible. It would mean either the complete return to nature or the war of each against all. The other alternative, that of giving men completely to the state, was briefly realized in human history but suffered, in Rousseau's perspective, from a number of basic flaws.

As much as he might seem at times to prefer the ancient reign of virtue to modern liberalism, it would be wrong to assume that the former was the best or highest form that Rousseau envisioned for human society. Although the citizen-body was free, its members freed from a degrading life of toil and called to a strenuous life of public performance, particularity within it remained relatively undeveloped. The moment of absolute freedom and independence that the bourgeois world asserted for its members, standing outside society and judging its usefulness to them, had not yet dawned. Nor was equality (or freedom) realized in all the parts of the social organism of the polis.

In addition to being an insufficient substitute for the equality and freedom of nature, the city-state also contained the sources of its own destruction. First of all, as was already the case with Athens, it was susceptible to the growth of enlightenment and individualism, to the separation and growing antithesis of public and private spheres through the growth of commercial relations. Sparta was in a way the exception in the ancient world to the rule represented by Athens: 'The difference between human art and the work of nature is felt in these effects. Citizens have only called themselves members of the state in vain; they could not unite as true members are united in the body; it is impossible to make it so that each one of them would not have an individual and separate existence, through which he could alone adequately look after his own conservation' (*EG* 298). Individualism of the modern kind, the striving for self-sufficiency of the particular interested in his self-preservation and the maximization of his power, was already present in the expansionist city-state. The unity of life to which the polis aspired Rousseau conceived of as the differentiated wholeness of an organism, for which the separation of public and private already means its hidden decline. Spartan practice is for Rousseau the highest expression of political virtue rather than the theory of Aristotle's politics. For Aristotle there is no opposition in principle between public and private, but rather a unity in their distinctness.[24] The appearance of this distinction for Rousseau already spelled the beginning of the end.

If the polis were not undermined by commercial expansion, it could be destroyed by other tensions inherent in its organization. For the polis is an organization determined by its specialization for war. In the case of Rome war led to the destruction of freedom in the citizen-body through the development of empire and the emergence of despotism. The Spartan organization, on the other hand, truly demanded the 'changing of human nature' (*SC* 32). Sparta suppressed not only the particularity of the absolute ego that was to appear in bourgeois society but also the particularity of nature as expressed in the affective, passionate, erotic ties that bind the family. And Eros is governed by laws of its own, not easily made subject to the call of virtue or glory. The model of ancient virtue finds itself in contradiction with the laws of nature, with the erotic passions expressed within the family. As Hegel would see in Antigone the 'revenge of the family,' the inability of the immediate unity of the polis to give expression to and incorporate particularity,[25] Rousseau sees the member

24 For an interpretation of Aristotle along these lines see Arendt, *Human Condition*, 22ff.
25 The phrase 'revenge of the family' belongs to A. Kojève, *Introduction to the Reading of Hegel*, 276; see G.W.F. Hegel, *Phenomenology of Spirit*, 278-89; J.N. Findlay, *Hegel: A Re-examination*, 116-19.

of the 'natural community' inevitably finding himself in irreconcilable conflict with the laws of the city:

Plato only sought to purge man's heart; Lycurgus turned it from its natural course.
 A Spartan mother had five sons with the army. A helot arrived: trembling she asked his news. 'Your five sons are slain.' 'Vile slave, was that what I asked thee?' 'We have won the victory.' She hastened to the temple to render thanks to the gods. That was a citizen. (*E* 8)

The ancient reign of virtue, in which civic freedom depended on the prior cultivation of virtue as the unself-conscious, unreflective, and complete identity of the universal and the particular (*PE* 251-2) remains less than complete as a model for a fully human civilization. The particularity of custom gives way before the concrete form of extreme particularity, the particularity of bourgeois egoism, and the particularity of a banished, unincorporated force of nature - eros. The reign of virtue in its modern form begins not with freedom as the outcome of a virtue conceived as the identity of will and custom (or, in Hegelian terms, with the community as an immediate substantial unity), but with the absolute freedom of the particular will and with the idea of virtue as moral autonomy - as the universalization of the particular. But whether freedom and virtue can be reconciled under this formula is a question that can be answered only after a prior examination of the form of social life based upon egoism.

CHAPTER FIVE

Anthropology as History: The Critique of Bourgeois Society

> La première difficulté revient toujours, et ce n'est que
> de l'ordre social établi parmi nous que nous tirons les idées
> de celui que nous imaginons. Nous concevons la
> société générale d'après nos sociétés particuliers.
> Rousseau, Geneva Manuscript

The Form of Social Labour in Bourgeois Society

According to Rousseau's anthropology, an understanding of human nature was predicated, among other things, upon an understanding of the social relations into which men enter in order to transform external nature. Accordingly, what defines civil society for Rousseau is precisely its economic form. Civil society for Rousseau resembles very closely the notions of it later held by Adam Smith, Kant, Hegel, and Marx, and previously by the Physiocrats.[1] Under this form of society men are united essentially through a form of exchange in which each regards the other as primarily a means to the satisfaction of his own need. Society is a vast 'system of needs,' from the operations of which no single individual can exempt himself. As Hegel puts it, 'civil society is the tremendous power which draws men into itself and claims from them that they work for it, owe everything to it, and do everything by its means.'[2] In Marx's

---

1 On Physiocracy, see eg, Martin, *French Liberal Thought*, 228-35; Laski, *Rise*, 119-23; on Smith's and Kant's 'basic model of society' see Colletti, *From Rousseau to Lenin*, 156-66; on Hegel's idea of civil society and the system of needs see Shlomo Avineri, *Hegel's Theory of the Modern State*, 141-54.
2 Hegel, *Philosophy of Right*, add. to sec. 238, p 276

words 'the reciprocal and all-sided dependence of individuals who are indifferent to one another forms their social connection.'³ Modern society presents itself similarly to Rousseau as the all-encompassing interdependence of free producers: 'Free and independent as men were before, they were now, in consequence of a multiplicity of new wants, brought into subjection, as it were, to all nature, and particularly to one another; and each became in some degree a slave even in becoming the master of other men; if rich they stood in need of the services of others; if poor, of their assistance; and even a middle condition did not enable them to do without one another' (*DOI* 156). In one sense, of course, men remain free and independent, in that in civil society there is no authoritative allocation of work and reward. In another sense, the objective interdependence of individuals relative to a primitive existence grows.

The increase of objective interdependence cannot take place without the introduction of a new dynamic into the development of needs. Needs do not arise spontaneously, as it were, out of any natural insatiability. In *human* beings, needs and their modes of satisfaction are not naturally given. Even in primitive society they arise out of taste and reflection, out of cognitive processes bearing on aesthetic value and instrumentality, processes that are inseparable from the process of labour itself. Work, as the naturally imposed condition of human existence, contains its own moment of liberation from nature. Thus even in primitive society needs are not given and fixed once and for all, yet there is a qualitative difference with respect to bourgeois society. In society structured as a *system* of needs, each man

must now, therefore, have been perpetually employed in getting others to interest themselves in his lot, and in making them, apparently at least, if not really, find their advantage in promoting his own. Thus he must have been sly and artful in his behaviour to some, and imperious and cruel to others; being under a kind of necessity to ill use all the persons of whom he stood in need ... In a word there arose rivalry and competition on the one hand, and conflicting interest on the other, together with a secret desire on both of profiting at the expense of the other. (*DOI* 202-3)

It is not simply the growth in the division of labour as such that subjects men to the system of needs, not simply the matter of physical survival that increases objective dependence. Rather, the inherent dynamic of civil society compels all the actors to foster actively the proliferation

3 Marx, *Grundrisse*, 156

of needs in the other. Hegel was to remark upon this very same dynamic.[4] Nor is Rousseau's complaint directed, as some would have it,[5] simply at the division of labour as such, but at a form of social organization in which the development of skill, technique, productivity, and the refinement of need go hand in hand with the absolute impoverishment of some, the relative impoverishment of many more, and the disintegration of the human personality under the impact of what Rousseau was wont to call the 'empire of public opinion.' 'And what is the price of those cruel luxuries which the few purchase at the expense of the multitude ... if a few men are happier the human race only has more to be sorry about. In multiplying the commodities of life for a few rich individuals one has only forced the majority of men to feel themselves to be miserable' (*LM* 1089).

The civilized corruption that Rousseau was so fond of denouncing turns out not to be the simple expression of *amour-propre* but its formation and inflammation in the social relations of bourgeois society, that is, society established as a network of economic exchanges. This represented to him, if not the single most important of his discoveries, at least the one that was most 'cruel and astonishing' (*PN* 137).[6] If the critique of

4 Hegel, *Philosophy of Right*, add. to sec. 191, p 269; cf Marx, who, unwittingly harking back to very Rousseauan language, expands at some length on just this aspect of civil society in the section on 'Need, Production and the Division of Labour' in the *Economic and Philosophic Manuscripts*, in *Early Writings*, 358-9: 'Under the system of private property ... each person speculates on creating a new need in the other, with the aim of forcing him to make a new sacrifice, placing him in a new dependence and seducing him into a new kind of enjoyment and hence into economic ruin. Each attempts to establish over the other an alien power in the hope of thereby achieving satisfaction of his own selfish needs. With the mass of objects grows the realm of alien powers to which man is subjected, and each new product is a new potentiality of mutual fraud and mutual pillage ... Lack of moderation and intemperance become its true standard. Subjectively this is manifested partly in the fact that the expansion of production and needs becomes the inventive and ever calculating slave of inhuman, refined, unnatural and imaginary appetites – for private property does not know how to transform crude need into human need. Its idealism is fantasy, caprice and infatuation.'
5 See, eg, Starobinski, *Transparence*, 23-4, 286-328.
6 On this point cf *DOI* 222-3: 'That *men* are actually wicked, a sad and continual experience of them proves beyond doubt: but, all the same, I think I have shown that *man* is naturally good. What, then, can have depraved him to such an extent, except the changes that have happened in his constitution, the advances he has made and the knowledge he has acquired? We may admire human society as much as we please; it will be none the less true that it necessarily leads men to hate each other *in proportion as their interests clash*, and to do one another apparent services, while they are really doing every imaginable mischief. What can be thought of a relation, in which the interests of every individual dictates rules directly opposite to those the public reason dictates to the

advancing civilization centred on any particular quality it was on this fundamental structuring of social relations as the self-seeking of isolated, unattached individuals:

Our writers all look upon it as a masterpiece of modern policy, that the sciences, arts, luxury, commerce, laws and our other connections, by drawing together the bonds of society by personal interest, lay all under a mutual dependence and by reciprocal wants unite them in one common interest; by which means individuals are obliged to concur to the public good, in order to promote their own ... It is to be sure a very wonderful thing to have laid mankind under the impossibility of living together, without being under the necessity of supplanting, deceiving, betraying and destroying each other! It is necessary for us never to appear what we are; as, for every two men whose interests may coincide, there are an hundred thousand, perhaps, whose interests are totally opposite: nor are there any means for any one to succeed without deceiving or ruining the rest. Such is the fatal source of outrages, robberies, villainies and the horrors of all sorts which are inseparable from a state, in which everyone pretending to promote the reputation and fortune of others, endeavours in reality only to promote his own, and that at their expense. (PN 127-8)[7]

Lucio Colletti was quite right to see in this passage a moralistic critique of bourgeois society that answers in advance the arguments of men such as Adam Smith and Kant concerning the salutary effects of the division and competition of interests as the motor of progress in human affairs.[8] The point, however, is that Rousseau's critique and understanding of bourgeois society does not stop with an abstract denunciation of economic rationality from the point of view of moral feeling. We must examine further both his idea of civil society and earlier forms of society before restricting the source of his insights to a purely backward-looking, moralistic critique of economic development.

Social corruption, which is ultimately a form of personal derangement

---

community in general – in which every man finds his profit in the misfortune of his neighbour ... we find our advantage in the misfortunes of our fellow creatures, and the loss of one man almost always constitutes the prosperity of another' (emphasis added).

7 The following passage also tends to confirm the close association in Rousseau's mind between civilized corruption and specifically bourgeois social relations: 'c'est ainsi que les mêmes causes qui nous rendent méchant nous rendent encore esclaves, et que notre faiblesse naît de notre cupidité; nos besoins nous rapprochent à mesure que nos passions nous divisent et plus nous devenons ennemis, moins nous pouvons passer les uns des autres' ('Fragments Divers,' in *Political Writings*, ed. C.E. Vaughan, 1.323).

8 Colletti, *From Rousseau to Lenin*, 160-1

or self-estrangement, reaches its apogee with the liberation of the system of needs from any form of traditional restraint. The development of civil society as a dynamic system of exchange relations does not take place immediately. A number of other elements are presupposed. In the second *Discourse* Rousseau presents the emergence of civil society out of the state of nature as a historical process. However, his actual presentation is only pseudo-historical. The evolution of civil society that occupies a central place in the second *Discourse* would perhaps be better regarded as the mythic form of the analysis of a dynamic totality. The linkage between the various moments of the whole of the structure of civil society is delivered as a vaguely chronological, vaguely causal account, apparent chronological priority corresponding with logical priority. But it is more illuminating to look at the 'developmental stages' in that account as moments abstracted from the larger whole of the structure of civil society. Rousseau is not so much giving a historical account of the rise of bourgeois society as a figurative representation of a network of logical relations. The process is not complete until the establishment of the state; in other words, the state for him is an essential precondition of the existence of civil society.

We have seen that for Rousseau civil society is a network of instrumental exchanges among producers who take each other to be naturally independent. This system presupposes the liberation of private property, in the sense that property no longer represents a right merely to dispose of the product of one's own labour but an exclusive right to productive resources and the right to alienate or exchange goods and labour.[9] The right of private property includes the right to alienate one's labour. The emergence of private property also presupposes a certain level of technological development and a corresponding increase in the division of labour. For Rousseau the invention of agriculture and metallurgy are necessary conditions.

The de facto establishment of true private property and market-exchange relations brings in its train certain unforeseen consequences:

In this state of affairs equality might have been sustained, had the talents of individuals been equal, and had, for example, the use of iron and the consumption of commodities always exactly balanced each other; *but as there was nothing to preserve this balance*, it was soon disturbed, the strongest did most work;

---

9 This is clearly implied in the passage in which Rousseau criticizes Puffendorf's argument justifying slavery (*DOI* 211; see also 201, where Rousseau attempts to distinguish between the extended rights of property in civil society and the natural right to dispose only over the fruits of one's labour.

the most skillful turned his labour to best account; the most ingenious devised methods of diminishing his labour ... while both laboured equally, the one gained a great deal by his work, while the other could hardly support himself. Thus natural inequality unfolds itself insensibly with combination, and the difference between men, developed by their different circumstances, becomes more sensible and permanent in its effects and begins to have an influence, in the same proportion over the lot of individuals. (DOI 201-2; emphasis added)

In other words, simple exchange, in which there is by definition no authoritative distribution of reward and/or no commutative system of just exchange, cannot long remain in existence unchanged. Once access to the means of production is effectively barred as a result of the whole of the land being owned, 'one man could aggrandize himself only at the expense of another' (DOI 203). Society tends to bifurcate into two distinct classes of men, the 'rich,' those with exclusive access to the means of production, and the 'supernumeraries,' those without access or who are driven off the land and 'were obliged to receive their subsistence or steal it from the rich' (DOI 203). Production for exchange creates a class of landless labourers who can find a subsistence existence only in the sale of their labour.[10]

This preview of the separation of capital and labour is signalled by and solidified in the increased circulation of money, which becomes a fund of capital and no longer merely a medium of exchange: 'Poverty did not make itself felt ... until money began to circulate there. It created the same inequality in resources as in fortunes: it became a great instrument of acquisition which was inaccessible to those who had nothing' (CPC 297-8).[11] Production is no longer conceived of as an exchange of equivalents, itself defined by the agreement of free contractors, but is best conceived of as the expanded reproduction of capital: 'Strange and fatal must be that constitution, in which the accumulation of riches always facilitates the means of farther accumulation, and in which it is impossible for him that has nothing to acquire anything; in which an honest man hath no means to extricate himself from poverty' (PN 139). What began as simple exchange between free and equal producers, who recognized each other as equals, ends up as systematic exploitation. While the appearance of reciprocity is preserved, the substance of reciprocity disappears.

Thus, if the system of needs makes each of society's members dependent

10 Rousseau, PC 920
11 I have modified Watkins's translation here slightly.

on the rest; if, to repeat Hegel's words, it 'draws men into itself and claims from them that they work for it, owe everything to it, and do everything by its means,' it does not distribute its burdens or rewards evenly or equitably. There are increasing numbers who, in order to subsist, must sell their labour. And these do not have equal bargaining power with those who employ them. As Rousseau says, 'in every kind of commerce, it is always the less downtrodden who dictates to the other' (*CAC* 283).[12] And it is of course the 'rich' who are the least pressed. Thus the labour contract establishes a relation in which the appearance of an exchange of equal values obscures the reality of systematic, continuous exploitation:

Another no less important fact is that the losses of the poor are much harder to repair than those of the rich, and that the difficulty of acquisition is always greater in proportion as there is more need of it. 'Nothing comes out of nothing' is as true of life as in physics ... The terms of the social compact between these two estates of men may be summed up in a few words: 'You have need of me because I am rich and you are poor. We will therefore come to an agreement. I will permit you to have the honour of serving me, on condition that you bestow on me the little you have left in return for the pains I shall take to command you.' (*PE* 264)

It should be clear that Rousseau is not referring to the relations of personal dependence enjoined, under feudal social arrangements, upon persons of different status, but to a relation among legal and political equals. The poor man has need of the other for no other reason than that he is poor and the other rich. The right of command is established only through the consent of the poor man in the bargain.

Civil society is therefore a dynamic system in which men are related primarily through an economic system of needs. It presupposes a relatively high degree of technological development and division of labour, while the co-ordination of the various technico-productive functions takes place via the medium of universal exchange in the market. The formal equality and reciprocity of the market, whatever real meaning they may have had at first, become little more than an ideological veil concealing the exploitation of an increasing pool of landless labourers. Rather than universalizing wealth, the increasing productive power of the system universalizes scarcity in different forms for different classes. The universalization of scarcity, in the form of absolute need for the propertyless

12 As in n 11

and relative but unlimited need for the 'middle condition' and the 'rich,' provides the momentum that propels the unlimited accumulation of 'wealth.'

The lynchpin of the entire system is true private property, which Rousseau calls the 'last point of the state of nature' (*DOI* 192). The reason for it being called the last point might seem to be that Rousseau is following Locke in assuming that a complex money economy is 'natural' and can develop in a state of nature – that is, either historically prior to or theoretically abstracted from political society and the power of the state.[13] But if the evolution of civil society that he presents in part 2 of the second *Discourse* is regarded as a mythic, pseudo-historical form of the analysis of the dynamic process of civil society, it appears that Rousseau is pointing to the institution of property as that which makes possible *both* civil society and the state, as well as their characteristic relationship. There are actually two quite distinct states of nature in the second *Discourse*, or two distinct uses of a single terminology. One state of nature is historical and is used in connection with Rousseau's anthropology. The other is strictly a juridical concept used primarily in a critique of formal equality.[14] Ironically, the historicization of the state of nature is also an implicit critique of its usage as a juridical form. But Rousseau goes on to employ the juridical state of nature in order to be able to criticize the theory of natural rights, and primarily Locke, in its own terms, internally.

Civil Society and the State

The state, for Rousseau, continuously arises from the relations of civil society, and it is in turn an essential condition of the continuation of those relations. Civil society as bourgeois society does not arise first, is not a natural growth to which the state is a later afterthought, however much the following famous passage might superficially suggest that:

The first man who, having enclosed a piece of ground, bethought himself of saying 'This is mine' and found people simple enough to believe him, was the real founder of civil society. From how many crimes, wars and murders, from how many horrors and misfortunes might not anyone have saved mankind, by

---

13 Rousseau, *DOI* 201; for Rousseau, evidently, private property is a purely conventional relation that develops only in the context of the expanded use of certain productive techniques.
14 Cf Plattner, *Rousseau's State of Nature*, 99

pulling up the stakes, or filling up the ditch and crying to his fellows: 'Beware of this imposter; you are undone if you once forget that the fruits of the earth belong to us all, and the earth itself to nobody.' But there is great probability that things had then already come to such a pitch, that they could no longer continue as they were; for the idea of property depends on many prior ideas. (*DOI* 1972)

It is from the preceding discussion of the dynamics of bourgeois society (which in Rousseau's text follows the above-cited passage) that we can understand to what pitch 'things' had been brought and how.

We have seen that the system of social relations as exchange relations among independent property owners leads necessarily in Rousseau's eyes to a condition of universal disorder, competition and exploitation. 'The new born state of society thus gave rise to a horrible state of war; men thus harassed and depraved were no longer capable of retracing their steps or renouncing the fatal acquisitions they had made, but labouring by the abuse of the faculties which do them honour, merely to their own confusion, brought themselves to the brink of ruin' (*DOI* 203-4). This state of war is not a simple condition but is in fact doubled, at once a war of each against all and a 'class war' of rich against poor. This notion appears less difficult if we assume that by the term war Rousseau was not necessarily referring to actual struggles but, like Hobbes, to 'a known disposition thereto.'[15] Yet it is the very *appearance* of the struggle as simply a war of each against all that guarantees the apparent legitimacy of the state that evolves from this particular form of society. The state becomes necessary in appearance to guarantee the 'safety' (*DOI* 205) of individuals both rich and poor, to ensure 'protection for their lives, liberties and properties, which are, so to speak, the constituent elements of their being' (*DOI* 208). Given the relations of civil society, this apparent necessity is also, of course, real. The state's supervision of the relations of civil society is necessary to the continuation of those relations. The appearance is not absolutely false. We would say that it is ideological. It merely abstracts from the group conflicts that are also generated by the relations of civil society.[16] The appearance also abstracts from and thus represses its own history by treating those relations as natural and given. These men are no longer capable of retracing their

---

15 Hobbes, *Leviathan*, ed. Macpherson, 186
16 It abstracts, as Marx said in *The German Ideology*, from the 'life process of definite individuals ... as they operate, produce materially, and hence as they work under definite material limits, presuppositions and conditions independent of their wills' (*Reader*, 118).

steps. By this Rousseau does not merely indicate that the steps cannot be retraced in practice but that they have not been or cannot be retraced theoretically or consciously. What is in reality a process in which consciousness plays an important role is frozen in appearance into a static, given, and natural condition.

The whole of the second *Discourse* is testimony to Rousseau's understanding of ideology as imputed nature. It is an attempt to retrace those steps ignored by all previous theorists of natural law, who, 'every one of them ... constantly dwelling on wants, avidity, oppression, desires and pride, has transferred to the state of nature ideas which were acquired in society; so that in speaking of the savage, they described the social man. It has not even entered into the heads of most of our writers to doubt whether the state of nature ever existed' (*DOI* 161). Thus Hobbes, whom Rousseau honours for having 'seen clearly the defects of all the modern definitions of natural right,' in not admitting in the human soul an innate knowledge of virtue, none the less 'improperly admitted, as a part of savage man's care for self-preservation, the gratification of a multitude of passions which are the work of society, and have made laws necessary' (*DOI* 181). The state of nature that Rousseau presents is, on the contrary, aimed at elucidating the difficult question of distinguishing 'properly between what is original and what is artificial in the actual nature of man' (*DOI* 155). It is therefore transparently a 'conjecture' or 'hypothesis' arrived at not by considering the men of bourgeois society in abstraction from the state but by abstraction from a 'long process' (*DOI* 163) of social development inseparable from his actual nature. But once the actual is thus understood as the product of a process, it is no longer nature, at least in its prescriptive sense. The theorists who are ignorant of the historicity of human nature reproduce at a higher level of 'scientific' sophistication the 'seductive' speech of the 'rich' founder of political society, who, 'after having represented to his neighbours the horror of a situation which armed every man against the rest, and made their possessions as burdensome to them as their wants, and in which no safety could be expected either in riches or in poverty, he readily devised plausible arguments to make them close with his design' (*DOI* 205). The imputation of 'viciousness' to nature serves as the ideological justification of the state that arises in bourgeois society and that guarantees the position of the rich man, of him who is 'destitute of valid reasons to justify and sufficient strength to defend himself' (*DOI* 204).

The same fundamental notions of equality and reciprocity that legitimate and are ostensibly embodied in the system of needs also serve as ideological underpinnings of the state. That Rousseau sees this is clear from the words he puts in the mouth of the mythical founder of the class state:

> 'Let us join,' said he, 'to guard the weak from oppression, to restrain the ambitious, and secure to every man the possession of what belongs to him: let us institute rules of justice and peace, to which all without exception may be obliged to conform; rules that may in some measure make amends for the caprices of fortune, by subjecting equally the powerful and the weak to the observance of reciprocal obligations.' (*DOI* 205)

The product of the combined forces of each is thus put at the service of the rich through the enforcement of the sanctity of contracts – especially the labour contract, which has the same appearance of equality and reciprocity but which, as we have seen, is for Rousseau the illusory form of substantive inequality and exploitation.

The bourgeois state is therefore the epitome of bourgeois society at the same time that it is represented as a power over and beyond it. The equality and reciprocity that ostensibly reign in the state in the form of equality before the law are intended to be a new, if not higher form of the equality and reciprocity found in the state of nature. In the same way the equality and reciprocity of the fully developed market is in appearance quite consistent with the equality of fully independent producers. The state is supposedly the *restoration* of the equality of nature and the termination of the state of war; but in reality it guarantees the perpetuation of inequality in civil society at the same time that it introduces a new form of inequality, political inequality, and transfers war to another level. At the political level inequality is expressed in the form of the cycle of regimes:

> If we follow the progress of inequality in these various revolutions, we shall find that the establishment of laws and of the right of property was its first term, the institution of magistracy [that is, of a separate administrative and/ or legislative organ] the second, and the conversion of a legitimate into arbitrary power the third and last; so that the condition of rich and poor was authorized by the first period; that of powerful and weak by the second; and only by the third that of master and slave, which is the last degree of inequality, and the term at which all the rest remain, when they have got so far, till the government is either entirely dissolved by new revolutions, or brought back again to legitimacy. (*DOI* 214–15)

Equality before the law, guaranteed by the force of the state, is the answer to the war into which the state of nature tends to degenerate. Conventional equality in political society is the illusory restoration of that natural equality that in the sphere of civil society has been transformed into inequality. The state is the ideological restoration of community that has been dissolved in the relations of civil society. 'It is to law *alone* that men owe justice and liberty' (*PE* 240). This notion of equality is the theory, or rather the ideal, that one class in civil society produces for itself and for the rest of society for the purpose of stability and legitimacy. In fact, since 'the flaws which make social institutions necessary are the same as make the abuse of them unavoidable' (*DOI* 215), the reality is quite different.

The bourgeois state fixes and makes permanent the state of war by compelling its members to use only peaceful means in the struggle. Contracts and commerce once again replace 'usurpation' and 'robbery.' At the same time a new division is created in society, a division that, although it owes its existence to the division and competition of interests and classes, once established acquires a life of its own. This is the division into 'weak' and 'powerful' and authorizes the political-bureaucratic class, the 'magistracy,' which tends to gain in strength and independence in proportion to the 'dissension' and 'division' reigning in civil society. When dissension and division wax to their fullest, the tendency to despotism receives its fullest expression. And despotism is the perverse inversion of the state of nature, a condition in which 'all private persons return to their first equality, because they are nothing' (*DOI* 219).

A perfect parallel in the political realm, which realizes its term in despotism, is thus established with the realm of civil society, where the equality and reciprocity of the state of nature receive their inversion in the exploitation of labour. Thus behind the ideal of conventional equality, expressed in political society and law, lie the true functions of the state and law in bourgeois society, 'Which bound new fetters on the poor, and gave new powers to the rich; which irretrievably destroyed natural liberty, eternally fixed the law of property and inequality, converted clever usurpation into unalterable right, and, for the advantage of a few ambitious individuals, subjected all mankind to perpetual labour, slavery and wretchedness.' (*DOI* 205).

Civil Relations as Relations of Alienation

Depotism and its inversion, the state of nature as a state of war, constitute the horizons of bourgeois society. Normally it is located well within these extreme terms. This is, of course, not to say that in normal times the existence of men in bourgeois society is harmonious. This existence is perceived by Rousseau as, even in the best of times, a fragmentation of personality into antithetical and unrelated aspects. The most celebrated aspect of this process is the division of social existence between the roles of private and political life, the split between man and citizen: 'Render man whole and you will make him as happy as he can be. Give him entirely to the state or leave him completely to himself. But if you divide his heart, you rend it.' (CG 7.202-3). That split between interest and duty that takes place in civil society is, however, something new and unique, not to be found in the same form in earlier types of society. The reason for this lies ultimately in the economic structure of civil society, which takes hold of and distorts an egoism that Rousseau conceives of as inherent in all social relations.

Civil society is that objective structure that enjoins upon its members the necessity of acting upon specific rules of self-interest in the instrumental reciprocity of the market; it is based upon that 'relation in which the interest of every individual dictates rules directly opposite to those the public reason dictates to the community in general – in which every man finds his profit in the misfortune of his neighbour' (DOI 222-3). It should be clear that for Rousseau the relation between interest and duty is a variable and historical one, in which both aspects in their relation to each other are deeply affected by 'the methods of life men adopt in society.' The vices of civil society thus 'belong not so much to man in himself, as to man in a state of society ill-governed' (PN 139).[17]

The exchange relations of civil society presuppose equality and reciprocity; their legitimacy rests upon the equality of the persons contracting. Yet the developed condition of exchange relations enjoins upon each the necessity of exploiting all those within reach, upon pain of destitution. Thus civil society dictates to each his interest. But this interest can only be pursued upon formal terms of political equality, an equality that is preserved in the state as the rule of law that 'subjects equally the powerful and the weak to the observance of reciprocal obligations' (DOI 205). Thus civil society also dictates to each the form of his duty. This is how men come to be 'forced to caress and destroy one another at the same time' (DOI 223). These specific, historical forms of duty *and* of interest both have their grounds in the logic of social relations as exchange relations. And Rousseau is aware that this has not always

17 Cf *Discourse on the Origin of Language*, in *Origin of Language*, trans. J.H. Moran and A. Gode, 30-1: 'When one wants to study men, one must consider those around one. But to study man, one must extend the range of one's vision. One must first observe the differences in order to discover the properties.'

been the case, since the development of exchange relations is a particular and historical event. In summarizing the evolution of society as he had presented it in the second *Discourse*, Rousseau in his *Lettre à Christophe de Beaumond* refers to pre-modern societies as having not yet crossed the threshold to a condition in which the opposition of interests outweighs 'the public reason': 'So long ... as the opposition of their interests is less than the concurrence of their knowledge, men are essentially good' (*LCB* 251). Although egoism, arising out of social relations as such, may be transhistorical, it is not an essence. It is always constituted, extended, relaxed, and transformed in the particular social relations of given historical forms of society.

Civil society produces a peculiar form of self-interest and a corresponding form of duty. Thes are antithetical to each other even though both are grounded, paradoxically, in a notion of equality. Yet this is not the only way in which the existence of men in civil society is alienated, fragmented, and at odds with itself. For civil society is the realm of universal exchange where all values can be reduced to a single form of expression in money. In this case again it might seem that Rousseau's critique is purely moralistic, an inheritance perhaps from Christian (or even Stoic) condemnation of earthly striving after wealth in favour of a transcendent virtue. Thus Rousseau characterizes the modern Europeans as all dreaming 'only of luxury, and [they] know no passion except the passion for money; sure as they are that money will fetch them everything they fancy, they will sell themselves to the first man who is willing to pay them. What do they care what master's bidding they do, or what country's laws they obey?' (*GP* 12). Surely there is nothing striking in the opposition of venality and virtue. Yet we have also seen that the terms of Rousseau's discussion of civil society are not exclusively moral ones but also moral metaphors in which the amoral logic of abstract social relations is expressed. The logic and dynamic of civil society, in and of themselves, demand venality as the overriding form of the expression of self-interest. For money is no longer a simple means of exchange: as society evolves from a form of simple exchange between independent producers into a more complex relation between owners and non-owners of the means of production, money becomes not an object of use but primarily a means to further accumulation. As such, money seems to take on a life of its own, as more and more of the independent producers (those of the 'middle condition') are, in the maelstrom of the system of needs, deprived of their independent status: 'Under this administration money, being the principal necessity, would form the immediate object of work ... consequently all work that could not produce it would necessarily be neglected' (*PC* 925). In civil society, therefore, the primary necessity is the necessity for money.

The expansion of needs becomes the impoverishment of human need as activity is characterized universally by having money as its overriding object. Since money is the universal medium of exchange and anything can be exchanged for money (except life and liberty, which remain constituent elements of man's being), need is reduced to a single need, a need that tends to exclude all other needs and one that has no limits:

One can make men act only by appealing to their self-interest. That I know. Of all interests, however, that in pecuniary gain is the most evil, the readiest to be corrupted, though also – in the eyes of one who has knowledge of the human heart ... the least important and compelling. In the heart of every man there is a natural reservoir of several strong passions: if in any man only the passion for money remains alive, that is because the remaining passions, which should have been awakened and developed in him, have been starved or stamped out. (*GP* 70)

The member of that society organized as a system of needs is therefore not to be condemned from a transcendent moral vantage point. If anything he is an object of something like pity as he is buffeted by the winds of chance that blow incessantly in the market:

It is not only that money is a sign, but also that it is a relative sign, in practice effective merely by reason of its unequal distribution. (*CPC* 304)[18]

Pecuniary wealth is purely relative. According to the circumstances (which may change for any one of ten thousand reasons), one can with one and the same amount of money, be rich for one moment and poor the next. But with one and the same amount of real goods no such thing can happen; they are directly useful to man, and so have an absolute value that the operations of the market cannot affect. (*GP* 73)[19]

18 This is a slight modification of Watkins's translation.
19 The following passage from Marx, *Economic and Philosophic Manuscripts*, in *Early Writings*, 358, deserves comparison here: 'Man becomes ever poorer as a man, and needs ever more money if he is to achieve mastery over the hostile being. The power of his money falls in inverse proportion to the volume of production, i.e. his need grows as the power of money increases. The need for money is for that reason the real need created by the modern economic system, and the only need it creates. The quantity of money becomes more and more its sole important property. Just as it reduces everything to its own form of abstraction, so it reduces itself in the course of its own movement to something quantitative.'

Money as the source of power and as the necessary means of increasingly more satisfacton is inherently unreliable. As the primary tie among individual men in society, its possession seems to express power but in reality expresses powerlessness in the face of a greater, capricious, unknown being – a set of circumstances that is the 'operations of the market.' There is no possibility of individual control over this capricious external power, while collective control remains impossible so long as communal life is organized as a state that guarantees its operations or tampers with them only to ensure their fundamental continuance.

The power of money for Rousseau is not only an expression of individual and collective powerlessness, another expression of social alienation, but a universal solvent in which all other human powers are resolved by the power of exchange. Rousseau recognizes four kinds of 'forces' that can be predicated of men in society. These are riches, nobility or rank, power (by which is meant political power), and personal merit (by which is meant not only moral goodness but excellence pertaining to any of the faculties of body or mind). A society, he says, can be judged according to the relationship among these four forces. Civil society represents the 'extreme term of corruption,' since in the grip of its dynamic, 'among these four kinds of inequality, personal qualities being the origin of all the others, wealth is the one to which they are all reduced in the end; for, as riches tend most immediately to the prosperity of individuals and are easiest to communicate, they are used to purchase every other distinction' (*DOI* 216-17). In civil society it is not a matter of priorities. The value of pecuniary wealth is not that it can provide a foundation for power or personal merit, as it might have for an Aristotle, but rather that the intrinsic value expressed in human differences is lost. They are all 'reduced' to riches. The universality of exchange value takes the place of the particularity of concrete human qualities. Hence the term *corruption*, in its original meaning of the decomposition or dis-integration of an organic body articulated into functionally discrete parts, is especially apt. What takes place is not merely moral depravation – the very grounds of moral and other forms of discrimination are undercut in the homogenization of all value.[20]

---

20 Marx, in the section on 'Money' in the 1844 manuscripts, offers a similar understanding of the human meaning of money: 'Since money, as the existing active concept of value, confounds and exchanges everything, it is the universal confusion and exchange of all things, an inverted world, the confusion and exchange of all natural and human qualities ... If we assume man to be man, and his relation to the world to be a human one, then love can be exchanged only for love, trust for trust, and so on. If you wish to enjoy

It is extremely questionable, however, whether the conditions of existence enforced in civil society are appropriate grounds for the creation of 'real personal qualities.' As we have seen in chapter 3, the ego for Rousseau is not an origin. Savage man living in the pure state of nature is not a human individual but a purely natural being. Individuation is a necessary aspect of the historical evolution of culture through the process of social labour. The form, therefore, of social labour is something internal to the ego as such and also to particular forms of the self corresponding to specific societies. In civil society the ego tends to be conceived of as an abstract origin, a substantial essence, whose relations with others are purely external and instrumental. Social development adds nothing to it but additional means to attain objects that are already given by nature. The additional means themselves are merely modifications, as with Hobbes and Locke, of what is enjoined upon every rational agent by natural law. Rousseau's critique of Hobbes and Locke is therefore not restricted to their misplacing the origin of moral evil inside the human subject as such, but reaches down into the very constitution of the ego. Thus these philosophers are 'obliged to make man a philosopher before he is a man' (*DOI* 158). And not only do they make him a philosopher; they make him a bourgeois philosopher, 'for whom liberty itself is nothing but a means of acquiring without obstacle and of possessing securely.'[21] The abstract, atomic egos that are the points of origin of civil society are necessarily equal in their very abstractness and are thus eminently suitable to enter into the relations of ostensible instrumental reciprocity that are the essence of civil society.

If the bourgeois form of social labour is captured unawares in the modern philosophical consciousness of the ego, and if that consciousness is ideological in its repression of the historicity of the self, the latter does none the less express a crucial truth concerning the actual egos constituted in the relations of civil society. Thus although Hobbes 'improperly admitted as a part of savage man's care for self-preservation the gratification of a multitude of passions which are the work of society, and have made laws necessary' (*DOI* 181), these passions are no less real for being 'unnatural' or 'factitious.' And Rousseau's critique thus negatively accords Hobbes high honour for accurately describing the actual

---

art you must be an artistically educated person; if you wish to exercise influence on other men you must be the sort of person who has a truly stimulating and encouraging effect on others. Each one of your relations to man – and to nature – must be a particular expression corresponding to the object of your will, of your real individual life' (ibid., 379).

21 Cited in Gossman, 'Time and History,' 339 n 1

system of relations among men in civil society. These relations are, in a sense, summed up in the term *amour-propre*, which in Rousseau's usage shares a fundamental similarity with the picture of social relations drawn by Hobbes. In Hobbes's view power (and the search for power) is primarily relative; it is always gained at the expense of another. This being the nature of power, it follows that, in the absence of any countervailing factor, social relations will be a continual and unlimited struggle for predominance. Such a struggle is and can be seen to be ultimately self-defeating. The solution therefore lies in the creation of one massively superior power that will maintain the delicate equilibrium among power-seekers and effectively contain the permanently incipient state of war from disrupting their instrumental relations.[22]

Rousseau is in fundamental agreement with Hobbes that the relations of civil society are in fact such a struggle for predominance, in which power is gained only through a corresponding loss of power on another's part. We have seen how this is anchored in the economic relations of civil society. At the same time it is expressed psychologically as a 'universal desire for reputation' (*DOI* 217), a desire that is inherently unlimited precisely as a result of its depending upon recognition on the part of the other. Those who assume the role of superior, the 'few rich and powerful men,' pursue luxury, wealth, and office, not for anything they might offer in themselves but as signs of power; they 'prize what they enjoy only insofar as others are destitute of it; and because, without changing their condition, they would cease to be happy the moment the people ceased to be wretched' (*DOI* 217).[23] At the same time it is clear that this struggle for recognition is not restricted to the rich and powerful but permeates all the relations of civil society.[24] However, in civil society this dynamic is not recognized for what it is, since that

---

22 On the subject of Hobbes's political theory reflecting the social and economic relations of bourgeois society, see Macpherson, *Individualism*, esp. 17-76, 106.

23 Cf *PE* 268: 'They must know but little of mankind who can imagine that, after they have been once seduced by luxury, they can ever renounce it: they would a hundred times sooner renounce common necessaries, and had much rather die of hunger than of shame.'

24 See Rousseau, *DOI* 202: all members of civil society, including those of the middle conditions and the poor, are brought into subjection to one another through the establishment of the market; also, 215: 'Besides, individuals only allow themselves to be oppressed so far as they are hurried on by blind ambition, and, looking rather below than above them, come to love authority more than independence, and submit to slavery, that they may in turn enslave others.' The dynamic of ambition also comes to command the highest and best activities of society, the arts, the sciences, and philosophy – on this point see not only *DAS* but also *PN* 129-37.

form of society is in theory based on the universal recognition of natural equality. These are men 'forced to caress and destroy one another at the same time' (*DOI* 223) because they are natural equals who in the dynamic of the system of needs are 'naturally' placed in the position of adversaries. Rousseau therefore recognizes in Hobbesian man not a fiction but a candid description of the reality of bourgeois society that he makes his own.[25]

The rationality of the abstract ego that naturally seeks to maximize its power therefore represents for Rousseau the moment of truth of liberal political thought. The difference, of course, is that for Rousseau it is only a moment. What it fails to recognize is that this form of freedom contains its own negation. In the economy all are subject to the laws of the market, while certain men are in fact subjected to other men as well, in being forced to labour for them. In the rule of abstract value embodied in money, real personal qualities are reduced to fungible commodities. In the political realm the equality of the state of nature returns ultimately as an equality of mistreatment in despotism, while preceding stages institute a milder form of class rule. And by no means least is the negation of freedom in the psychological or moral realm. The free, rational individual, the ideal-typical member of civil society, who in the consciousness of his freedom has seemingly arrived at the height of self-consciousness, whose relation to society and the state is itself instrumental, is psychically a non-being. This man, who conceives his freedom to lie in a relative lack of external constraint and who is conceived as self-identical across shifting relations, has in reality perfectly internalized systemic constraint and is now subject to the whole of society, the particulars of which he is driven to dominate. He 'lives constantly outside himself, and only knows how to live in the opinion of others, so that he seems to receive the consciousness of his own existence merely from the judgement of others concerning him" (*DOI* 220).

The highest irony, therefore, is in the near-complete subjection in reality of the being who appears most free. And there is equal irony in the fact that the conscious assertion of this freedom is a crucial factor in subjection. The self-sufficient, self-identical subject of reason, the bourgeois, free from all personal domination, whose essential self-expression is the domination of nature and the erection of social arrangements based on scientific knowledge, has not escaped subjection to the power of either.

25 See Rousseau, *PN* 143ff. Rousseau believes that when 'vice' has progressed to a certain point, it becomes necessary to base political relations on the 'candour' of science. This preserves society from total disintegration and the individual from complete degradation, 'for in a country where there should be neither probity nor morality left, it would be still better to live among knaves than among ruffians' (144).

If anything he has internalized them. They have become an integral part of his false freedom.

Psychically, however, the integrity of the member of bourgeois society is a fragile and dependent thing, caught on the one hand between the warring claims of interest and duty and on the other between the demands of nature and the impositions of culture. Always compelled to act in accordance with the shifting social forces bearing down upon him, he unwittingly identifies his freedom with the most thoroughgoing control. In a striking metaphor Rousseau compares the member of civil society to a spider totally enveloped in a web he himself has spun:

> When I see each one of us, ceaselessly taken up with public opinion, extend his existence, so to speak, all about him while keeping hardly anything in his own heart, I believe I see a small insect forming from his substance a grand web, by the threads of which alone he appears sensitive, while one believed him to be dead in his hole. The vanity of man is the spider's web that he stretches over everything that encloses him. The one is as solid as the other; the least thread that one touches puts him in movement; he would die of exhaustion if one left the web in peace, and when with a finger one tears it, he will completely exhaust himself in order to have it rebuilt instantly. (LM 1112)

In civil society the self-identical subject is necessarily divided not only from other individuals and from society as a whole but also in his psychic integrity. The ego becomes merely the node of a web of external forces, but forces that were his own to begin with, 'formed from his substance.'

Rousseau, in holding that 'there is nothing more truly beautiful than power and independence' (CPC 326), was in fundamental agreement with liberalism and the Enlightenment. But no one before him, and relatively few after, understood better the negation of power and independence contained in the very structure of civil society and in its premises. Civil society, although it ostensibly begins with independent (and therefore equal) centres of power, turns these powers into an alien power that is the negation of individuality.[26] If this is the inherent logic of civil society, of society structured and conceived of as a system of needs, it is not for Rousseau either the natural or final form of the development

---

26 Cf Marx, *Economic and Philosophic Manuscripts*, in *Early Writings*, 366: 'estrangement appears not only in the fact that the means of my life belong to another and that my desire is the inaccesible possession of another, but also in the fact that all things are other than themselves, that my activity is other than itself, and that finally – and this goes for the capitalists too – an inhuman power rules over everything.'

of human nature. History (and ethnography) at least offer him the example of fundamentally different forms. But it would at this point be premature to introduce his proposed 'solutions' to the human dilemma. For the history of the social individual has an added dimension not unrelated to the development of the forms of social labour. Each historical form of human collective existence is predicated upon a peculiar transformation of man's 'original' nature, an original nature that persists, if never unmodified, within the artifice of social institutions. For Rousseau the history of civilization is not only a history of deepening alienation but one of more and more severe repression.

Recapitulation: The Pattern of Human History

Rousseau's anthropology laid the groundwork for an understanding of human nature as constituted in the history of practical, social activity. Rousseau understands the historical transformation of nature as a succession of forms of social labour. Each form of social labour is expressed in and corresponds to a form of social individuality. Each form of social individuality in turn demands a particular modification of human instinctual life. The social modification of desire is predicated upon the existence of the quintessentially social passion – the desire for recognition – which in turn presupposes the ability to substitute symbolic gratification for the direct expression and satisfaction of the 'savage.' *Amour-de-soi*, the instinctual form of self-regulation that is pre-social and pre-individual, gives way to *amour-propre*, the desire for self-esteem symbolically mediated by another or others. But where *amour-de-soi* coincides with the immediate unity of self and other, *amour-propre* presupposes the disquieting separation of self and other; it is the impetus to a unification of subject and object that can never be satisfied: '*Amour-propre* is always irritated or discontented because it wishes that each preferred us to everything and to himself, which cannot be' (*RJ* 233). The ensuing struggle for recognition, itself already a transformation of the force of biological desire, supplies a large part of the momentum of all striving in human history.

Amour-propre is a necessary aspect of the perfectibility of the animal who is biologically formed to become social. *Amour-propre* is both the result of social evolution and one of its conditions: the result, because it is based upon the symbolic function developed in the course of the development of language and reason; and the condition because it is the 'motor of progress' in history. Perfectibility would not reach very far did it not give rise to and depend (in ontogenesis) on vanity. Thus

Rousseau is regretfully forced to admit that perfectibility, 'this distinctive and almost unlimited faculty, is the source of all human misfortunes; that it is this which, in time, draws man out of his original state, in which he would have spent his days insensibly in peace and innocence; that it is this faculty, which, successively producing in different ages his discoveries, and his errors, his vices and his virtues, makes him at length a tyrant both over himself and over nature' (*DOI* 219). Although it is a series of accidents that force man, in social labour, to separate himself from nature, his perfectibility will thenceforward be inseparable from his social second nature.

History is, then, the formation of the social individual. In the succession of social formations described above, in primitive, ancient, and bourgeois society, the self is mediated by the demands of society in such a way as to promote the reproduction of specific sets of social relations. The member of primitive society is not, for himself or his fellows, an instance of the abstraction man but a concrete individuality defined by his specific relations as father, brother, son, uncle, stranger. In the polis the citizen has extended the scope of the social tie to include all other free men, but his freedom is grounded in the unconscious unity of his particular existence with the universality of custom. In the bourgeois the self finally declares its self-subsistence as reason and appears to itself as absolute, while nature and other men become merely the stuff of its own instrumental activity. Yet the bourgeois knows that he cannot subsist or enjoy in isolation and that the only basis for sociability lies in the fundamental recognition by each of the freedom and equality of all the others. Relations of instrumental reciprocity therefore appear to the bourgeois as natural relations, and it is upon these that he proposes to erect all his social institutions. But we have seen that these relations are in substance the negation of the autonomy that is their principle.

The history of the forms of social labour is an epic in miniature of the development of the freedom of the particular, at first from nature and then from the community a second nature, only to find, in the assertion of absolute freedom, a new subjection to the pseudo-nature of the market. The 'freedom' of the 'savage' lies in his immunity and utter insensitivity to an exterior will. But this immunity coincides with his own complete lack of self-consciousness. Negativity only arises under the necessity to produce his subsistance in relations with others. His freedom is therefore dialectically identical to his complete subjection to natural necessity. Paradoxically, freedom here, for the 'animal-man' *is* necessity. But it is also due to natural necessity that men gradually come to oppose their wills to nature. Significantly, it is not the individual man who accomplishes this feat. Freedom from nature may be a biological necessity for men, but it is enforced in different ways as a social necessity. Desire for the desire of others takes the place of unmediated instinctual desire and is won in labour, speech, and action. The desire for recognition, however, is in and of itself limitless and unsatisfiable. Therefore, in some instances a community of equals gives way to a society of masters and slaves, those who work and those who act. The former are reduced to being subhuman,[27] while the rest, who do not work, are free only as a caste of warriors imprisoned by their own ethos. Freedom here is not identical to natural necessity but to social force, which appears as second nature.

War produces empire and empire, despotism. Under the despot all are equal and discover their equality. The citizen-warrior and the slave give way to the bourgeois. Now, the bourgeois is someone who works, but not in direct personal submission to another. The bourgeois works for himself and exchanges his products for those of another. All are free and equal – free to enter into exchange or not, equal in that exchanges among equals are exchanges of equivalents. The bourgeois is a creature of the market, and the relations of the market are the nature of this creature, his nature in two senses: because he acts as though the needs created in production for the market were his own authentic needs and because he recognizes relations of exchange among free and equal producers as natural relations. But the freedom and equality of the relations of instrumental reciprocity give rise through the operations of the market itself to subjection to a new nature – the pseudo-nature of the market. Freedom here turns out to be the subjection of persons to a blind and mechanical economic dynamic. It is at the same time the erection in the political sphere of a Hobbesian sovereign out of the appearance of atomized conflict in civil society. This Rousseau calls a return to a 'new state of nature' (*DOI* 219).

History, however, does not simply take on the pattern of a development of free particulars, gradually differentiating themselves from their natural and communal backgrounds only to find themselves still subjected to blind impersonal forces. History is also a process of increasing inner misery. What could be at once more insulting and more paradoxical to the enlightened mind than the demonstration that man in a state of nature, whose life is admittedly solitary, poor, nasty, brutish, and short, has no reason to envy the civilized man?

---

27 Rousseau often maintains that a slave (or anyone reduced to being a natural condition of production) is less than human.

A famous author, reckoning up the good and evil of human life, and comparing the aggregates, finds that our pains greatly exceed our pleasures: so that, all things considered, human life is not at all a valuable gift. This conclusion does not at all surprise me; for the writer drew all his arguments from man in civilization. Had he gone back to the state of nature, his inquiries would clearly have had a different result, and man would have been seen to be subject to very few evils not of his own creation. It has indeed cost us not a little trouble to make ourselves as wretched as we are. When we consider, on the one hand, the immense labours of mankind ... and, on the other hand, estimate with ever so little thought, the real advantages that have accrued from all these works to mankind, we cannot help being amazed at the vast disproportion there is between these things, and deploring the infatuation of man, which, to gratify his silly pride and vain self-admiration, induces him eagerly to pursue all the miseries he is capable of feeling, though beneficent nature had kindly placed them out of the way. (*DOI* 222)

Civilized wretchedness is a 'moral,' psychic misery, a suffering of the soul that is quite distinct from a state of physical privation.

Why is it then that we 'see around us hardly a creature in civil society, who does not lament his existence' (*DOI* 180)? The key (but not the solution) is to be found in the psychic life of savage man. The savage supplies a prototype, in the immediacy of his psychic life, of human happiness. It should be understood that a prototype is not an ideal but an original pattern. Rousseau's ideal of human happiness – as it will be encountered in *Emile* – is a dialectical return to the psychic equilibrium of the savage, but after the limitations of savage existence have been overcome, a return that incorporates the extension of the human spirit developed in history.

The psychic life of the savage is essentially peaceful because he 'lives within himself'; his indifference to the exterior world makes even Stoic *ataraxia* a pale shadow of the original (*DOI* 220). His psychic life is peaceful because it is unified. Having not yet encountered the necessity to oppose himself to either internal or external nature in either labour or social life, his desire is always commensurate with his power. The savage is, as it were, self-identical along several dimensions. The demands of his internal nature are pre-adapted to the exigencies of external nature. Thus, temporally, there is no need to delay the expression of instinctual needs; correspondingly, there is no need to alter or modify the instinctual expression of need in either its aims or its object. Desire receives immediate expression both temporally and psychologically. His self-regulation is automatic and instinctual. Psychoanalytic psychology would call him pre-ambivalent. Time and the external world are to him strictly irrelevant.

Social man, by contrast, retains the fundamental aim of the instinctual life of the savage, but the conditions of fulfilling these aims are no longer present. *Amour-propre* has as its aim the re-establishment of the unity of self and other now denied to social man by the necessity to oppose himself to external and internal nature in labour and to internal nature in relations with human others. The exigencies of culture simultaneously inflame his passions but demand that these be subjected to the control of reason, delayed, deflected, and modified to correspond to social goals. And in a sense, through the evolutionary development of intelligence and imagination, culture supplies him with the means to accomplish this partially. But the perpetual transition from biological to cultural life that human beings undertake depends on harnessing the force of biological desire in the interests of culture. Nature is never annihilated, but remains the principal condition and well-spring of culture: 'The state of society that constrains all our natural inclinations cannot however annihilate them. In spite of our prejudices and in spite of ourselves, they still speak in the depths of our hearts and often lead us back to the truth we abandoned for the sake of chimeras' (*EG* 305).

In social man instinctual self-regulation gives way to self-regulation based upon the adoption and internalization of cultural demands. This is accomplished via the substitution of the desire for self-esteem for the unmediated desires of the purely biological. But the desire for self-esteem is mediated by the other. Self-esteem is dependent upon recognition. Introduced into the psyche of the social man is a specialized agency through which the demands of society – that is, virtue – come to be identified with the nature of the individual. The psychic life of social man is thus divided against itself in its mediation by the other. Or, in other words, both the (false) happiness and the misery of social man are inextricably caught up in *amour-propre*. He is made susceptible to psychic misery by (necessarily) depending for his happiness on a self-esteem that is subject to the demands of culture but that may have completely lost touch with his original nature – a nature that he continually keeps *and* continually transforms.

It is therefore the very striving for the wholeness of the pre-cultural self through the attempt to reduce the other to the guarantor of one's self-esteem that opens the self to identification with cultural demands. Now, for Rousseau, culture seems above all to demand two things – labour and morality or virtue. Both of these are predicated on the social denaturing of the individual through the regulation of self-esteem. Both therefore presuppose a kind of repression of nature, understood as the abstract force of biological desire.

The history of civilization is, for Rousseau in the second *Discourse*, largely the development of increasing 'labour, slavery and wretchedness': 'Civilized man ... is always moving, sweating, toiling, and racking his brains to find still more laborious occupations: he goes on in drudgery to his last moment, and even seeks death to put himself in a position to live, or renounces life to acquire immortality' (*DOI* 220). In civil society, as opposed to very primitive human society, the 'idleness that nurtures passion is replaced by work, which represses it. Instead of being concerned with living happily, one had to be concerned with living. Mutual need uniting men to a greater extent when sentiment has not done so, society would be formed only through industry' (*EOl* 47). Increasing civilization demands increasing self-instrumentalization in more and more dangerous, unsatisfying, and degrading forms of labour (*DOI* 226). We have already seen how the division of labour, the regime of private property, and the system of needs bring this about. Instead of freeing men from unnecessary labour, the advance of the arts and sciences seems only to hold out the prospect of extending and deepening the sphere of necessity. A simple comparison 'without partiality of the state of the citizen with that of the savage' leads to pessimistic conclusions, since if 'you reflect on the mental afflictions that prey on us, the violent passions that waste and exhaust us, the excessive labour with which the poor are burdened, the still more dangerous indolence to which the wealthy give themselves up, so that the poor perish of want and the rich of surfeit; if you reflect but a moment ... you will see how dearly nature makes us pay for the contempt with which we have treated her lessons' (*DOI* 224-5). The revenge of nature is expressed not only in the pseudo-nature of the economic determinism that rules civil society but in increasing 'mental afflictions': 'It is in vain that one thinks of annihilating nature; it is reborn and shows itself where one expected it the least. The independence men are deprived of takes refuge in societies; and these great bodies, left to their own impetus, produce things more terrible in proportion to the degree in which their mass prevails over individuals' (*EG* 296).

Work for Rousseau is one of the principal and crucial demands of culture, and a demand that, as a result of a semi-independent sociocultural dynamic, is in the course of history increasingly severe. But it is imposed on the individual not simply through natural necessity, nor is it imposed, in bourgeois society, simply by physical force or the threat of starvation. Both 'civilized' work and the repression it demands are enforced by a social morality within the individual that is the internalization of the conditions of self-esteem. Thus, in the end, the form of social labour is seen to be an essential component in the vicissitudes of the instincts. As civilization advances and as cultural demand takes the place of more immediate and direct forms of the expression of desire, as virtue progressively supplants *bonté*, the burden of morality becomes heavier.

Virtue is the internalization of cultural demand. But virtue seems impossible without a sort of neurotic conflict. From a slightly different perspective it could be said that virtue, as an aspect of systems of political domination, is based upon, exploits, develops, and intensifies the capacity for neurotic conflict inherent in human-cultural existence. Slaves run to their chains only because they see in them their happiness. The extraction of obedience, just as much as toil, is a psychological process as important as it is obscure. In *La Nouvelle Héloïse* Rousseau presents a dramatic examination of the intertwined processes of psychological repression and political domination. Neither Rousseau's sense of the meaning of historical-cultural existence nor his 'program,' his understanding of the process and preconditions of emancipation, can be properly grasped without examining this novel from a perspective that is at once psychological and political. For in Julie the ghost of the *purity* of virtue, duty, conscience is finally put to rest.

CHAPTER SIX

Julie and the Pathology of Conscience

> He alone who could situate utopia in blind somatic pleasure,
> which, satisfying the ultimate intention, is intentionless,
> has a valid and stable idea of truth.
> T.W. Adorno

Social Unreason and Individual Pathology

Rousseau was among the first to articulate in some measure of their full complexity two complementary moments of the civilizational process: each step in the apparent advance of reason seemed to entail a corresponding regression and irruption of irrational forces. In preceding chapters we have seen that the history of the social forms of labour constitutes just such a process. The emergence of the rational, free member of bourgeois society from the trammels of the natural community entails as its obverse his immersion in the pseudo-nature of the market. The natural laws of the market society, however, are anything but rational in their effects on the individual. Increasing control over nature, freedom from superstition and myth, all seem to somehow conspire to render the beneficiaries of reason not only unfree but miserable. Civil society is a voyage to despotism in which all are united in their subjection to arbitrary power. Its final term is a parody of the state of nature.

Human knowledge in Rousseau's eyes is unsuited to attain absolute truth, to penetrate appearance to the level of ultimate realities, to reconstruct the world out of the apprehension of the intelligible essence of substances. More than this, reason is itself not fully autonomous. As both Condillac and Hume have proved, 'Since we are not wholly intelligence, we would be unable to philosophize with so much disinterestedness that our will does not influence our opinions a little. One can often determine the secret inclinations of a man by way of his purely speculative opinions ... In the long run reason follows the bent the heart gives it' (*LMF* 11377–8).

The constructs of human reason cannot be accepted as autonomous. Their roots lie in the hearts of men. As we have seen, however, the heart is itself informed by culture. Unlike the biologistic voluntarism of Condillac, the heart in its *inquiétude* is not taken by Rousseau to be final. Underlying the appearance of the autonomy of reason are the secret inclinations of the heart, but these themselves are historical. The history of philosophy is thus linked to the history of society, and the history of society is mirrored in the history of the human heart. The philosophy of enlightenment, for example, which takes its version of the triumphant march of reason to be the liberation of human nature, does not recognize itself to be a reflection of the logic of the member of the system of needs.

Philosophy for Rousseau is thus no proof against or transcendence of this double process in human civilisation. Philosophy, along with the arts and sciences, has been a part of its irrationality.[1] When it comes to the autonomy of practical reason, the picture is quite similar. The essence of political reason is the autonomy of the 'voice of duty.' The inner assent to the voice of duty embodied in the formation of the general will is the triumph of practical reason. Yet even here (see chapter 7 below) seeming progress is inextricably bound up with irrationality: 'Although in this the civil state, he deprives himself of some advantages which he got from nature, he gains in return others so great ... that, *did not the abuses of this new condition often degrade him below that which he left*, he would be bound to bless continually the happy moment which took him from it forever' (*SC* 16; emphasis added). It is only a suggestion, but the suggestion is clear: the citizen, the embodiment of human dignity, is as a matter of course degraded below the level of his existence in the state of nature. He is *not* obligated to bless that moment that precipitated him out of nature and made him 'instead of a stupid and unimaginative animal ... an intelligent being and a man' (*SC* 16). The dignity of reason is only the obverse of the degradation of irrationality. Natural man is neither one nor the other, neither rational nor irrational, neither degraded nor exalted.

1 See Rousseau, *PN* 135–7; and *LM* 1987–91.

Julie and the Pathology of Conscience / 137

But the history of civilization is only an apparent contradiction for Rousseau, because the bond between irrationality and reason is not necessary indissoluble. The dissolution of that bond, however, is predicated upon a real understanding of the historical process. One side of that understanding is to be sought in the history of the forms of social labour. But we have seen that each form of social labour, each epoch of human history, is maintained by the inculcation of a certain form of virtue, corresponding to the functional needs of that particular form. Each cultural form of virtue (excepting perhaps the primitive) is at the same time a partial denial of nature as desire, a systematic inability to incorporate desire into the sphere of cultural expression. Not only the theoretical but the real dissolution of the paradoxical bond between progressing reason and growing irrationality will therefore depend not only upon a historical reconstitution, a 'retracing of steps' directed at the historical forms of social labour. It is equally predicated upon a historical, genetic analysis of virtue, duty, and conscience. 'Society must be studied in the individual and the individual in society; those who desire to treat politics and morals apart from one another will never understand either' (*E* 197).

The paradoxical bond between the history of reason and the history of unreason is something that belongs not only to the species but to the individual. The relationship is more than a mere parallelism. The history of social unreason is unfolded inside the individual. Tension and contradiction, then, do not simply take place at an objective level in the structure of social institutions and at a conscious level for the individual. As we shall see, the conflict within the individual is primarily unconscious.

In calling for a study of society and the individual in each other Rousseau is proposing not simply a social psychology that proceeds at the level of consciousness. His anthropology has laid some of the foundations for an individual depth-psychology with an essential sociological dimension. Rousseau does not understand the human psyche in terms of external relations between an affective, desiring faculty and a cognitive, rational faculty. The affective and the cognitive are internally related in a developmental process. The course of human evolution has produced a creature who must understand and transform the world in order not only to satisfy his desire in it but also to survive. No longer a creature of instinct, he displays malleable drives organized, modified, and restrained in the interests of culture. Human cognition itself depends upon that first negation of desire made in recognition of the necessity to labour. A part of the cognitive apparatus is the 'faculty' of imagination, under the auspices of which desire may be displaced symbolically to non-'instinctual' aims and objects, one of which is knowledge itself (see chapter 3 above). On the most fundamental level, therefore, the human psyche is the result of a dynamic process. Thus, 'we must not confuse what is natural in a state of savagery with what is natural in civilised life' (*E* 368).[2]

The human psyche is the hidden battleground where the contestants, desire ultimately grounded in biology and the activities and apparatuses of culture, each depend upon the other for their existence: 'Our inner conflicts are caused by these contradictions. Drawn this way by nature and that way by man, *compelled to yield to both forces*, we make a compromise and reach neither goal. We go through life struggling and hesitating, and die before we have found peace, useless alike to ourselves and to others' (*E* 9; emphasis added); 'each man is a doubled being: nature acts within; the social spirit shows itself without' (*EF* 273). Thus nature not only refers to what exists at the origins but also to that which remains concealed in the process of development from origins. Nature and the secret inclinations of the heart are simultaneously linked and distinguished. The secret inclinations of the heart are the precipitates of the interaction of culture and nature, which remain unintegrated into cultural expression.

Human individuation and socialization depend upon some split between the demands of nature and the demands of culture. But the split itself, or rather the inner conflicts to which it gives rise, are not always conscious. Thus, 'we no longer dare seem what we really are, but lie under a perpetual restraint'; the norms, forms, rules of civilized behaviour are what 'we must always follow, never the promptings of our own nature' (*DAS* 122). It is only the social spirit that exhibits itself externally, to consciousness. Even to ourselves we dare not seem to be what we really are, literally creatures of conflict. Self-knowledge cannot, therefore, rest at the conscious level, or even with knowledge of our own social self-creation in the historical development of civilization. It is necessary to extend the sphere of knowledge into the secret history of the human heart:

In order to know a character well it is necessary to distinguish what is acquired from what is nature, to see how it has formed itself, what occasions developed it, what chain of secret affections rendered it so, and how that chain is modified,

---

2 Modified translation

in order to sometimes produce the most contradictory and unexpected effects. That which is seen is but the least part of that which is; it is the apparent effect whose internal cause is hidden and often very complicated. (*EC* 1149)

The Problem of Virtue

Central to the structure of character in any given individual is the formation of conscience. Virtue for Rousseau means adherence to the voice of conscience: 'Virtue! sublime science of simple minds ... Need we do more, to learn your laws, than examine ourselves and listen to the voice of conscience, when the passions are silent?' (*DAS* 142) A problem arises here, however, because Rousseau again and again identifies the voice of conscience with the voice of nature: 'There is thus in the depths of every soul an innate principle of justice and moral truth anterior to all national prejudices, to all the maxims of education. This principle is the involuntary guide by which, in spite of our own maxims, we judge our own actions and those of others as good or evil, and it is to this principle that I give the name conscience' (*LM* 1108). What could be a more categorical identification of conscience with a nature that transcends culture than those lines, or than these: 'do not confound the secret penchants of our heart that mislead us with this more secret dictate, even more inward, that beseeches and murmers against these interested decisions and leads us back in spite of ourselves to the route of truth. This interior sentiment is that of nature itself' (*LMF* 1138). If conscience, however, is an 'innate principle' anterior to particular cultures, which comes into conflict with the practical maxims of those cultures and which is equivalent to nature itself, is this not tantamount to saying not only that in the final analysis is it beyond the reach of culture but that it is a suprahistorical source of value? Conscience in this case would represent the natural core of absolute individuality, functionally comparable in Rousseau's thought to the earlier roles of natural reason and natural law. In this case virtue would be submission to a dictate of nature as opposed to the dictates of either socially mediated pressures or the pressures of a 'lower' nature.

Most scholars who have wrestled with the vagaries and logical inconsistencies[3] of Rousseau's doctrines of virtue and conscience have indeed assigned conscience a transcendent, suprahistorical status. Disagreement has centred upon the essence, or nature, of conscience and upon the abstract

---

3 For example, cf the differences between the Savoyard vicar's treatment of conscience in *Emile* (*E* 253) and Rousseau's in *LM* 1109.

conflict between virtue and inclination. There has for quite a while been controversy over whether Rousseau is essentially a sentimentalist or an intuitionist in ethics or whether the kernel of his doctrine is rationalist. The sentimentalist judgment seemed to hold sway throughout the nineteenth century, only to come under attack in the first half of the twentieth from the neo-Kantian revisionism of Ernst Cassirer. In Cassirer's hands Rousseau's ethics 'is not an ethics of feeling but the most categorical form of a pure ethics of obligation (*Gesetzes-Ethik*) that was established before Kant.'[4] Not only that, but 'in opposition to the predominant opinion of the century Rousseau eliminated feeling from the foundation of ethics.'[5]

Understandably, the interpretation of Rousseau as an ethical superrationalist was in turn subjected to a revisionist critique at the hands of Robert Derathé. For Derathé, however, Rousseau ends up holding two distinct moralities, one that affirms a victory of reason over the natural penchants, the other positing a morality of instinct (see chapter 1, notes 46, 47, 20). But Derathé believes that although for Rousseau these two moralities remain distinct, they are not irreconcilable. In the end, therefore, Derathé's position is fundamentally as rationalist as that of Cassirer. His criticisms of Cassirer are largely confined to a critique of Kantian intellectualism and legalism, whereas he wishes to grant feeling or sentiment a crucial but not equally dignified role in the formation of conscience in the civilized man. Reason, like society, is not in itself the source of error, even though it is dependent on feeling for maintaining its true course.[6] Accordingly, Rousseau's thought ends up in the paradox that man by himself cannot achieve moral liberty and must therefore subject himself to reason.[7]

In the debate on the nature of Rousseau's doctrine of conscience a consensus has been established, as it were beforehand, that whatever the true nature of the relation between feeling and reason, conscience itself, although not immune to external historical influence, constitutes an Archimedean point from which the political and personal world can be transformed. What is important is that on both sides of this debate conscience remains a permanently accessible, suprahistorical access to nature and, as such, becomes the pole around which social practice can and must reorient itself. Rousseau's reputation as a moralist is an accretion of tremendous historical weight precisely because he presents such a

---

4 Cassirer, *Question*, 96
5 Ibid., 99
6 Derathé, *Rationalism*, 167, 7–8; Pierre Burgelin has developed the most sophisticated reconciliation of feeling and reason along these lines in his *Existence*, esp. 311, 324–7.
7 Derathé, *Rationalism*, 123

complex problem for interpretation in terms of idealist philosophy. And Rousseau's best idealist interpreters have never been entirely comfortable in his company. This is exemplified, for example, in Cassirer's admission that Rousseau's thought 'persistently slips away from the strict line of argumentation'[8] towards the sundering of reason and conscience, virtue (and therefore conscience) and happiness, and away from an exaltation of human dignity towards an insistence upon feeling. In Cassirer's eyes these would constitute a capitulation, a submission to the felt pressure of phenomenal reality. Nevertheless, Cassirer is scrupulously honest in allowing that when Rousseau complains, 'All the evil I ever did in my life was the result of reflection; and the little good I have been able to do was the result of impulse,'[9] an important component of his thought remains unintegrated into the rationalist interpretation.[10]

When Rousseau is seen, however, as engaged in the creation of a historical anthropology in which the history of the human heart plays a large part, the issue of conscience becomes a problem of a different sort. If we are no longer obliged to sort out the abstract roles of faculties like reason and feeling in the formation or operation of conscience, it becomes possible to investigate Rousseau's thoughts as not governed by an abstract separation of nature and history. Conscience belongs to nature for Rousseau in so far as it transcends the limitations of a particular social ethic. It is not purely the product of a given environment and a given education. It retains within it a demand that belongs to the earliest stages of human existence – the 'primitive,' narcissistic demand for the identity of self and other.

Conscience, however, belongs just as much to history, in that as a psychological capacity it is the product of a historical evolution producing profound changes in the bio-psychological capacities and structures of the human animal. The history of conscience, however, does not stop with its initial appearance. As biological evolution gives way to cultural evolution, conscience acquires a history that is dependent on a relatively independent series of developments in social structure and organization. Conscience is dependent in its content and its dynamic functional role within the human psyche on the history of society. Just as the passions have their history, conscience too, which, if not one of them, is closely allied, has its own.

8 Cassirer, *Question*, 127
9 Quoted by Cassirer, ibid., 127
10 Derathé, *Rationalisme*, and Burgelin, *Existence*, are more successful in relating feeling and reason in the development of conscience, but neither is able to resolve satisfactorily the conflict between virtue and happiness, and both abstract from the history of society as mediating the forms of virtue.

The issue of conscience or of virtue for Rousseau can therefore be cast not so much as a philosophical issue with respect to the foundations of ethics but as a psychological and political issue. In his opposition to the growing moral relativism of the Enlightenment, Rousseau was concerned to oppose the pure environmentalism that tended to arise on the soil of Lockean empiricism. In opposition to the environmentalist contention that ethical systems were merely the product of local prejudices, Rousseau tended to fall back on the existence of a universal moral feeling underlying particular ethical systems (*LM* 1108–9). Behind history stood a nature that could be depraved but not destroyed. But this is not to say that what appears as conscience under any particular historical form is the pure, untouched voice of nature:

To exist for us is to feel; and our sensibility is incontestably anterior even to our reason. Whatever the cause of our existence may be, it has provided for our conservation in giving us feelings consonant with our nature; and one could not deny that at least these are innate. These feelings, with regard to the individual, are the love of self [l'amour de soi-même], the fear of suffering and of death, and the desire for well-being. But if, as one could not doubt, man is an animal sociable by nature, or at least made to become so, it cannot be so except by other innate feelings relative to his species. *And it is from the moral system formed by this double relation to himself and his fellows that the natural impulsion of conscience is born.* (*LM* 1109; emphasis added)

What Rousseau hints at but leaves out of the above list of natural sentiments relative to oneself is, of course, *amour-propre*. *Amour-propre* is a natural sentiment relative to the members of one's species. Under the sway of *amour-propre*, self-esteem, the cultural substitute for the feeling of existence that enveloped the natural man, is conditional upon the regard of one's fellows. Conscience is *born* from the double relation to oneself and one's fellows. Conscience, as we shall see presently in greater detail, is a specific internal psychic agency that regulates social behaviour by 'secretly' dictating the cultural conditions of self-esteem. Conscience is born partly, but necessarily, from *amour-propre*, the most social of the passions. The dictate ('le dictamen') of conscience is natural only in so far as man is an animal made (by himself) to become sociable. When Rousseau therefore exalts conscience as a 'divine instinct' and seems to link it to a transcendent nature, he is disguising in the terms of providential-teleological thinking a challenge to transcendent moral systems as serious as that posed by his contemporary environmentalists.

At the same time, however, conscience is not linked to a transcendent reason or divine will. If conscience therefore takes up the role but not the metaphysical status of natural law, it is through its relation to *amour-de-soi*, which is the 'nature that can be depraved but not destroyed.' Virtue becomes both the internalization of social demand and a possible source of resistance to it. *Amour-propre* internalized in conscience can be set up against *amour-propre* that operates as the conscious desire for self-esteem mediated by the uninternalized other. Against the sort of stimulus-response slavery recommended by the early utilitarians as the essence of a rational social education, Rousseau's psychology of virtue aims at preserving a dimension of personal autonomy from the immediate social environment.[11]

Rousseau's glowing paeans to conscience must also be seen in relation to his equally forceful misgivings about its severity and the malaise to which it is linked under civilized conditions. The Spartan mother mentioned above (see page 107) is a paragon of virtue; so is Brutus: 'Brutus having his children killed could be nothing but just. But Brutus was a loving father; in order to do his duty he tortured his heart, and Brutus was virtuous' (*LMF* 1143). All that may be required to learn the laws of virtue is to listen to the voice of conscience when the 'passions' are silent. But to act virtuously and to maintain a virtuous intent is to be engaged in 'a state of war' (*LNH* 682).[12] The voice of conscience, to be effective, must be enforced: 'This word virtue signifies *force*. There is no virtue without combat; there is none without victory. Virtue does not simply consist in being just but in being so in triumphing over one's passions, in ruling over one's own heart' (*LMF* 1143). The force turned against one's own desire is one's own force and it is also the force of nature: 'Only through passion can we gain mastery over the passions; their tyranny must be controlled by their legitimate power, and nature herslf must furnish us with the means to control her' (*E* 292).

Virtue lends itself through a mysterious dynamic towards extending its sway over the whole of life. It has its own laws, which lead the individual 'to fight his dearest desires and to rend his heart in order to fulfil his duty' (*RJ* 209). As for those under its sway, 'they have hardly any other good rule of justice but to resist all their inclinations and always to

---

11 See, eg, *LMF* 1139: 'Eh qui ne sait que, sans le sentiment interne, il ne resteroit bientot plus de traces de vérité sur la terre, que nous serions tous successivement le jouet des opinions les plus monstreuses, à mesure que ceux qui les soutiendroient auroient plus de genie, d'adresse et d'esprit, et qu'enfin reduits à rangir de notre raison même, nous ne saurions bientot plus que croire ni que penser.'
12 In full it is: 'un état de guerre, et pour y vivre on a toujours quelque combat a rendre contre soi.'

do the opposite of what they desire, solely because they desire it' (*RJ* 209-10). Desire in itself eventually seems to call up a compulsive passion aimed at checking it. Virtue seems to feed on itself, extending its empire into realms to which it is totally alien. Thus the 'bright illusion' comes into existence which 'by virtue alone pretends to render us happy' (*EP* 15). It is crucial therefore not to 'exaggerate matters beyond the truth, nor to confound, as the stoics did, happiness with virtue' (*CG* 6.227). It is crucial, too, to limit virtue in its own interests, to avoid repeating the error of Christianity: 'Christianity, by exaggerating every duty, has made our duties impracticable and in vain' (*E* 337). In the eyes of Rousseau's best developed paragon of virtue, Julie, it appears as a jealous and demanding but false diviity: 'Mad and ferocious virtue! I obey its undeserving voice; I abhor it while I do everything for it. What use are its vain consolations against the distressful agonies of the soul? No, the sullen idol of wretches, it only increases their misery by depriving them of the resources which fortune offers them' (*NH* 3.3).

The language Rousseau uses in describing the psychic experience of virtue is laden with terms of aggression. War, force, combat, triumph, rending, and ferocity are all terms used to describe virtue or its results, while Julie accuses it of being 'insane.' How very much unlike the gentle yielding to an inner urge that it seems to be when Rousseau states that, to learn its laws, all we must do is listen to the voice of conscience in the silence of the passions. Conscience is itself one of the more ferocious of the passions.

A fuller understanding of conscience and virtue and their roles in civilized wretchedness must await a careful examination of Julie's case history in *La Nouvelle Héloïse*. The same is true of an understanding of the role that excessive denaturation plays in creating the internal requisites of political domination, and vice versa. Before I examine Julie's case history, it will be useful to catalogue the functions of conscience, the internal agency of social control as Rousseau presents them elsewhere than in *La Nouvelle Héloïse*.

Unlike the utilitarians, whose split between moral intent and moral goodness accommodates itself so well to the theory of the hidden hand, Rousseau believed that the moral life is centred in the inwardness of human purpose: 'All the morality of human life is in the intention of man' (*LM* 1106). This emphasis on intent, purpose, and wilfulness has been taken as another way in which Rousseau anticipates Kantian ethical voluntarism. But for Rousseau, unlike Kant, the experience of duty does not constitute evidence of the supersensible world. And Rousseau inverts the Kantian proposition by making the existence of God, or at least the belief in his existence, a practical condition of morality: 'all formulas in matters of faith only appear to me as so many chains of iniquity, of falsehood, of hypocrisy and of tyranny. But let us never be unfair, or aggravate the evil by taking away the good. To take away all belief in God from the hearts of men is to destroy virtue' (*LMF* 1142). Rousseau's emphasis on intent points to the inner life as the arena in which conflicting impulses and desires play out their drama. Conscience is oriented towards the world of 'secret penchants of our heart,' towards hidden, secret, unconscious wishes. Conscience is a 'more secret,' 'even more internal dictate' that is also a feeling (*LMF* 1138). The virtuous soul is involved in a strenuous battle of guarding against these secret desires: 'One must be incessantly on guard. The instant of enjoyment passes and never returns; that of doing evil passes and returns endlessly. One forgets oneself for a moment and is lost' (*LH* 667).

Conscience is therefore an internal, secret, omnipresent monitor and judge, 'this interior voice that judges me in secret and makes itself ceaselessly heard in my heart' (*LM* 1104). This judge is the source of punishment in the form of powerful feelings of guilt: 'One speaks of the wail of remorse that secretly punishes hidden crimes and so often brings them to light. Alas, who of us has never known that importunate voice. I speak from experience and would like to erase that involuntary feeling that gives us such torments. But if we obeyed nature we would know with what kindness she approves of what she has commanded and what charm one finds in enjoying the inner peace of a soul content with itself' (*LM* 1107). But conscience establishes its control, not only through the threat of punishment but also through the promise of intense rewards, the provision of which seems to restore almost as complete a sense of interior peace and security as that enjoyed by savage man. The enjoyment of the rewards of conscience has the force of sensuous experience: 'This moral sentiment ... this exquisite feeling of beauty, of truth, of justice, which is always reflected on ourselves, holds the soul of whoever is endowed with it in a continual ecstasy that is the most delightful joy' (*CG* 19.212). In being able to avail itself of such powerful rewards as well as punishments, conscience as an internal agency becomes the pre-condition of independence from the immediate environment. The weight of external pleasures *and* pains tends to diminish in importance, the more active is the voice of conscience:

These interior preparations independent of fortune and of events made more of a lively impression on me to the extent that my inclination to the contemplative and solitary life gave them room to develop. I felt in me, as it were, the counterweight to my destiny ... In seeking the principle of this hidden force that thus balanced the empire of my passions, I found that it came from a secret judgment that I made, without thinking, of the acts in my life and on the objects of my desires. My troubles tormented me less in imagining they were not at all my doing. And my pleasures lost all their value when I saw with composure in what I had made them consist ... I saw that it was vain to search out happiness afar when you neglect to cultivate it in yourself. (*LM* 1102).

But this description of the main features of conscience is incomplete in so far as it is abstracted from the social context in which conscience develops. Conscience is born of the double relation between ourselves and others, and it represents the turning of nature against itself. How this is accomplished and what its significance is can be approached through a reading of Rousseau's most detailed and complex instance of a 'virtuous soul' in Julie.

Conscience and the Psychodynamics of Excess Denaturation in Julie

In Julie Rousseau demonstrates that virtue is itself not pure but follows from the internalization of an external authority. The novel has often been interpreted as a sermon for the victory of the ethical will over the 'assaults of feeling'[13] or as a lament over the eternal, unresolvable, tragic conflict between duty and inclination.[14] It has also been approached as a lyrical celebration of Platonic love, in which the lovers are engaged in a process of mutual improvement in virtue. In the latter interpretation the history of Julie becomes a reconquest of rational order over the disorder of the heart, and Julie herself a symbol of non-alienated virtue (non-alienated because reunited with love), through sympathy with whom we the readers are to be led to virtue.[15] *La Nouvelle Héloïse* has characteristically been seen by Jean Starobinski as a long reverie on the theme of transparency and the veil. Torn between the demands of carnal love and the need for order, Rousseau creates in Julie's history a dialectic in which the two are finally reconciled as a benevolent sympathy. For Starobinski the society that grows up around Julie is Rousseau's utopian dream of transparent erotic relations, but one that remains an illusion. It is illusory because Julie's Clarens expresses merely the wish for innocence. The society of Clarens is the appearance of innocence elebrating itself and is similar to Hegel's notion of the cult of beautiful souls. But

---

13 Cassirer, *Question*, 94; see also 92-4.
14 Shklar, *Men and Citizens*, 62
15 Burgelin, *Existence*, 118, 264-6, 332-3, 348, 350, 384, 387, 391-400

Julie and the Pathology of Conscience / 147

behind the veil of transparency lies the inability of the soul obsessed with its own innocence to realize its utopia practically. According to Starobinski, Clarens is a marvelous despotism in which equality is regained only as a 'sweet illusion' in the revelry of the communal feast. The wish for transparency remains unrealized because beautiful souls do not muddy their hands; they do not labour. Transparency itself becomes an ideology supporting inequality since 'il suffit à Rousseau que l'égalité se réalise comme état d'âme collective.'[16] The order of nature is dialectically reconstituted, but only as a game.[17]

The pages of *La Nouvelle Héloïse* have also been ransacked for quotations that, when removed from the context of the novel's development, can be used to present a Rousseau who is wholeheartedly on the side of either reason or feeling, virtue or the heart. Many approaches to *Julie* are in effect denials of it as a dramatic whole and a process, from which Rousseau stands apart. But when it is grasped in that way, the illusion of an abstract opposition between feeling and reason, eros and virtue, and their subsequent dialectic should be seen not to be the message of the novel but its theme, its topic. Rousseau is not espousing here an illusory dialectical solution to an unresolvable problem but disinterring the social and psychological roots of just such illusions. Among other things Julie is, I think, the case history of the institution, progress, and resolution of excessive repression maintained in the interest of domination.

The immediate content of the novel is both simple and familiar: the progress of an unhappy and socially disruptive romance between two lovers, Julie and St Preux. Their romance faces seemingly insurmountable difficulties, undergoes various transformations, and resolves itself with the death of the heroine. At the centre of the novel, however, is not so much the affair between the two lovers as the manner in which Julie handles the conflicts to which the affair gives rise and the manner in which her false resolutions of her conflicts support the false social order both within and without her through the operations of conscience and virtue.

From the start Julie's attraction to St Preux is the occasion of a conflict within her. The conflict appears to her as one between the erotic demands of her nature and the socially recognized demand for pre-marital chastity. The conflict is at first fully conscious on Julie's part and centres around her sense of self-esteem. Honour and its opposite, shame, are deeply

16 Starobinski, *Transparence*, 123
17 Starobinski's interpretation of *La Nouvelle Héloïse* is to be found in *Transparence*, 99–150; see also Berman, *Authenticity*, for an interesting interpretation along similar lines.

important to her; her idea of happiness, the 'happiness of a rational being,' coincides with the sense of self-esteem (*NH* 1.24). For Julie, 'no one can be happy unless he enjoys his own esteem' (*LNH* 224). She insists on her nobility of soul, since she places shame and honour above mere sensuality. 'Mere pleasure' is not happiness since happiness depends above all on virtue:

That sweet enchantment of virtue is vanished like a dream. Our passions have lost that divine ardor which gave vigour to them by purifying them. We have sought pleasure, and happiness has fled us. Recall once more those delightful moments in which our hearts fused the more we respected each other, in which our passion drew from its own excess the strength to conquer itself, in which our innocence consoled us for our restraint, in which the homage paid to honour turned everything to the profit of love ... now, given up to the delusions of the senses, we are nothing but common lovers, sufficiently happy if jealous love still condescends to preside over the pleasures which even the most brutish mortal can enjoy. (*NH* 1.32)

The illicit and secret union she is carrying on with St Preux is a violation of noble virtue because it requires dishonesty and dissimulation, whereas virtue requires complete honesty and frankness. (*NH* 1.35).

Yet Julie's own arguments do not fully convince her. She continues to meet with St Preux even as her arguments become more strenuous in aiming to convince him that their relation ought to change into one that lacks sensual expression. At the very moment when she insists most stridently on honesty and frankness, she makes use of the occasion of her parents' absence to arrange a tryst with St Preux in a mountain chalet. As soon as the external source of authority removes itself from the field of supervising her behaviour, she succumbs to the demands of nature. Inside their retreat, under the sovereignty and protection of 'nature's laws,' she complains that the openness that exists between lovers is forced into disguising itself in order to survive (*NH* 1.36). In moments of clarity she is thus quite aware that what separates her from St Preux are the laws of society, prejudices that she calls 'infernal monsters': 'what infernal monsters are these prejudices, which deprave the best hearts and silence the voice of nature at every moment? ... Do you know what has happened within me because of so many contradicting emotions which destroy each other? A sort of stupidity which renders me almost insensible and permits me to use neither my passions nor my reason' (*NH* 1.63). Julie's conflict, for all its debilitating effects, is still conscious and she is capable of listening to arguments, of judgment, and able at times to see through the vanity of her sense of honour.

St Preux represents and takes up the other side of the argument, speaking on behalf of nature, spontaneity, and feeling: 'Do you not know,' he addresses Julie, 'that there is a time when no one's reason resists any longer, and that there is no man in the world whose good sense may then prevail?' (*NH* 1.21) Finding Julie 'too perfect for a mere mortal' (*NH* 1.38) and being the only character in the book with a sense of humour, he complains to her that 'all the morality you have offered is very good, but the chalet is still better' (*NH* 1.45). These and other arguments, some of them abstruse and philosophical, are transparently ploys in a developing struggle between the two lovers themselves. The conflict between desire and the sense of honour is at first transferred into their relationship.

At the beginning of their relationship St Preux had been led to believe that Julie's hesitations issued purely from a sense of moral uprightness, but it soon becomes clear that what she fears is parental rejection. It is the opinion of her father above all that is crucial to her self-esteem (*NH* 1.44). Julie then avails herself of St Preux's need for her own esteem to manipulate him gradually into renouncing their worldly and carnal relation in favour of a sublime friendship.[18]

Julie's effort to manage her conflict turns from an attempt to hide their relation into an attempt, at one and the same time, to banish St Preux (the occasion of her desire) and to manipulate the world into accepting their marriage. In an effort to allay the anxiety caused by the growth of her inner conflicts, she orders St Preux out of her vicinity. He is to take up residence in a neighbouring town. Accusing him of having seduced her, she represents herself as a humiliated creature who must be paid in the coinage of respect; a commerce in respect is proposed in place of their erotic exchanges (*NH* 1.50). This effort on Julie's part to displace St Preux geographically is her first attempt to repress the conflict. Further geographic displacements, to ever greater distances, serve to represent more strenuous and temporarily successful attempts at repression.[19] As long as the force of Julie's rational arguments is insuf-

---

18 *NH* 1.42-3: 'What a strange control is the one you exercise over me, which can make disappointment as sweet as pleasure and give obeying you the same charm one would find in self-gratification.' See also 1.2, 7, 10.

19 I do not mean to suggest that Julie ever really accomplishes a successful repression of her conflict, but only that at this stage her conflict is not so intense, or Julie so weak, that the attempt at repression is anything more than tentative and conditional. It has, moreover, a plausibly realistic aim. Not only does St Preux's presence intensify her anxiety, but it threatens her realistic efforts to persuade her father to sanction their marriage. Yet Julie is still so dependent on self-esteem mediated by her parents that it is equally plausible that her supposed effort to convince them is an excuse to begin to remove the occasion of her anxiety from consciousness. Probably both motives are present, but what is important is that a solution to the conflict has not yet been found and

ficient to condemn her desire, however, St Preux is kept relatively close by and the conflict remains conscious. It will not be the weight of judgment or rational argument that is finally responsible for achieving the repression of the conflict. Only an equally powerful emotion will suffice to erect this barrier.

Her conflict now appears to Julie not simply as an abstract opposition of inclination and duty but rather involves a passionate longing for her beloved on the one side over against her love for her father, duty, and 'nature' (in a quasi-Platonic sense) on the other (*NH* 2.4). Yet in reality the only thing standing between the two sides is Julie's father, the Baron d'Etange. All the efforts made to bring him to agree to their marriage remain unsuccessful, however, since the baron had already promised her hand to a man to whom he owes his life, and of course such a dutiful promise cannot be abandoned. Shunning all suggestions that she elope with St Preux, Julie reaffirms her commitment not so much now to her parents but to her father's 'house.' Seeing her obedience to nature now in opposition to her obedience to love, she identifies nature with the laws of reciprocity that bind society together. Her identification with her father's house is based upon the honour bound up with it. She now feels that her honour can be restored only through maintaining the honour of her father's house, by honouring the most basic of society's laws: the keeping of promises.

Yet this stage of attempting to manage the conflict is so riddled with contradictions that it cannot last long. St Preux is sent further off, to Paris, in return for the flimsy hope that success in a career might turn the baron's will in his favour. St Preux and Julie continue their communication in an attenuated form; even this exchange of letters is at Julie's insistence to remain secret. Julie's compromise is of course also a refusal to choose either side of her dilemma. She will distance herself from St Preux but cannot refuse him finally; she will serve her father's 'illusions,' his concept of duty, in this way (*NH* 2.6), but she will refuse to marry without St Preux's consent. The sublimity of her affection for St Preux is at its height; they are 'united at a distance' (*NH* 2.16), while Julie is able for a short while to exult in the freedom that her stoic courage seems to have won her.

Julie's desire has not yet been debarred from consciousness. In psychoanalytic metapsychology, 'topographical' notions are spatial metaphors used to describe the movement of psychic material from one part of the psychic apparatus to another, as in movement from the system Conscious to the system Unconscious; see Freud, 'The Unconscious,' 116-50; also Otto Fenichel, *The Psychoanalytic Theory of Neurosis*, 14-15; also C. Rycroft, *A Critical Dictionary of Psychoanalysis*, 91.

Julie's judgment and reason are not enough to destroy her conscious attachment to St Preux. Even at the great distance separating them there is still communication, if only in the form of a continuous flow of symbols. But with the sudden discovery of this hidden communication, a train of events is set in motion that will lead Julie to repress completely (but only for a time) her love for St Preux. The discovery of their secret letters leads to a second scene (the first resulted in St Preux's being sent to Paris) of violent recriminations between Julie and her parents, during which she comes to believe that her father has threatened her with death. Shortly after this her mother dies. For a long time already Julie had believed that her affair would mean the destruction of either her parents, her lover, or herself (*NH* 1.29). And she thus comes to blame her mother's death on herself. It is decided that in place of the veil that disguised their tenuously continued relation, an 'everlasting veil' will be placed over the whole affair: 'what use is it to go back over the past? It is now a matter of concealing this odious mystery under an everlasting veil, of effacing the slightest trace of it if possible, and of assisting the goodness of Heaven which has left no visible evidence' (*NH* 3.1).

Julie's desire for St Preux is no longer something that she can manage at the level of conscious compromise, assent, or condemnation. Julie now associates her desire for St Preux so closely with her mother's 'destruction' that she has come to identify it with a death wish, which has apparently killed her mother and now threatens her father. The tremendous anxiety generated by the new meaning of the conflict, her ambivalence towards her father (which is rooted in her dependence on him – her need for his esteem), can only be allayed by a thorough repression of her desire for St Preux. At the same time, it is only the force of this *new* element that is sufficient to effect that repression.

The institution and the ramifications of this repression as they appear in the novel are complex, comprising a number of separate moments. First of all Julie begins to identify with her dead mother, who appears to her to be the epitome of Christian humility and gentleness. This identification means, at first, submitting to her father's wishes as her mother had done all her life; but the identification is only completed at the end of the novel, when Julie dies for the sake of her child as she imagines her mother died because of her. In the final analysis only this expiation will remove both the burden of guilt she has acquired and the legitimation of her desire for St Preux.

In the second place, identifying with her mother and submitting to her father's wishes means marrying Wolmar. The marriage ceremony is itself for Julie more than a ceremony. It becomes an epiphany (*NH* 3.18).

At the moment of taking her vows it suddenly becomes clear to her that by marrying Wolmar she is fulfilling her noble destiny, affirming her ties to the past, the traditions of her father's house, and accepting the demands of society while taking her place in it. More than that, however, she experiences the marriage vow as a rebirth and renewal of her nature. It is felt as an act of expiation that is simultaneously a bestowal upon her of grace, a God-given deliverance, she is convinced, from her guilt. Addressing St Preux after the ceremony, she writes:

I shall love you always, do not doubt it. The sentiment which attaches me to you is still so tender and lively that another woman would perhaps be alarmed by it; as for me ... I feel that its nature has changed ... I know that exacting decorum and the external show of virtue would demand still more and would not be content until you were completely forgotten. I think I have a more certain rule and I abide by it. I listen secretly to my conscience; it reproaches me for nothing; and it never deceives a heart which sincerely consults it. If that is not enought to justify me before the world, that is enough for my own tranquility. How has this change come about? I do not know. What I do know is that I have ardently desired it. God alone has done the rest. I should think that a soul once corrupted is so forever ... unless some unexpected revolution, some abrupt change of fortune and situation suddenly alters its connections and, with a violent shock, helps it to recover a desire for good. All its habits being broken and all its passions modified in the general revolution, it sometimes recovers its primitive character and becomes like a new creature recently formed by nature's hands. Then the memory of its former baseness can serve as a deterrent against a relapse. Yesterday we were abject and weak; today we are strong and highminded ... My marriage has made me experience something like what I am trying to explain to you. This bond, so feared, delivers me from a servitude much more fearful and my husband becomes dearer to me for having restored me to myself. (*NH* 3.18)

Julie's happy marriage will be based not on love, which is, she thinks, unnecessary, but on honour and virtue. Her desire for St Preux seems destroyed and replaced with a pure and tender affection. Yet it is not replaced by desire for her husband. Julie's desire is now desire for God, the source of peace, renewal, and absolution. In a sense Julie, the new Héloïse, by marrying has taken the veil.

Her marriage to Wolmar is simultaneously the birth of a religious vocation. The philosophic virtue that she displayed earlier will be 'refined,' she says, with Christian virtue. The veil she adopts in her new calling is in a sense the same as the everlasting veil that now shrouds her desire for St Preux. The feeling of union, of harmony and tranquility, that she earlier sought in a lovers' retreat is now to be found inside the protective walls of the nunnery of her marriage, in a union with God. All this is predicated upon a strenuous denial (but one that is *no longer conscious*) of her feeling for St Preux (the memory of 'former baseness' serves 'as a deterrent against a relapse'). For his part St Preux, in symbolic obedience, leaves Paris for a period of exile at the other end of the world. By displacing him to the greatest distance possible, Julie is attempting to deny the memory that is linked in her mind to shame, dishonour, guilt, and abandonment by her two fathers, her real father and God the father. Through the internalization of the demands of father and society Julie has rendered her conflict and her guilt unconscious. She has temporarily replaced them with the rewards of conscience, with its other side. In place of the feelings of annihilation that accompanied her guilt over her mother's death, she enjoys the exquisite grace of God.

The socialization of Julie's unruly desire is in this case also its harnessing to a political need. It now becomes possible for her to assume her social functions at Clarens, Wolmar's model estate, which serves as a model of enlightened despotism and where her husband plays the role of philosopher-king, of Truth, while Julie is Beauty; she is the 'garland of flowers' thrown over the chains of this community where the weight of authority is experienced as pleasure. The harmony established at Clarens only appears, however, to be stable. It is based on Julie's spiritual balance, something that Wolmar knows clearly. Just as the first half of the book (parts 1 to 3) is the history of a repression, the second half is a history of the return of the repressed. St Preux returns from exile after a number of years, and with his return Julie's conflict is also renewed; it threatens to overwhelm her with all the intensity it had at the time of her mother's death.

The past now begins to torment her: 'It is not, you know, that my heart still feels the effects of old wounds; no, it is cured. I feel it. I am very sure of it; I dare believed myself virtuous. It is not the present which I fear; it is the past which torments me. There are memories as fearful as the original sensation' (*NH* 4.1). Julie's religious devotion seems to wane in proportion to the growth of the threat from the past. Her much discussed garden, an artificial Elysium that is the most subtle imitation of nature, is where Julie begins to seek her peace of mind because she feels obsessively unable to set foot again in the nearby grove where she first embraced St Preux (*NH* 4.11). Julie's obsession with her garden is a perfect symbol *and* symptom of neurotic conflict, as it both expresses and denies the repressed desire. The happiness Julie expects to experience in her garden, removed from Clarens in the midst of it, removed from 'all that artificial order of society which had made me so unhappy' (*NH* 4.11), is the immediacy of spontaneous erotic fulfilment as she had once experienced it. Yet it functions just as much to deny her links with St Preux, the renewal of which would not only endanger her marriage but unearth her guilt and anxiety in all its original intensity.

Wolmar, whose one passion is 'to read the hearts of man' (*NH* 4.12), understands something of Julie's position and intends to 'cure' both her and St Preux of their desire for each other. Cured of their conflicts, they will be able to devote their energies to Clarens. Wolmar intends to restore St Preux's confidence in himself: 'we shall not leave so honest a man in doubt about himself. We shall teach him to have more confidence in his virtue, and perhaps one day we shall enjoy with more benefit the fruit of the trouble we are going to take' (*NH* 4.7). And he invites Julie to integrate her old passion into the new sterength of her ego (*NH* 4.12). Wolmar attempts to accomplish all this by compelling the former lovers to *remember* and to re-experience fully the entire force of their earlier passion, but in their new surroundings and in the light of their subsequent development. He expects that, although their desire has remained hidden and unabated in spite of their conscious denials, they have each sufficiently changed that once what has been repressed has been made conscious, its intensity will be seen to be much less than was expected. The force of rational judgment, of virtue, will then suffice to turn desire to new aims and objects, to their roles in the community of souls that is Clarens. For that reason Wolmar leads them into the original grove and persuades them to embrace and kiss before his eyes (*NH* 4.12). Shortly afterwards, recalling that time when Julie and St Preux met in the mountain chalet in her parents' absence, Wolmar leaves Clarens. Julie and St Preux return to the cliffside where the latter had spent the beginning of his period of exile and there seem to re-experience their desire for each other together with an immediate and cathartic purging of that desire (*NH* 4.17).

Wolmar's therapy by way of anamnesis[20] does appear to take effect in the case of St Preux. He becomes more tractable, appears as a 'slave' now in the service of Wolmar (*NH* 4.9), considers the latter to be like a god, calls him father, and offers him gifts 'as to God himself' (*NH*

---

20 This remarkable anticipation of psychoanalytic technique has already been noticed by others, eg, Shklar, *Men and Citizens*, 142, but they have not noticed how the rest of the book, with its anticipations of psychoanalytic *theory*, is tied up with it.

4.8). Sure of being 'cured,' he takes pleasure in so considering himself a 'child of the house.'[21]

Julie's progress is, however, not assured. Although Wolmar has no doubts about her ultimate success, she herself does not remain at peace. She begins to have disturbing dreams, urges her friend Claire to marry St Preux, since she is not sure of her own sentiments (*NH* 5.13). Although she assures St Preux that they have been cured, thanks to Wolmar, she fears for her virtue and urges him likewise to marry Claire (*NH* 5.13).[22] This desire to have the two of her friends married is her last attempt to again displace St Preux, to erect a final barrier to consciousness of her renascent desire for him.

Julie's death is not delayed for very long. Its cause is ambiguous. After diving from a great height into a lake to save the life of her son, she falls seriously ill. Whether her death had as sufficient cause her fall or whether while on the way to recovery she simply resigns from life, we cannot know. In Julie's own eyes her death is simply the unfolding of her destiny; she attributes the cause to God (*NH* 6.12).

It is only on her deathbed that it finally becomes clear to Julie that she still loves St Preux. It appears that she can finally make this admission to herself because she now knows that she will die and accepts her death, even welcomes it, as expiation of the guilt she still suffers over the death of her mother. Wolmar's cure must be accounted a failure. To the reader who pays close attention to the progress of Julie's commitment to virtue, *La Nouvelle Héloïse* cannot consistently represent a dialectic of passion and the demand for social order, synthesized in a sexually purified and tender sympathy. This is, certainly, what Julie and her friends would *like* to believe about the society of Clarens, that it is the expression of friendship, of a sublime, virtuous, and chaste love. But in terms of the development of the novel this appearance, this veil that Julie has thrown over the past, like Penelope's shroud for Laertes, begins to unravel almost as soon as it has been constructed. As the action moves towards Julie's death, her anxiety becomes almost frenzied, and if there is a moment in which she experiences peace, it is only when she knows she is going to die (or when she decides to die).

Wolmar *could not* have cured Julie since her problem was not so much

---

21 Rousseau, *NH* 5.2. One could say that in St Preux's case, Wolmar, making use of the transference, has become a 'parasite of the super-ego'; on the latter concept see Fenichel, *Neurosis*, 109.

22 See also *NH* 6.6-8.

desire for St Preux in itself as it was the unconscious guilt over her mother's death and over the ambivalence she felt towards her father that was associated with the affair. Or rather, he could not cure Julie without dissolving their marriage and threatening the stability of Clarens, of the whole community. For her marriage to him was in the first place a part of an unconscious strategy to expiate her guilt. Had he attempted to dissolve that guilt, he would have undermined the very basis of their relationship, and with it an important part of his power over the whole community.

At the same time, we know that the whole development could have been very different, that there had been nothing but the *force* of Julie's fear of loss of honour (loss of the father's esteem) preventing her elopement with St Preux at an early stage. Instead, Julie succumbed to the demand for a renunciation of a perfectly legitimate desire in order to satisfy her need for self-esteem, a need apparently not mediated by another but answering to a pure code of honour. Her seeking after happiness in honour and in religious devotion in turn led her to instrumentalize herself, her nature, her desire, in the interest of maintaining Wolmar's rule over Clarens. Indeed, Clarens will go on, although in Julie's death its heart has died. Her last letter is a sort of testament:

What advantage was left for me to derive from life? By depriving me of it, Heaven no longer deprives me of anything regrettable and instead protects my honour ... After so many sacrifices, I consider as little the one left for me to make. It is only to die once more ... You are losing of Julie only that which you have for a long time lost. The best of her remains for you. Come, rejoin her family. Let her heart dwell among you. Let all those she loved gather together to give her a new existence. Your duties, your pleasures, your friendship – all will be her work. (*NH* 6.12)

Julie's death is also the beginning of her apotheosis. The memory and the worship of her saintliness will bind the community together as her presence did in life. Julie's death, if anything, serves to absolve the sense of conscience itself and to shift responsibility to fate. What she leaves behind her is a new body in the form of a priesthood and a congregation.

Julie: The Theoretical Yield

The first thing to be noted from the consideration of the *Nouvelle Héloïse* as Julie's case history is that, for Rousseau, the notion of a pure morality is an illusion. Rousseau's doctrine of conscience cannot be adequately understood as a reorientation of ethics away from the utilitarian hedonism of the Enlightenment towards a conception of the autonomy of the moral will, à la Kant. Julie's history, the memory of which includes Wolmar's use of therapeutic anamnesia, testifies to the mediacy of duty. But the illusion of the autonomy of duty and conscience is not merely an illusion. It is an ideological illusion bound up with the legitimation of social domination. The issue is not so much whether Clarens is or is not the just society. The point is that Julie's implicit belief that adherence to duty transcends both her desire and her social environment, her belief that adherence to duty is adherence to a higher nature, is an instance of the sundering of nature and history, or the naturalization of the historical, that is at the bottom of ideology.

If, however, conscience is at bottom not merely the pure and simple voice of nature that transcends both egoism and external authority, what is it, and how does it come to be? When conscience is seen as the opposite of egoism (*amour-propre*), which is the usual view, no answer to the above questions can be found. Conscience inside that problematic is reason or feeling or some combination of the two, or even something ultimately mysterious, a secret 'dictate' that functions like a positive version of Socrates' *daemon*. But with Julie, in place of the spectacle of the pure moral will and unmediated eros in opposition to each other, or need on the one side and duty on the other, we have the spectacle of duty as mediated by the historical need of society, of conscience as a kind of super-ego, an internalized regulation of self-esteem, of an agency originally located in the exterior internalized by the agent.

In the previous chapter I maintained that *amour-propre* is not to be separated from *amour-de-soi* but is a necessary outgrowth of it in the transition from nature to culture. *Amour-propre* has as its aim the restoration of the original narcissistic feeling of wholeness proper to *amour-de-soi*. Under cultural conditions the desire for self-esteem is in varying degrees substituted for the unmediated desire of simple biological life. The feeling of self-esteem is in turn mediated by the other in symbolic terms. In this way the forces of biological desire is harnessed to the demands of culture. Biology lends culture its force by way of the symbol and imagination. Social control can therefore operate with the force of biological desire.

When Rousseau opposes conscience to 'opinion,' he is not opposing conscience to *amour-propre* as such but only to *amour-propre* that operates at a conscious level. But conscience is not a truth and a nature that transcends opinion; it is only an inner opinion that opposes an outer opinion. It thus renders the individual to some extent autonomous, relative to external social authorities. But it does this at the cost of transplanting external authority within the self.

It was shown above that for Rousseau conscience is a judgment, or a dictate set up secretly against other secret penchants, accompanied by either a feeling of worth and intense pleasure or a feeling of worthlessness accompanied by intense displeasure; that it is an ever-present monitor and judge. But in the case of Julie we are actually given a remarkable insight into the history and the mechanisms of the acquisition and operations of conscience inside the psyche perceived as a dynamic system. When Starobinski asserts that 'il fallait Freud pour penser les sentiments de Rousseau,' he is referring primarily to the possibility of understanding Rousseau's theoretical and literary work in terms of his own neurotic afflictions. Others have noted the resemblance of Wolmar's 'cure' of Julie to psychoanalytic psychotherapy. But the resemblance does not end there, nor is it fortuitous. Julie offers more than a case of unsuccessful therapy. And in some sense Rousseau displays an uncanny depth-psychological perception that must be accounted much more than mere sentiment.

In the period before the crisis that ends up with Julie's marriage to Wolmar and her discovery of divine grace, she shares some crucial characteristics with the pre-Oedipal child. She is heavily dependent on her parents' esteem and love; at the same time she has a tendency to follow her own wishes when her parents are not present. The episode in the mountain chalet is testimony to this. She has not yet fully internalized the external authority. As a consequence her suffering at that point is not neurotic, nor is it unconscious. There is a serious conflict between her own wish for St Preux and her wish to retain her parents' and primarily her father's esteem. She is fully aware of this conflict, and her attempts to resolve it centre around convincing her father to give in to her wishes.

At this point, however, a series of fortuitous events intervenes that places Julie in the position of the Oedipal child. The frustration of her desire by her parents coincides with a perceived threat on her own life issuing from her father and with the death of her mother. Julie has previously given many signs of ambivalence, especially towards her father. Her desire for his love has been combined with the extreme frustration of his denial of her wishes. But now her situation has become intolerable. Her desire is identified with an aggressive urge towards both parents. She believes that it has killed her mother. At the same time she believes she has sunk so low in her father's esteem that she is threatened with death, with annihilation.[23]

In a sense it matters little that the frustrated wish in question is Julie's desire for St Preux. In psychoanalytic terms this can be seen as a wish for a father substitute. From the moment that Julie perceives her mother's death as the responsibility of her wish (for a father substitute) we are no longer dealing with the 'normal' story of unrequited love. Nor does it ultimately matter that Julie is in late adolescence when this episode takes place. Under the extreme pressure of her conflict with her parents over St Preux, Julie can be seen as undergoing an unconscious regression to the stage of Oedipal conflict.

Julie's conflict in this new situation is no longer amenable to the type of rational, practical solution she had earlier sought. Instead she unconsciously attempts to allay the intense anxiety caused by her ambivalence by throwing an 'everlasting veil' over the whole affair. Julie must repress her desire for St Preux in order to conquer her ambivalence towards her father, and both the force and the occasion are supplied by the introjection of both her parents, now operating much more effectively as conscience. It is therefore possible now to see what Rousseau indicates by saying that 'nature herself must furnish us with the means to control her.' The super-ego derives its force (and to a certain extent its severity also) from nature itself: 'the anti-instinct forces have an instinctual character because they are derivations of instincts. The instinctual attitudes of the children toward their parents are turned into forces hostile to the instincts by an introjection of the parents. Thus through the influence of the external world instinctual impulses have been transformed into anti-instinctual impulses.'[24]

In Julie's case the 'resolution' of her Oedipal conflict results in a much more conscientious character. Wolmar was perfectly justified in his confidence in her virtue when he left the ex-lovers alone. But Julie's virtue and especially her *love* of virtue were not as well founded as Wolmar

---

23 See Fenichel, *Neurosis*, 105: 'The "loss of the superego's protection" or "the inner punishment performed by the superego" is felt as an extremely painful decrease in self-esteem and in extreme cases as a feeling of annihilation. It has been stated repeatedly that small children need some kind of narcissistic supplies for maintaining their equilibrium. The privilege of granting or refusing these supplies now taken over by the superego. The fear of being punished or abandoned by the superego is the fear of annihilation through lack of these supplies.' See also 132-6 on the role of the superego in defence.

24 Ibid., 103

supposed. Julie's virtue is and remains essentially reactive and defensive, at once a reaction-formation, a denial of her aggressive wishes towards her father, and an identification with her mother. And Julie's *love* of virtue also remains defensive. In loving virtue she feels that she merits the love of God, which in turn, through the miracle of divine grace, recaptures for her the marvellous sense of self-esteem she once enjoyed when she merited her parents' love.

The veil of repression that Julie casts over her very carnal desire for St Preux is at the same time a taking of the veil in a different sense. Julie's marriage is parallel to the entrance of the first Héloïse into a nunnery. It is the transformation of carnal love into Christian love. Rather than loving one man, she has a tender love for all beings. In a very real sense it is this affection that holds the community of Clarens together – all its inhabitants bask contentedly in the recognition it affords them. Julie becomes the whole community's conduit for love from God – the one thing that Wolmar, the atheist, philosopher, and man of reason, is unable to supply by himself.

The pleasure of identification with her parents through the route of virtue, the gain in self-esteem that is made by finding a father substitute in God, is the 'economic' reason why the repression can maintain itself for any length of time without rendering Julie incapable of functioning. But since Julie's love of virtue is in large part a defence, it has its own unconscious dynamic, which resists Julie's attempts to assuage her guilt feelings. In marrying Wolmar and giving up St Preux, in taking the veil and renouncing carnal love, Julie has made a childish attempt to expiate her remorse over the death of her mother. But in the process she has truly acquired a conscience. And in Freud's words:

Originally, renunciation of instinct was the result of fear of an external authority: one renounced one's satisfactions in order not to lose its love. If one has carried out this renunciation, one is, as it were, quit with the authority and no sense of guilt should remain. But with fear of the super-ego the case is different. Here, instinctive renunciation is not enough, for the wish persists and cannot be concealed. Thus in spite of the renunciation that has been made, a sense of guilt comes about. This constitutes a great economic disadvantage in the erection of a super-ego ... Instinctual renunciation now no longer has a completely liberating effect; virtuous continence is no longer rewarded with the assurance of love ... conscience ... is indeed the cause of instinctual renunciation to begin with, but ... later the relationship is reversed. Every renunciation of instinct

Julie and the Pathology of Conscience / 161

now becomes a dynamic source of conscience and every fresh renunciation increases the latter's severity and intolerance.[25]

Julie's wish cannot, indeed, be successfully sublimated. And each attempt seems to bring a fresh onset of guilt. After five years of marriage to Wolmar Julie allows herself the complaint that 'my husband understands me, but he does not respond enough to my liking. His head is not turned by love as mine is ... I desire one more animated and more like my own' (NH 4.1). Julie still harbours an 'odious secret,' the concealment of which leads her conscience to interpet her husbands 'marks of respect and consideration ... as opprobrium and signs of contempt' (NH 4.1). Her conscience now begins to upbraid her for having banished St Preux to the ends of the earth, where he was certain to have met an undeserved death. And this turning of conscience towards St Preux magically coincides with his return in fact. Julie's guilt has thereby come full circle. Continual renunciation presses guilt forward until the repressed reappears in quite a dangerous form. Blaming herself for St Preux's death is quite close to conscious recognition of her death-wish for her father. At the same time it is the return of desire in its relatively unsublimated, carnal form. In a sense the dynamics of conscience finally undo the renunciation that conscience at first imposes. Julie is forced once again by her own conscience to confront what she is unable to accept.

Driven by her conscience,[26] Julie's character becomes dominated by defensive patterns. Indeed, her behaviour throughout the book reads like a catalogue of defence mechanisms. When faced with the loss of her father's esteem early on, she denies the existence of carnal desire on her part – it was St Preux who seduced her. Thus her denial corresponds with a simultaneous projection. Her sexual needs in regard to St Preux are later handled by repression. The veil that is cast over her affair is a form of forgetting. The forgetting cannot be complete in this instance, however, so it is accompanied by the isolation of affect. If erotic desire is handled in this way, Julie's aggressive urges are handled by a reaction-formation – her Christian gentleness and submission to the wishes of father and husband take the place of and oppose her 'destructive' rebelliousness. In her final act of self-sacrifice, the wish to expiate the responsibility for her mother's death is an example of undoing. Indeed,

25 Freud, *Civilization and Its Discontents*, 74–5
26 On the role of the superego in the aetiology of neurosis, see Freud, *The Ego and the Id*, espec. 46, 48–9; also Fenichel, *Neurosis*, 132–6, 291ff, 397ff.

the crisis that precipitates Julie's fresh access of conscience over the death of her mother precipitates a classic regression.

Julie's death is not accidental, nor is it the tragic outcome of the clash of irreconcilable forces. Today she would perhaps be diagnosed as a case of pathological self-esteem-regulation manifesting itself in a fate-neurosis.[27] But her significance is larger than that. Julie's death is a symptom of civilization itself. Freud, seeing a danger in the relentless demands of civilization for the sublimation of libido, recognized that the ego in 'its struggle against the libido exposes itself to the danger of maltreatment and death.'[28] He understood it to be his task 'to represent the sense of guilt as the most important problem in the development of civilization and to show that the price we pay for our advance in civilization is a loss of happiness through the heightening of the sense of guilt.'[29] *La Nouvelle Héloïse* is in some respects a similar indictment, but in figurative, pre-theoretical form. Julie's death is the figurative equation between civilization and the subordination of Eros to Death.

It is possible now to see closer to the root of Rousseau's 'hesitations,' as Cassirer would have them, about virtue, conscience, and duty. If Rousseau's central indictment of human civilization was its fostering of and dependence upon *amour-propre*, that indictment was not restricted to the demoralizing effects of the symbolic mediation of self-esteem at a conscious and social level. Conscience turns out after all to be nothing else, and nothing less, than the internalization of self-esteem-regulation, the quite Freudian super-ego. Under certain 'civilized' conditions, conscience itself becomes 'ferocious' and 'insane.' What is more, these conditions are linked to the advance of civilization itself. Julie is a paragon of civilization in this sense because she is identified with both the Platonic and the Christian traditions. As in the former tradition she identifies happiness with virtue, and as in the latter she has exaggerated all her duties. She is a blending of philosophic reason and Christian morality. She is the unself-conscious representative and victim of the arrogance and contempt with which Rousseau feels advancing civilization has treated nature. In her eyes the repression of nature has no limits. According to Julie, 'All these pretended needs do not have their source in nature but in the voluntary debauchery of the senses ... desires constantly repressed become accustomed to remaining at rest, and temptations are multiplied only by the habit of succumbing to them' (*NH* 2.27).

27 On pathological self-esteem regulation see Annie Reich, 'Pathological Forms of Self-Esteem Regulation.'
28 Freud, *Ego*, 46
29 Freud, *Civilization*, 81

For Rousseau it would be as senseless to attempt to annihilate conscience as it would be to attempt to return to the forest and take up the life of savage man once again. But this does not mean that duty and virtue are the true, central, and ultimate ends of human existence, nor that they are to be identified with happiness. Conscience and virtue are central moments in the social life of civilized human beings. They demonstrate once again that the human individual is already the social individual under each and every form of society. Moreover, they serve to demonstrate that the social self is a dynamic process constituted within particular forms of the social life-process: 'Because, although one cannot overturn the order of nature, one gives to the trunk of the tree an oblique direction and to man inclinations modified according to the conditions in which he is found, according to the civil institutions in which he lives. We are not precisely double, but compound' (*EMF* 273).

Freud saw the increasing malaise in civilization not simply in terms of the repression of sexuality but as increasing unconscious guilt. For this reason he understood it to be the task of his therapy often to 'oppose the super-ego' and 'endavour to lower its demands.'[30] What was true of the individual super-ego was also true of the 'cultural super-ego.'[31] Something of the same understanding is present in Rousseau. Thus he opposes virtue in the name of *bonté*,[32] because 'When man ... strives to be more than man he is weak indeed' (*E* 45). For the same reason virtue is opposed to wisdom: 'Virtue is nothing but the force to do one's duty in difficult situations; and wisdom, on the contrary, is to dispel the difficulty of our duties. Happy is he who, contenting himself with being a benevolent man, has put himself in a position never to have need of being virtuous' (*CG* 10.291).

For Freud, the increasing unconscious guilt accompanying the development of civilization was largely the result of the force of innate aggression. Since interest in work and the common good were insufficient in his eyes to give rise to or guarantee the survival of large social units he speculated that in order to restrain aggressive behaviour and forge links between individuals in large groups, innate aggression must be

30 Ibid., 90
31 See ibid., 86–91; also, eg, 'Civilized Sexual Morality,' and 'Five Lectures on Psychoanalysis,' espec. 86.
32 See *DOI* 184–5; cf *RJ* 271: 'L'instinct de la nature est moins pur peut-être, mais certainement plus sur que la loi de la vertu'; and *LMF* 1142–3: 'Faire le bien est l'occupation la plus douce d'un homme bien né. Sa probité, sa bienfaisance ne sont point l'ouvrage de ses principes, mais celui de son bon naturel. Il cède à ses penchans en pratiquant la justice comme le méchant cède aux siens en pratiquant l'iniquité. Contenter le goût qui nous porte à bien faire est bonté, mais non pas vertu.'

turned against the self. This is the work of the super-ego, which by upholding high moral ideals and fostering the repression of sexuality at once holds down violence and creates that 'aim-inhibited love' that binds together groups larger than the family.[33]

Rousseau was unencumbered by the hypothesis of a death instinct. Aggression in his eyes, although it remained 'natural,' was largely the result of frustrations created by social forms themselves.[34] He therefore conceived of the increasing demands of virtue as the outcome of a political struggle: 'we were meant to be men, laws and customs thrust us back into infancy' (*E* 49). What better example of this than Julie? Accordingly, he could not conceive of the history of civilization in terms of the immense dualism of metaphysical forces, of the interaction of eros and death, in the way that Freud came to in later life.[35] The conflict of nature and culture at this level was therefore an artificial, potentially transient episode, subject to the possibility of historical, practical intervention: 'The voice of nature and that of reason would never have found themselves in contradiction if man had not imposed on himself duties that he was subsequently always forced to prefer to the natural impulse' (*OCI* 250).

The history of Julie, the paragon of virtue and reason, comes to parallel the history of the species. The advance of reason in virtue once again results in a regression and the dominance of the irrational. Julie's virtue, because it is primarily defensive, a continual escape from unconscious anxiety, is civilized unreason unfolded inside the individual. For all of Julie's claims to be a paragon of sublimation, she is, after all, not much different from the 'civilized man' who 'goes on in drudgery to his last moment, and even seeks death to put himself in a position to live, or renounces life to acquire immortality' (*DOI* 220; see above, page 133). Julie in the end seeks death as a release from the forces that had been preventing her expression of desire. The question therefore arises whether the claims of nature and the claims of culture are reconcilable and what it is that is necessary to bring about the reconciliation. The history of Julie supplements the critical work of the *Discourse on the Origins of Inequality* in showing that politics is at least in some large degree responsible for the 'contradiction' between reason and nature. Julie's

---

33 Freud, *Civilization*, 5–7
34 Although Freud recognized this, as in *Civilization*, 77, he did not follow up on its implications, as a result of his inability to conceive of the abolition of alienated labour. On this last point see G. Horowitz, *Repression*, espec. 176.
35 Freud saw possibilities for reform but not the possibility of the transcendence of the struggle between Eros and Death. Although he was sympathetic to critics of civilization, he was unwilling to offer any such 'false' consolation; see *Civilization*, 91–2.

neurotic, compulsive virtue is not only her own affair, after all, but also her 'voluntary' subordination in the interests of maintaining the social order. And Julie's history also deepens the understanding of the civilized wretchedness that attends the perfectible animal of the second *Discourse*. If civilization for Rousseau is essentially a process of denaturation, the possibility of which is already contained in the nature of the human animal as artificer, civilized wretchedness is at least partially the result not of denaturation as such but of the excessive denaturation required to sustain social inequality. The culture of social inequality necessitates the imposition of a set of duties that, in order to be accepted, are predicated upon excessive denaturation. Julie must seek her happiness in virtue and in the divine absolution that follows from it rather than in the realization of her desire in the world.

The reconciliation of reason and nature will therefore require a twofold reform of society in the individual and the individual in society. The *Social Contract* represents one of Rousseau's efforts in that direction, but as we shall see, its conclusions are far from being entirely positive – it develops the possibilities of political reform within the limits of bourgeois society. Political reform within these terms is found wanting. Yet in *Emile* Rousseau takes up the other side of the problem, the reform of society in the individual. This will require something very different from the type of political solution and the type of political education envisaged in the *Social Contract*. It will require, for lack of a better term, a redressing of the balance in favour of *instinct*: 'does one dare take the part of instinct against reason? This is precisely what I wish' (SGP 62-3).[36] But this taking the side of instinct will turn out not to be a repudiation of reason, but its potential fulfilment.

---

36 Quoted by Strauss, *Natural Right*, 262 n 22

CHAPTER SEVEN

'A Masterpiece of Modern Policy': The *Social Contract*

> The general is the illusory form of communal life.
> Marx, *The German Ideology*

Position and Premises of the *Social Contract*

Whether it is cherished as one of the founding documents of modern democratic theory or reviled as the totalitarian instrument of an authoritarian personality, the *Social Contract* is usually taken to be the prescriptive centrepiece of Rousseau's work. Following upon the ambivalence of the second *Discourse* and preceding his 'retreat' into apologetic introspection and mystical experience in his autobiographical writings, the *Social Contract* appears to embody his most thoroughgoing attempt at a solution to the problems of modern men. The loss of liberty and equality, happiness and individual dignity, in the growth of civilization is now to be redeemed in a new form of association among men.

In the second *Discourse* Rousseau displays no great love for the state, the Dedication to the Republic of Geneva notwithstanding. And yet that dedication, with its effusive and glowing praise of a 'democratic government, wisely tempered' (*DOI* 145), clearly foreshadows an attempt on Rousseau's part to transcend the limitations of the Lockean state he criticizes in the second part of the *Discourse*. There can be little doubt that the *Social Contract* is just such an attempt. It claims to be and is a serious and realistic attempt at a solution, but it is not, as I wish to demonstrate, the best solution, or the ultimate solution of the deepest problems set forth in the *Discourse*. Although the *Social Contract* offers a solution, without a doubt, and although that solution elevates the state to levels of importance only darkly hinted at in the *Discourse*, the solution itself has problems of its own that are not accidental or contingent but given in the structure of the solution itself; further, it is abstracted from a larger historical process and consequently either begs the question of its finality or limits the terms of its applicability; and it must therefore constantly be judged with an eye to the dissonances that all too clearly exist between it and Rousseau's other major writings.

The solution that the *Social Contract* offers to the sorry condition of modern society is unfolded on three distinct levels simultaneously. The first level is the ideal and pertains to the ultimate resolution of the historically developed conflict between individuality and community. At this level the *Social Contract* projects a model of social individuality of which it could be said that the essence is the mutual recognition on the part of each member of the inherent non-fungible value of all others. At this level the political community of equals as 'ends-in-themselves' is perceived by its members to be the condition of the free development of each and all.

The second level is the practical. Here Rousseau is concerned to demonstrate two things: first, that the ideal is not simply a static, timeless form but a real possibility emerging from a definite set of historically evolved social relations. Also, the ideal must be rooted in the *interests* of individuals, as these interests are formed in their patterned interactions. Possible members must have a compelling interest in this form of community, and they must be persuaded that it can be made to work in durable institutions.

The third level, the least explicit, is the reflective, and it appears not only in the juxtaposition of the two previous levels but in Rousseau's sometimes desperate regressions to archaic and authoritarian practices such as the civil religion, censorship, and the Legislator. At this level Rousseau indicates the historical limits imposed upon the project in question. The reflective juxtaposition of the two other levels is not artificial, precisely because the ideal is not conceived of as the brainchild of transcendent philosophical knowledge but as the common knowledge of the potential members raised to a higher degree of awareness.

These levels are not parts or sections of the *Social Contract*. The work as a whole, at any point, contains all of them to a lesser or greater extent. When the assumption is suspended that the second *Discourse* is simply superseded, answered wholly or in part in the *Social Contract*, a different understanding of its significance becomes possible. It may be read not simply as a prescriptive ideal but as a *continuation*, in a hypothetical mode, of the general critique of bourgeois society that Rousseau had in the second *Discourse* grounded in a historical anthropology. The sovereignty of the general will, derived from principles inherent in modern social life, represents the best polity that a society patterned upon market relations can conceive and attempt to realize. Yet since in that society this ideal remains unattainable, life under the sovereignty of the general will amounts to the alienation of communal life in the state. This is at best an ambivalent solution since it announces the project of human mastery over a previously reified history, but under conditions in which that project must, in perpetually failing, reproduce reification. The solution itself begs for a solution – and the outlines of this become visible only in *Emile*.

The problem of the *Social Contract* actually divides itself into three inseparable but distinct questions: what exactly *is* the problem for which Rousseau poses the *Contract* as a solution; what is the solution itself; and finally, what is the status of the solution? The problem of the *Social Contract* is certainly the *outcome* of the historical process analysed in the second *Discourse*, but the *Contract* itself is, precisely because of that fact, less than a full resolution of the dilemma posed in the earlier work. In the second *Discourse* Rousseau had based his critique of bourgeois society and of the bourgeois conception of the state on an anthropology that placed the historicity of human nature at its centre. And it was the historicity of nature that was precisely what the theorists of bourgeois society could not accept. Only so long as nature was static and transcended the historical process itself (either as laws of nature or as the telos of a history of progress) could it perform due service as the ultimate justification of bourgeois social relations. But by finding in the history of human nature the key that upset and unravelled the theory of bourgeois society, Rousseau was posing a problem that was simultaneously larger and deeper. His solution to the question concerning inequality thus posed the much more complex, subtle, and intractable problem of historicity. Although the *Social Contract* offers, in terms compatible with bourgeois natural right, a solution to the problems of modern society, its status with respect to the dilemma posed by human historicity remains to be discussed.

Ancient Virtue, the Modern State, and the Will

The state envisioned in the *Social Contract* has often been seen as an attempt to revive the classical notion of citizenship.[1] But the ancient

---

1 This is seen positively by, eg, Barker, *Political Thought*, 520-1, and negatively, as the regressive longing of an authoritarian personality by Shklar, *Men and Citizens*.

reign of virtue was based on the substantial unity of the community, a unity upheld through the relatively complete identification of the individual with his customary status and role. Freedom was also expressed in this political community as the absence of personal dependence on the part of the citizens – but this in turn was based on the immediate identity of the individual citizen with the whole. The ancient polis was in Rousseau's eyes not in essence a suitable model for his contemporaries. In his *Lettres de la Montagne*, for example, he admonishes the once great Geneva of the dedication to the second *Discourse* for comparing itself with lowly Athens, let alone with Sparta, the prototype of ancient virtue: 'Let these great names be. You are merchants, artisans, bourgeois always occupied with private interests, with trade, with profit; people for whom liberty itself is nothing but a means of acquiring without obstacle and possessing securely.'[2]

Subjective, egoistic freedom was also manifested in the polis, but it was anything but the *basis* of the common existence. The communal life of the citizen body Rousseau envisioned as entirely given and unwilled. The appearance of subjective freedom constituted rather a threat primarily met through ancient civic education, which instilled the public ethos in the individual without reflection and will playing any part. The ancient citizen did not submit his membership in communal life to his own conscious judgment or choice. Correspondingly, there was an absence of differentiation of public and private spheres.[3]

The *Social Contract* is based first of all on the premise that the ancient reign of virtue cannot be integrally recreated. Progress in enlightenment and the emergence of market relations have rendered that impossible. Enlightenment overthrows the authority of custom and tradition and submits every feature of social existence to the scrutiny of reason. Reason in bourgeois society is the subjective, instrumental reason of the maximizer of utilities. To be sure, separate features of the classical polity can be drawn upon and imitated, but the basis of social existence now lies in the supposedly originary will of the abstract individual.

---

2 Quoted by Gossman, 'Time and History,' 339 n 3
3 This is substantially the view that Hegel has of the Greeks 'in the first and genuine form of their freedom': 'we may assert, that they had no conscience; the habit of living for their country without further reflection, was the principle predominant among them. The consideration of the State in the abstract – which to our understanding is the essential point – was alien to them. Their grand object was their country in its living and real aspect; this actual Athens, this Sparta, these Altars, this form of social life, this union of fellow citizens, these manners and customs. To the Greek his country was a necessary of life, without which existence was impossible' (*The Philosophy of History*, 253).

The only legitimate basis of the modern state that Rousseau is discussing in the *Social Contract* is the will, the absolutely free will that is presupposed in the act of alienation by which, according to Rousseau, a people 'becomes a people; for this act, being necessarily prior ... is the true foundation of society' (SC 11). Society is therefore to be established by convention and does not issue any longer from nature. The family does not supply a model of political authority since it is sustained past the period of the children's maturity only by a convention and voluntarily (SC 4-5). In the same way nature does not provide the basis of the state in so far as force, superiority in wisdom, and fact are not recognized as legitimate sources of political authority. Force is a physical power that has no moral effect; it creates no right and is not a legitimate source of political authority (SC 6). In the same way, the existence of any given political order says nothing about its legitimacy. Grotius's method of reasoning from fact to right is entirely illegitimate: there is none 'more favourable to tyrants' (SC 4). As for the reasoning that asserts that there are natural classes of superiors and inferiors, masters and slaves, this is the reversal of cause and effect: 'If then there are slaves by nature, it is because there have been slaves against nature. Force made the first slaves, and their cowardice perpetuated the condition' (SC 5).

The modern state has this essential difference from the polis, that it must be essentially grounded in a conscious and rational act of will. What differentiates it from the polis is not, then, the absence of personal dependence. The ancient citizen was not dependent upon a personal superior. Personal dependence characterizes the relation of master and slave, absolute monarch and subject, lord and vassal. The ancient city shares with the modern state the characteristic that its citizens are not personally bound to a superior but impersonally bound by law. It is in their relationship to law, however, that the essential difference appears. In the one case it is the immediate expression of the communal interest and is also identified with a nature that transcends the day-to-day practices of the city, its conventions. The pagan city held its laws from its gods; it 'made no distinction between its gods and its laws' (SC 107). In the second case law is the expression of the communal interest reflected through the independent will of a rational subject who stands outside his own creation and judges it.

Both forms represent expressions of political liberty since both are governed by the expression of the communal interest in the form of law. But the second is only possible after its way has been prepared by a long history of social development: 'It takes a long time for feeling so to change that men make up their minds to take their equals as masters, in the hope that they will profit by doing so' (SC 106). In this way the modern state does, to an extent, represent the potential perfection of the first. Liberty in the modern state would be in a sense greater or more genuine since it would now follow from the fully conscious choice of each individual citizen. The ancient citizen obeyed the law because he could not separate his own existence from the existence of the city. In the modern state the citizen ideally will obey the law because 'the mere impulse of appetite is slavery, while obedience to a law which we prescribe to ourselves is liberty' (SC 16). If the modern state is to share with the polis an ethical mission, this does not mean that it will be a recreation of the immediate ethical life of the Greeks.

Individual Will and Political Sovereignty

That the modern state issues from the freedom of the rational will implies that it has its origins and foundations in a convention, that political society is a human artefact. But in referring the foundations of the civil power back to an original convention Rousseau is doing no more than joining with the liberal orthodoxy of the age. The revolution that separated natural law from theology had already been accomplished in the previous century by Grotius and Puffendorf.[4] Had Rousseau done nothing more than reaffirm along with them that sovereignty resides *originally* in the people, the *Social Contract* would be a minor work deserving little attention. Rousseau's historically important revolution in political theory lies rather in his forcefully drawing the democratic conclusion out of the premises of liberalism.

All the natural-law theorists since Hobbes had agreed that sovereignty derives from the individual wills of the members of society; but all of them had likewise agreed that sovereignty is to at least some degree alienable. The degree to which sovereignty is alienable was supposed to be based on the consent, explicit or tacit, of the members and fixed in its forms by the pact of submission that transferred sovereignty or a part of it to the Prince. This way of formulating the question allows for both absolutism and limited government, as exemplified in the work of Hobbes and Locke respectively.

Rousseau's central criticism, in the *Social Contract*, of earlier contract theories lies in his equation of the alienation of sovereignty with the

4 Derathé, *Science Politique*, 39. Derathé is in general indispensable for an understanding of the relations between Rousseau and early liberalism. See also Cobban, *Rousseau*; G.D.H. Cole, introduction to his *The Social Contract and Discourses*, v–xl; and Colletti, *Rousseau*.

renunciation of individual will, or liberty. Implied early on in the first book, in Rousseau's critique of Grotius's justification of slavery, is the notion that sovereignty is inalienable. This principle does not await the introduction of the contract itself. Grotius's justification of slavery had rested on the assumption that any contract in which there was an equivalent exchange is valid, and he had argued analogously that if a man could alienate his liberty to a master, then a whole people could alienate its liberty in transferring sovereignty to a Prince. For Rousseau, however, there is a crucial difference between alienation and renunciation: 'To alienate is to give or to sell' (SC 7). In politics, whether it be the relation of master and slave or that of people and Prince, 'to say that a man gives himself gratuitously, is to say what is absurd and inconceivable ... he who does it is out of his mind ... and madness creates no right' (SC 7). Yet a Prince has nothing of equal value to exchange for the right of command that is acquired when the will is alienated. Any convention, then, according to which sovereignty is alienated, is void by virtue of the fact that it is not alienation but renunciation that has taken place:

To renounce liberty is to renounce being a man, to surrender the rights of humanity and even its duties. For him who renounces everything no indemnity is possible. Such a renunciation is incompatible with man's nature; to remove all liberty from his will is to remove all morality from his acts. Finally, it is an empty and contradictory convention that sets up, on the one side absolute authority, and on the other, unlimited obedience. Is it not clear that we can be under no obligation to a person from whom we have the right to exact everything? Does not this condition alone, in the absence of equivalence or exchange, in itself involve the nullity of the act? (SC 8)

Political authority, then, is legitimate when it follows from a real 'alienation,' when it accomplishes a real exchange of equivalents. But this does not take place *between a people and its government*, whether that government be embodied in a natural individual or a representative assembly.

This distinction in Rousseau's eyes renders all previous versions of the social contract invalid, for they all amount to a renunciation of liberty. Any contract that transferred liberty from the people to a Prince would be an 'empty and contradictory convention.' It would be contradictory because freedom of will cannot be renounced. The alienation that takes place in political society is therefore not an exchange between a people and its Sovereign. It is an exchange that each individual makes for himself, or that the individual makes *with* himself in two different capacities:

'each individual, in making a contract, as we may say, with himself, is bound in a double capacity' (SC 13). For Rousseau any theory that founds the legitimacy of government on the will of the individual is inherently a theory of popular sovereignty.

It is inherent in the nature of human will that it cannot be renounced. To renounce one's will, to will merely the will of another, is a contradiction:

it cannot say: 'What he wills tomorrow, I too shall will' because it is absurd for the will to bind itself for the future, nor is it incumbent upon any will to consent to anything that is not for the good of the being who wills. If then the people promise simply to obey, by that very act it dissolves itself and loses what makes it a people; the moment a master exists, there is no longer a Sovereign, and from that moment the body politic has ceased to exist. (SC 20)

To remain free, therefore, is always to have at least the right to exercise one's will. Consent is no longer sufficient to establish the legitimacy of the acts of the Sovereign. Sovereignty is the power to make law, and 'laws are, properly speaking, only the conditions of civil association. The people, being subject to the laws, ought to be their author: the conditions of the society ought to be regulated solely by those who come together to form it' (SC 31).

It has often been noted that the theory of the social contract tends inevitably in the direction of political democracy, but most of the early modern practitioners of the theory, Hobbes, Grotius, and Puffendorf, were absolutists.[5] Even in Locke's case it was anything but clear whether sovereignty ultimately resided in the people or whether it was shared in balance among the permanent interests of the kingdom. From the premises that political society has its foundations in a convention rather than in nature, divine will, or force, and that a convention is a human act of will, notions that in the *Social Contract* Rousseau chooses to share with his predecessors, he feels ready to move immediately to the notion that sovereignty is essentially inalienable and inherently absolute and indivisible. Unlike his predecessors Rousseau believes that the distinction between the source and the exercise of sovereignty is illegitimate. With one stroke therefore Rousseau condemns absolutism, constitutional monarchy, and representative government. At the same time government is immediately transformed into a trust, and one that is unconditionally revocable (SC 76). The transformation that takes place is also the

5 Derathé, *Science Politique*, 42ff

substitution of a body of active citizens for the essentially passive subjects of even the most limited governments.

The *Social Contract*, Rousseau's proposed solution to the problem of politics in civil society, transcends previous solutions, but paradoxically, by driving through to the extreme conclusions inherent in their premises. Hobbes had begun by grounding political obligation in, to use Rousseau's phrase, the 'absolute and naturally independent existence' (SC 15) of the individual. Rousseau pushes this idea to its logical extreme with the insistence that will cannot be renounced. Locke's government was legitimate when it was based on popular consent – albeit a popular consent that was largely tacit. Rousseau insists that consent that cannot be brought into question at any time is specious. If sovereignty cannot be renounced, then it is in the nature of things that in point of right it always resides in the will of the populace. If tacit consent is meaningless, then the only genuine form of consent is active participation. Upon the basic premises of early liberalism Rousseau constructs a democratic polity of active citizens rather than an aggregate of passive subjects.

Sovereignty and Contract

The essence of Rousseau's political doctrine in the *Social Contract*, the idea that the only 'legitimate rule of administration' (SC 3) is expressed in the inalienable, indivisible, and absolute rule of the popular will, does *not* in and of itself require a contractualism. The contract itself does not follow from the essential notion that the 'will does not admit of representation' (SC 78). What does, however, require the notion of a contract is the problem of the formation of a popular will in the first place. Or rather, the formation of such a will, in the absence of the prior existence of a *people*, requires the notion of a contract. The doctrine of inalienable popular sovereignty is *not* inextricably linked with the notion of a fundamental contract. The contract that Rousseau constructs is thus compatible with the doctrine of popular sovereignty but is not necessary to it. All that is needed in order to assert that doctrine is his distinction between alienation and renunciation, which is announced early on in the first book and precedes the actual contract. Since that distinction already proclaims the notion of inalienable sovereignty, the contract, which is introduced for a different function, is rendered consistent with it by the reduction of the *pactum societatis* and the *pactum subjectionis* into one single compact. The contract itself is a fictitious and figurative device that will legitimize only a specific sort of popular will that cannot be represented.

The doctrine of the sovereignty of the popular will and the doctrine of the popular will as a 'general will' in the specific sense of the *Social Contract* are thus in principle separable. However, Rousseau does not in fact separate them. Although it appears from the arrangement of the text that popular sovereignty follows from the nature of the contract, that is in fact not the case. The contract follows from the inherent validity of popular sovereignty, once the assumption is made that the basis of the modern state is will.

Certainly in the case of the polis, which was a historically legitimate form of political association, the popular will was not a general will in the sense given to that term in the *Social Contract*. In the polis, at least for Rousseau, government was legitimate when it was the government of laws, even though those laws were essentially the customs and traditions of a culturally unified people. Sparta did not need a theory of a contract, although it might be possible to read one back into the Spartan polity forcefully. In the modern state, however, the fundamental laws of the social body are eternally open to question, and the constitution is re-created anew with every act of sovereignty (SC 44) and even in the tacit consent of the people to the decrees of government (SC 20-1).

Thus legitimate government is republican government and a republic is 'every State that is governed by laws' (SC 30). 'To be legitimate, the government must be, not one with the Sovereign, but its minister' (SC 31 n 1). When the popular will or the public interest is not constituted by the self-subsistent autonomous reason of monadic individuals, it is embodied directly and immediately in the customs of the people, its habits and traditions, its 'manner of existence.' Even the modern state must in the end acknowledge this power, which Rousseau calls a fourth form of law, after constitutional, civil, and criminal law, and which 'forms the real constitution of the State, takes on every day new powers ... and insensibly replaces authority by the force of habit' (SC 44).

Certainly, also, once a genuine popular will can be brought into existence, it cannot be maintained in existence unless it, and not the Prince, is Sovereign. But for this no contract is necessary. In fact it is the mistaken notion that there is a contract between a people and its government that must be defeated. If, then, legitimate government is based on convention, which is an act of will, and if the will cannot in its nature be transmitted or renounced, and finally, if there exists no popular will already embedded in a network of customary relations and rules, it would not be possible to speak of legitimate government. Thus the question par excellence in the modern world becomes the formation of society.

In the ancient city the existence of a popular will as a product of habit, as something that appeared natural, as an ethic that was lived aesthetically and pre-reflectively, prevented the emergence of the absolute individual will that was the foundation of bourgeois society. Once that will emerged fully, however, the rule of custom, which could over the generations create a *people*, was no longer possible. In a sense, once the supremacy of the individual will is recognized, the question of the proper relation of government and society is settled forthwith; but the problem of the formation of society itself becomes more intractable than ever. Once the will is made the ultimate foundation of political authority, it follows for Rousseau immediately that the will must *remain* Sovereign. Anything less than continuous and effective self-determination constitutes a self-renunciation on the part of the will, a denial of its own essence. But at the same time, the will that has emancipated itself from the authority of custom and nature, conceived of teleologically, is the will that has nothing in common with other wills except the similarity of need and an abstract equality. Thus the foundation of inalienable popular sovereignty is simultaneously a mortal danger to itself.

This is the problem upon which earlier modern natural-law theory had so far morally foundered. It recognized the supremacy of the will, but in opting for monarchical absolutism, it betrayed its own fundamental principle; it sought in the sovereignty of a particular will the solution to the problem of society, of the plurality of wills. This is seen most clearly in Hobbes, who shares with Rousseau the doctrines of a single contract and of an inalienable and absolute sovereignty but for whom the state of war could be transformed into a settled social condition only when the will is, in Rousseau's terms, totally 'renounced.' Bourgeois society is not naturally republican. It takes a long time for men to decide to take their equals as masters 'in the hope that they will profit by doing so.' The *Social Contract* is an attempt to face this problem squarely, in a sense to compel the bourgeois to live up to the implications of the principles upon which his existence is based. But if bourgeois society must no longer rely on the rule of a master in order to live with itself, then 'it would be better, before examining the act by which a people gives itself to a king, to examine that by which it has become a people; for this act, being necessarily prior to the other, is the true foundation of society' (SC 11). However, in order to understand this act, it is necessary to examine more closely its premise. The act is a response to a predicament. The major premise of the social contract is a certain historical predicament.

The Major Premise: The State of Nature

From the start of the *Social Contract* Rousseau informs us that he is concerned not with the state or politics as such but with a problem specific to a definite historical epoch. His purpose is to inquire if 'in the civil order, there can be any sure and legitimate rule of administration, men being taken as they are and laws as they might be' (*SC* 3). The phrase 'men being taken as they are' might seem to refer either to human nature or a human essence in the abstract sense, or to human nature in the sense that follows from Rousseau's historical anthropology. If it is understood in the former sense, then Rousseau's idea of social relations will appear to be inherently bourgeois and he will be guilty of the mistake he attributes, in the second *Discourse* and elsewhere, to the theorists of natural law – that they read definite historical sets of social relations back into nature.[6] Once it is understood in the latter sense, however, then it is clear that the scope of the *Social Contract* is restricted on the whole to that specific historical form of social labour that Rousseau was at pains to analyse in the second *Discourse*. It is difficult on the basis of the *Social Contract* alone to settle this question. But if the second *Discourse* is understood as the foundation of a historical and social ontology according to which nature is unfolded inside the matrix of human historical activity, then there are strong reasons for presuming that the starting point of the *Social Contract* is just that historical predicament analysed in the *Discourse* and that this predicament is what delimits the boundaries to the solution proposed in the *Contract*.

Curiously enough, the *Social Contract* has virtually no discussion of the state of nature that precedes the contract itself. But the first version of the *Contract*, the so-called Geneva Manuscript, does have a rather lengthy chapter aimed at elucidating the question of whence 'the necessity for political institutions arises' (GMS 157). The society in which Rousseau's version of the social contract is a necessity and first becomes a possibility he calls there 'la société générale du genre humain.' It is a general society because it is composed of the independent, abstract individuals of civil society. Its existence presupposes a long historical development:

---

6 This is the case with both conservative and radical readings of Rousseau. See, for example, two recent articles: Arthur M. Melzer, 'Rousseau and the Problem of Bourgeois Society,' and Yoav Peled, 'Rousseau's Inhibited Radicalism: An Analysis of His Political Thought in Light of His Economic Ideas.'

Man's force is so proportioned to his natural needs and his primitive state that the slightest change in this state and increase in his needs make the assistance of his fellow men necessary; *and when his desires finally encompass the whole of nature*, the cooperation of the entire human race is barely enough to satisfy them ... Our needs bring us together in proportion as our passions divide us, and the more we become enemies of our fellow men, the less we can do without them. Such are the first bonds of the general society. (GMS 157-8; emphasis added)

The general society of the human race, which is composed of men who are independent and politically equal, is just that system of needs that constitutes the last term of the state of nature as it was described in the second *Discourse*. In it men are joined together exclusively or primarily through their instrumental relations with one another. The social bond is predicated upon a dynamic expansion of private needs, so that as the bond becomes stronger, so does the opposition of interests.

Earlier contract theorists and others had made it a part of their accounts of the state of nature to postulate a natural sociability among men that would moderate its strife. Puffendorf, for example, thought that human sociability assumed two forms, both of which were natural. The first was based upon an immediate, intuitive consciousness among human beings of the identity of their nature and led to a disinterested impulse to come to the aid of others, ultimately developing into a general kindliness on the part of each for all. The second was the usual form of interested, utilitarian, instrumental relations.[7] For Rousseau, the second truly described the society of the times, while the first was a fiction invented by the philosophers (GMS 158). In that state of nature that is the outcome of a social order based on instrumental relations of independent agents, the existence of each depends entirely on his constantly shifting relations with others. And in such a relation:

nothing is permanent except the misery that results from all these vicissitudes ... The kind of general society that mutual needs can engender does not, therefore, offer any effective assistance to man once he has become miserable, or at least it gives new force to him who already has too much, whereas the weak man – lost, stifled, crushed ... finally perishes as a victim of the deceptive union from which he expected happiness ... far from proposing a goal of shared felicity from which each individual would derive his own, one man's happiness is the other's misfortune. (GMS 158)

---

7 See Derathé, *Science Politique*, 142ff.

In such a condition, *pitié* is no longer effective. And even if it were, it would pose too great a danger to the one who felt it: 'Thus nature's gentle voice is no longer an infallible guide for us, nor is the independence we have received from her a desirable state' (GMS 158). In the same way, the 'natural law,' to the extent that it is developed in the individual in conjunction with the social development of the understanding, is rendered ineffective: 'concepts of the natural law ... begin to develop only when the prior development of the passions renders all its precepts impotent' (GMS 159).[8] This state of things, if it could subsist at all, would be nothing but 'a source of crimes and miseries for men, each of whom would see only his interest, follow only his inclinations, and listen only to his passions' (GMS 158).

It is not at all difficult to recognize in the 'general society' both the dissolution of all traditional social orders and the state of war that was the basis of the state in the second *Discourse*. The state of nature that is the major premise of the contract is thus the historical successor of the savage, primitive, ancient, and feudal orders that preceded bourgeois society. It is a return to nature in the sense that all recover their original absolute liberty. But at the same time it is a social state of nature in that none can survive, being subjected to a set of continually expanding social needs, without commerce with the others. Nothing unites the members of this society but their private interests, in relations of exchange that are inherently conflictual. It is a state of war that vindicates Hobbes's description: 'Hobbes's mistake, therefore, is not that he established the state of war among men who are independent and have become sociable, but that he supposed this state natural to the species and gave it as the cause of the vices of which it is the effect' (GMS 162).

How is a popular will to be formed out of this situation without the will being renounced? And what sort of will can it be that is to issue from an atomized aggregate of self-interested individuals enjoying perfect liberty by nature? If the alienation of liberty to a governing power, in whole or in part, amounts to a renunciation of will that contradicts its very essence, how then is a body politic to be formed? It would seem that in such a situation an overwhelming power standing outside of society capable of imposing unity and order would have to precede the act by which a people becomes a people. But it is just such a solution that Rousseau rejects, because the existence of such a power implies a previous renunciation of will. This would be the relation of 'a master and his slaves, and certainly not a people and its ruler' (SC 11).

8 Modified translation

In the face of the historical dissolution of all traditional solutions, that is, once bourgeois society has undermined the natural quality of traditional social relations and subjected political relations themselves to the private calculus of the abstracted individual, the problem takes on the following form:

as the force and liberty of each man are the chief instruments of his self-preservation, how can he pledge them without harming his own interests, and neglecting the care he owes to himself? This difficulty ... may be stated in the following terms:

'The problem is to find a form of association which will defend and protect with the whole common force the person and goods of each associate, and in which each, while uniting himself with all, may still obey himself alone, and remain as free as before.' This is the fundamental problem of which the *Social Contract* provides the solution. (SC 12)

Despite the historical predicament into which mankind has brought itself, Rousseau none the less believes that it is still possible to find a basis for political society *in* existing historical conditions and that this polity will be at least relatively legitimate and more than a mere aggregate. Rousseau's claim is extreme, but the extremity of the claim establishes the very critical distance from the proposed solution that Rousseau, I believe, wishes the reader to maintain. That the ultimate status of this solution is open to question is indicated throughout the *Social Contract* by his interjections, asides, qualifications, and the tone of pessimism that especially informs the second half.

In the Geneva Manuscript Rousseau's claim is, if anything, even more extreme. There he contrives a fictional interlocutor, an echo both of Thrasymachus and of Hobbes, who takes up the part of the stronger member of the general society and pleads that, although he is fully cognizant of the rules of natural justice, he sees no reason why he should limit his natural right in the absence of secure guarantees that others will likewise limit theirs. Even more, he claims that even an assurance of *justice* is insufficient: 'Furthermore, it will be my business to get the strong on my side, by sharing with them the spoils from the weak. This would be better than justice for my own advantage and for my security' (GMS 160).

It is this man's reasoning, as the hardest case, to which the contract as a whole is addressed. And far from being pessimistic about his ability to convince his fictional interlocutor, Rousseau claims that it is out of material composed of just such men that he will erect his solution:

But although there is no natural and general society among men, although men become unhappy and wicked in becoming sociable, although the laws of justice and equality mean nothing to those who live in the freedom of the state of nature and subject to the needs of the social state ... let us attempt to draw from the ill itself the remedy that should cure it. Let us use new associations to correct, if possible, the defect of the general association. Let our violent interlocutor himself judge its success. Let us show him in perfected art the reparation of the ills that the beginnings of art caused to nature ... Let him see the value of good actions, the punishment of bad ones, and the sweet harmony of justice and happiness in a better constituted order of things ... If my zeal does not blind me in this undertaking, let us not doubt that with a strong soul and an upright mind, this enemy of the human race will at last abjure his hate along with his errors; that reason which led him astray will bring him back to humanity; that he will learn to prefer his interest properly understood to his apparent interest; that he will become good, virtuous, sympathetic, and finally ... rather than the ferocious brigand he wished to become, the most solid support of a well-ordered society. (GMS 162-3)

It is certainly a prodigious, Herculean task that Rousseau is setting for himself in the above passage, that of transforming a ferocious brigand into a contented and model citizen, and without the intervention of any external agency. The remedy is to come out of the evil itself; the very reason that misled him is to restore him to humanity. Rousseau is here proposing what he himself denounces in the *Preface to Narcissus*, that is, 'a masterpiece of modern policy' (see above, chapter 5, page 111), which will unite men by exploiting the very private interests and reciprocal needs that define them in the system of needs of civil society.

What enables him to propose such a solution is that he perceives both sides of the relation of instrumental reciprocity subsisting among agents in the marketplace. Relations of exchange are already relations among putative, formal 'political' equals. As we have seen above (chapter 5, pages 125-6), civil society dictates both a form of interest and a form of duty. The instrumentalization of the other and the reciprocity that formally obtains between two agents in the marketplace - both follow from the absolute liberty that belongs to the second, bourgeois, juridical state of nature. If it is reason that accomplishes the separation of man from nature *and* the emancipation of the individual from any natural form of traditional community, reason likewise enjoins the recognition of the inherent equality of abstract individuals upon those same individuals. Civil society has the basis for a specific morality of its own. Even the 'violent interlocutor,' the man who is 'enlightened and independent' (GMS 160), knows this as the rules of natural justice. His problem is a different one: 'It is not a matter of teaching me what justice is, but of showing me what interest I have in being just (GMS 161). The morality that reason in civil society enjoins could be phrased in a different way, and one that, not surprisingly, anticipates one of Kant's formulations of the categorical imperative: 'Man ... is a being far too noble to be obliged to serve merely as an instrument of others, and one ought never to employ him for one's own convenience without referring to that which is agreeable to him' (*LNH* 536).

Each may serve as instrument for the other on the same terms that the other serves as instrument for him. Thus the general will transposes into the public sphere the same logic embodied in the morality of the relation of instrumental reciprocity:

Each man, in giving himself to all, gives himself to nobody: and *as there is no associate over which he does not acquire the same right as he yields others over himself*, he gains an equivalent for everything he loses, and an increase of force for the preservation of what he has. (*SC* 12; emphasis added)

Why is it that the general will is always in the right, and that all continually will the happiness of each one, unless it is because there is not a man who does not think of 'each' as meaning him, and consider himself in voting for all? This proves that equality of rights and the idea of justice which such equality creates originates in the preference each man gives to himself, and accordingly in the very nature of man. (*SC* 24-5)

The popular will in civil society takes the form of a general will that legislates universally, because in civil society each man has a natural preference for himself and simultaneously recognizes the absolute liberty and equality of the other.

Thus the very historical predicament that implicitly settles the problem of the relation of government and people, but that also poses the problem of the foundation of society in its most acute form, seems to contain the basis, or at least the principle, out of which society may be formed. Without this society, all that may be expected of the state is the forcible pacification of an aggregate of isolated antagonists – Hobbes's solution, perhaps tempered or moderated to a greater or lesser extent. But once it is recognized that equality provides a foundation for law, the possibility of bringing a people into existence becomes real once again. But before that act may take place, another condition must be added.

If we take the violent interlocutor as representative not even of the majority but of a substantial minority of men in the state of nature –

that is, in civil society abstracted from the state – it should be clear that that condition could be nothing else but a state of war identical to that described by Rousseau in the second *Discourse*. Were this not the case, were not even the stronger member of civil society threatened by the absence of a pacifying power, the contract would not be possible. As it is, all must feel a deadly insecurity; they must recognize not only a certain inconvenience but that 'the human race would perish unless it changed its manner of existence' (*SC* 11). Thus the very condition that makes the principle of the contract possible, the existence of perfectly independent and sufficiently rational individuals who are subjected to an ever-expanding set of social needs, also makes it necessary. Rousseau's major premise has only two important differences from Hobbes's state of nature. First, Rousseau quite acutely and accurately detects a greater *potential* for moral insight on the part of the bourgeois who are party to the contract. The principle of this morality follows from the very conditions of existence of the bourgeois individual. Second, because of this, Rousseau sees the possibility that the will, which is the basis of the modern state, need not be renounced, and therefore that sovereignty need not be transferred, so long as the Sovereign is absolutely no one in particular, and all in general. Thus it seems that a simple act is all that will be necessary in order to solve, in one master stroke, the problem of restoring the will to itself. This restoration of the will to itself, its return from the possession of a master, is to be found in the social contract. This contract, however, is nothing else than an act of 'total alienation,' but one in which each will remain as free as before. The return from alienation presupposes an extreme act of 'alienation.'

The Contract and Its Accomplishment: 'A World out of Nothing'

The historical predicament that makes the social contract both possible and necessary is the existence of civil society. The existence of absolutely independent individuals, for whom the only grounds of obligation lie in their private wills, makes the contract necessary, because such individuals have an absolute need for protection from their equals – a need that, like all their other needs, presupposes its formation at the hands of society. Yet the contract is possible because these same individuals recognize their antagonists as their equals – none claims any *a priori* right to rule, but only to fight. Under these conditions social existence must assume the form of a contract. It must be a contract since an act of exchange is the only relation among absolutely independent individuals that is legitimate. Yet this contract cannot amount to a renunciation of the will that is its foundation. The contract cannot, therefore, be an engagement with a third party or on behalf of a third party.

The solution that Rousseau proposes closely parallels the contract of Hobbes, with the exception that it is not undertaken on behalf of a third party, nor is liberty 'renounced': 'Each of us puts his person and all his power in common under the supreme direction of the general will, and, in our corporate capacity, we receive each member as an indivisible part of the whole' (SC 13). The community thus created is not a party to the contract. There is no problem or discrepancy created if one of the parties involved in the exchange is created by the exchange itself, for the community is not involved in the contract.[9] The contract itself is, like Hobbes's contract, an agreement among all the individuals concerned among themselves. It is an agreement to alienate, but not renounce, all their rights to a corporate body in which each will have equal shares. It is not an exchange *between* community and individuals but an agreement among individuals to subordinate their existence as separate beings on behalf of another mode of existence. Nevertheless Rousseau does speak of a 'mutual undertaking between the public and the individuals,' but this is not the contract itself. It is included in the contract. Rousseau's term is 'renfermé,' which can mean included, enclosed, comprised, concealed, or hidden. Thus the contract *gives rise* to a set of obligations of the members to the corporate body and of the corporate body to the several members. But there is no contractual relation with the corporate body as such.

The several members are obligated in so far as they have mutually undertaken to alienate their liberty in its entirety. The corporation is obligated to the members in so far as they are the authors of its being and have agreed that the corporate body should act only under the direction of the general will and 'receive each member as an indivisible part of the whole.' Thus, although the general will is conceived of as 'indestructible' no matter to what extent it is encroached upon through the capture by particular interests of the state (SC 85-6), the corporate body is not indestructible, either actually or morally (SC 12, 14).

The creation of the Sovereign through the contract is not a renunciation of liberty on behalf of a third party, nor is it an exchange with a third party. Yet it is an act of total alienation. In order to be legitimate this act of total alienation must involve a fair exchange. What is being

---

9 For diametrically opposite views on this question compare Cole, introduction, xviii, and Althusser, *Politics and History*, 125-35; cf Levine, *Autonomy*, 35-40, who wisely de-emphasizes this aspect of their reading.

exchanged is not, as was the case with previous versions of the contract, one incommensurable with another; it is not an exchange of liberty for peace and security. What is being exchanged is one mode of existence for another. A conscious act of self-transformation is required. The corporate mode is possible only when the renunciation is total; otherwise 'each, being on one point his own judge, would ask to be so on all; the state of nature would thus continue, and the association would become inoperative or tyrannical' (SC 12). And the corporate mode constitutes a fair exchange because each party to the contract recovers liberty, security, property, and power. Total alienation, far from being a renunciation, involves an advantageous exchange:

> the position in which they find themselves ... is really preferable to that in which they were before. Instead of a renunciation, they have made an advantageous exchange: instead of an uncertain and precarious way of living they have got one that is better and more secure; instead of natural independence they have got liberty; instead of the power to harm others, security for themselves, and instead of their strength, which others might overcome, a right which social union makes invincible. (SC 26–7)

Thus it seems that the original problem, the question of the formation of a society that would not rely on the renunciation of will, has been solved. Bourgeois society, in order to be true to itself and survive, rests on the formation of a sovereign popular will, in the form of a general will. Bourgeois society is inherently democratic, despite its past and despite the absolutist and despotic tendencies of its theorists. The general will is, if you like, the truth, in the Hegelian sense, of civil society.

The only legitimate popular will in bourgeois society is a general will. The popular will cannot be the immediate expression of a pre-existent community, since under the conditions of civil society the community has been dissolved. It is only through the general will, based on the total alienation of the natural and absolute liberty of the individual, that a community is reconstituted. And the community can be reconstituted only on the basis of equality.

It is equality that is at the heart of the general will and that is expressed in the form of law. This law is not the command of any actual superior, nor is it the customary law identified with a traditional community. The law, which is the real form of popular sovereignty, 'must be general in its object as well as its essence ... it must both come from all and apply to all' (SC 25). The natural equality of the contracting members is preserved in so far as, and only in so far as, their corporate existence is directed by the general will in the form of laws. The laws issuing from the Sovereign are to be strictly distinguished from decrees of magistracy, which pronounce upon particular events or persons. This applies likewise to the judicial function, which in the *Social Contract* is assimilated to the executive. Under the general will, equality is a function of the universality of the law, which 'considers subjects *en masse* and actions in the abstract, and never a particular person or action' (*SC* 30).

The community created through the social contract is a legislating body. It is well to note this point. It is not the community that legislates, but the community that is *constituted* and *reaffirmed* in the act of legislation itself. Of course the community is not constituted in any and every act that might pass as legislation, but only when its lawmaking follows the strict rule of producing a general will.

The solution to the problem posed by the supremacy of the individual will in bourgeois society is in the assumption of all its members of the lawmaking power, conceived as the power to make rules strictly limited by their universality. It is the unique property of this form of law that it both follows from and is the exact inverse of the relation that constitutes civil society. It follows from civil society since it recognizes the equality of all the members. It is the inverse of the usual relations subsisting in civil society, since under the law 'one cannot work for someone else without at the same time working for oneself' (GMS 175). In the system of needs, on the other hand, one supposedly works for others in working exclusively for oneself.

The problem and the solution are inseparable. Far from being a utopian work, the *Social Contract* is as strict as *Leviathan* in limiting itself to the materials at hand in erecting its solution. But this statement must be immediately qualified. The solution in principle, at the ideal level, is grounded in the conditions of civil society. But the same condition, the existence of absolutely free and therefore equal wills, sets definite limits within which the solution can be realized in practice. In this way the problem is taken up into the solution itself. And Rousseau persists in an attempt to examine the whole definite range of conditions under which the principle might be applicable. The second half of the *Social Contract* is not an addendum or afterthought or merely a form of wise counsel that might aid some prospective Legislator in carrying out his task.[10] It is an integral part of the whole work and attempts to establish, *a priori* as it were, the outcome of the concretization of the principle

---

10 Cf Masters, *Political Philosophy*, 306ff, who calls it a 'Handbook for Rulers' (311).

under different classes of conditions. All of these are incidental to the principle itself; almost all of them are capable of supporting the principle in some degree. Some will be more stable than others; some will be more adequate to the principle than others. But none can escape the inherent instability and tensions, not to mention contradictions, that follow from the same fundamental set of conditions that give rise to and sustain the principle in the first place.

The first and ultimately decisive condition is the retention of the sphere of particular wills, or rather, to be more accurate, the fact that a general will cannot exist except on the basis of a plurality of particular wills. It is interesting to note in this respect the shift that has taken place between the *Discourse on Political Economy* and the *Contract*. In the earlier work Rousseau was more than vague on the question of whether the general will must 'come from all' as well as 'apply to all.' What was crucial then was law in and of itself, in so far as law inherently tended to equity. Contract and popular sovereignty, although in retrospect seeming to wait in the wings, were in reality subordinated to a view of the state that approximated much more closely the model of ancient virtue. Thus, 'the rulers well know that the general will is always on the side which is most favourable to the public interest, that is to say, most equitable; so that it is needful only to act justly, to be certain of following the general will' (*PE* 242). In the *Contract*, however, the general will is much more clearly rooted in the will of the individual citizen. There is no general will that is not, in addition to being incidentally just, an outcome of popular sovereignty. By the time he came to write the *Social Contract* Rousseau had come to see that there was, in the interaction of particular wills that recognized themselves to be simply and only particular, a basis for law itself. The basis in principle for a community was present in what was earlier conceived of as the absolute negation of community, in limitless need, absolute fear, and thus in the perfect equality of persons.

The political community that arises through the contract has of necessity no autonomous existence. The state does not miraculously rescue the individual from the insecurity and moral degradation of the state of nature and deliver him to security, civil liberty, and the happiness of a rational creature. The state created through the contract is born out of the same muck and mire that could give rise to Hobbes's absolutism. The conditions that inspire it never disappear within it, although they are constantly negated by it. If Rousseau's citizen learns the benefits of civil liberty in the state, he never forgets the lessons of the state of nature. Rousseau is more than careful to preserve this tension throughout the

Contract, the realization of whose principle is always governed by the opposition of particular and general wills. The contract itself does not abolish civil society but only creates another sphere of relations that ought to be superior in fact, but whose superiority is in fact always in doubt. The ideal level and the practical level can only be separated abstractly, in theory. Although in some sense the particularity of the individual will is taken up into and included within the general will, this general will is never brought fully down into the particular but merely regulates it. In practice the general will is *reactive* and *defensive*, both in the interests of social equality and in its own interest. Community is expressed merely in the state, which in turn must see that the opposition of interests inherent in civil society never overflows and inundates its special province. But this task can never be adequately accomplished so long as the wills in which the general will originates are the absolute wills of bourgeois society. It is not a matter of accomplishing the perfect identity of particular and general will, for that is completely out of the question. Merely the adequate coincidence of particular and general wills requires a constant set of supporting circumstances not given in the principle itself. Before deciding what the status of the solution Rousseau proposes is, it is worth examining what follows from the structure of this act of association.

The act of total alienation creates the sovereign corporate entity whose essence is legislation as the production of an abstract and universal rule. This act also purports to accomplish the necessary transformation in the 'manner of existence' of the previously isolated individuals. The contract, which is a series of individual acts of will, creates a 'moral and collective body composed of as many members as the assembly contains voters, and receiving from this act its unity, its common identity, its life and its will.' (SC 13). But this moral and collective body exists both in place of and alongside the previous mere aggregation: it not only supplants the aggregation; it also both expresses and maintains it. Like the illegitimate state of the second *Discourse*, it not only transcends civil society but epitomizes one side of it and maintains the other side.

The manner of existence of the individuals is, however, not totally transformed by this act. What actually takes place is a kind of doubling of human existence. The Sovereign that is a moral and collective body leads an abstract and ideal existence:

It is apparent from this that the sovereign is by its nature only a moral person, that it has only an abstract and collective existence. (GMS 167)

But since the state has only an ideal and conventional existence, its members have no natural, common sensitivity ... how is it possible to be reassured that men who are constantly reminded of their primitive condition by nature will never neglect this other, artificial condition whose advantage they can only sense through consequences that are often far removed? (GMS 177)

Rousseau throughout the *Social Contract* draws attention again and again to the abstract and ideal nature of the Sovereign.[11]

It is, with hindsight, both ironic and perfectly apt that Rousseau should describe his solution to the problem of civil society as an 'alienation' rather than a 'renunciation.' For the *Social Contract* actually propounds the notion that the perfected political state, the absolute sovereignty of the general will, would, were it to be established, constitute the alienated expression of a communal life whose criteria of legitimacy could themselves not be realized. Rousseau's sense of alienation cannot be adequately analysed in quasi-Durkheimian terms as 'marginality.'[12] Nor is it simply the complaint of a petit-bourgeois against being pushed aside by the march of material progress. To characterize him as the 'Homer of the losers' is to miss the most illuminating insights he is capable of supplying.[13] Rousseau's understanding of alienation, whatever its psychological origins, is based on the notion that the social relations that themselves constitute individuals, that always render the will in determinate historical form, are the actual basis of those forces that escape human control. In the *Social Contract* the relations of instrumental reciprocity generate an ideal of social individuality that must be given some measure of real force in order to regulate the *bellum omnia contra omnes* that persists in the everyday world of private lives. Thus the membership of this polity must live a double life. The general will is no more nor less real than the particular wills. From the point of view of the particular bourgeois, he must continually submit to this community, which frustrates his private striving in the system of needs but which expresses both his social being and his need for security. From the point of view of the community, the sphere of instrumental reciprocity is an obstacle to and a condition of its being. The general will cannot be the communal life of serfs, helots, slaves, or aristocrats.

During his period of transition from radical democracy to communism Marx retrieved this level of meaning in the *Social Contract* when he

---

11 See, eg, SC 15, 22, 85-6.
12 B. Baczko, 'Rousseau and Social Marginality'
13 See Shklar, 'Equality.'

commended Rousseau for offering a good description 'of the abstraction of the political man.'[14] Yet Marx probably did not see that Rousseau also recognized that the abstraction and opposition of political forces to man's 'own forces' is the determinate production of bourgeois social relations.

That, at the reflective level, Rousseau does indicate that the contract is no more than the alienation of communal life in the state implies that he grasps the starting point, the historical problem of the *Social Contract*, as already constituting a condition of alienation. The only other readers of Rousseau who, to my knowledge, understand the historical grounds of the contract to be a condition of universal alienation are Althusser and, following him closely, Levine.[15] Rousseau does in fact specify that the social contract is both possible and necessary only at a certain point in the historical development of society: 'I suppose men to have reached the point at which the obstacles in the way of their preservation in the state of nature show their power of resistance to be greater than the resources at the disposal of each individual for his maintenance in that state. That primitive condition can then subsist no longer; and the human race would perish unless it changed its manner of existence' (SC 11). As Althusser points out, in this condition the forces of each individual are not the undeveloped powers of the pre-human savage but the capacities and powers of the civilized man as they have been historically developed in social relations with others. Opposed to the forces at the disposal of this social individual are the equally social and historically generated obstacles to his continued self-preservation in the 'primitive condition' of the state of nature. The obstacles to self-preservation are not natural, external dangers, but purely human dangers issuing from the social power that now stands outside of individual and collective human control. Thus both the 'forces' of the individual and the 'obstacles' to his preservation are functions of the relations subsisting among the same historical and social individuals. And the relations that generate this contradiction between the individuals and their own social powers arise in the course of their labour to produce the necessities of life as defined by the system of needs. The point in history from which the contract might issue is therefore conceived of by Rousseau as already being a condition of alienation. In it both the forces and the obstacles whose opposition constitutes a danger 'to the human race' are functions

---

14 Marx, 'On the Jewish Question,' in *Early Writings*, 234
15 Althusser, in *Politics and History*, 118-24; I am indebted to him on this point. See also Levine, *Autonomy*, 7, 27, 102 n 4.

The *Social Contract* / 191

and products of the historically developed relations of the market society.

Althusser, however, believes that Rousseau forecloses on the possibility of socio-historical change, of change in men as they are, and is therefore limited to an ideal solution to the problem of alienation. Althusser is thus forced implicitly to attribute the assumption to Rousseau that social relations as such, by nature, are bourgeois. But this is Rousseau's own critique of Hobbes, Locke, and the rest. In the *Social Contract* Rousseau does not foreclose on the possibility of such change. He is merely pessimistic about it. He abstracts from the possibility quite consciously and says so twice in the first few lines of the book.

The solution envisaged, the only one possible in civil society that does not contradict the supremacy of the will, is the total alienation that is the fundamental clause of the contract: 'they have no other means of preserving themselves than the formation, by aggregation, of a sum of forces great enough to overcome the resistance' (*SC* 11). This sum of forces is the force of the moral and collective body produced by the contract. The answer to the state of alienation is the state as the alienated expression of communal life. The contract thus becomes a compounding of alienation and not its solution.

Rousseau's critique of Christianity as a fictitious other world, opposed to the lived material world of the patria, has been seen to be the beginning of a theory of alienation and ideology.[16] But the critique of alienation and ideology permeates the *Social Contract* as a whole. What has obscured this is, primarily, that Rousseau must first unfold and develop the object of his own critique through a prior critique and transcendence of previous theories; and second, that he must in the end remain ambivalent about the status of the very solution he develops and criticizes. In this light any notion of contradiction or discontinuity between the second *Discourse* and the *Social Contract* disappears.[17] The former is not a defense of individualism while the latter is paradoxically staunchly collectivist.[18] They are both parts of a critique of bourgeois individualism grounded in a radical insight into the social history and historicity of human nature.

Marx's critique of Rousseau (among others) in *On the Jewish Question* was already present in Rousseau's work itself:

It is only in this way, *above* the *particular* elements, that the state constitutes

16 See Colletti, *Rousseau*, 176-9
17 Cassirer, eg, in *Question*, 52-4, sees a tremendous transformation of viewpoint between the two works.
18 See E.G. Vaughan, introduction, 4-5, 9-18, 39ff, 111, 115.

itself as universality ... The perfected political state is by its nature the *species-life* of man in *opposition* to his material life. All the presuppositions of this egoistic life continue to exist *outside* the sphere of the state in *civil* society, but as qualities of civil society.

Where the political state has attained its full degree of development man leads a double life, a life in heaven and a life on earth, not only in his mind, in his consciousness, but in *reality*. He lives in the *political community*, where he regards himself as a *communal being*, and in *civil society*, where he is active as a *private individual*, regards other men as means, debases himself to a means and becomes a plaything of alien powers.[19]

What Rousseau is describing in the *Contract* is the best possible polity that might be grounded in a society where the dominant form of relations is relations of instrumental reciprocity. He is describing the potential development in bourgeois society of a realm of value arising from the actuality of historically developed social relations, and also the perpetual defeat of this realm arising out of the very same soil. The whole of the *Social Contract* points backwards to the critique of its own major premise, the relations of civil society as the sphere where contradiction arises.

We have seen (in chapters 3 and 5 above) that one of the essential problems that lies at the heart of the second *Discourse* is the problem of alienation. Rousseau there conceived of human history as a whole as a process of the development of man's natural powers through various forms of social labour, which powers then assumed the form of an alien power over the individuals. In civil society this process reached its apogee in the extreme development of the isolated individual on the one hand along with its opposite, his powerlessness in the face of the alien power of the market, on the other. The *Social Contract* is an exploration of the limits of any attempted solution to that alienation within the alienation itself. This communal life is possible only as a legislative body in which each ideally recognizes in all the others his equal and in which each exercises his will only in so far as it is universalizable and its object is general. The split between the heavenly and the earthly life of which Marx spoke is not overcome. If anything the split is more intense because men are constrained to live both an earthly life and a heavenly life on earth.

As the 'obstacles,' however, are overcome only in an ideal fashion, they are never really overcome: 'The body politic, as well as the human body, begins to die as soon as it is born, and carries in itself the causes

19 Marx, *Early Writings*, 220

The *Social Contract* / 193

of its destruction.' (SC 73). The causes of the destruction of the state are rooted in the very presuppositions that make it possible and necessary.

Political Emancipation: The Defeat of the General Will through Its Own Pre-Conditions

That the perfected and democratic political state is perceived by Rousseau in the *Social Contract* as a compounding of the condition of alienation appears in the word-play surrounding the concept that is central to the contract: the concept of exchange. The contract is legitimate by virtue of the fact that it is a real exchange ('alienation') rather than a renunciation. It is possible because all must feel their survival threatened unless they enter into this exchange. At the same time this exchange is not an exchange of separate and different items; it is an exchange of one condition for another, a transformation: 'The passage from the state of nature to the civil state produces a very remarkable change in man, by substituting justice for instinct in his conduct, and giving his actions the morality they had formerly lacked' (SC 15). But it is only necessary to remind onself of the context in which this passage appears in order to sense its irony. Behind this transformation of the member of civil society, of the violent interlocutor, into a model citizen is an exchange of equivalents satisfying the rational self-interest of the bourgeois: 'What man loses by the social contract is his natural liberty and an unlimited right to everything he tries to get and succeeds in getting; what he gains is civil liberty and the proprietorship of all he possesses' (SC 16). The transformation is predicated upon an exchange of equivalents, and an equivalent is gained only in the transformation.

That the state leads an artificial, fictitious, and ideal existence is evident from the beginning in the distinction that remains between man and citizen. The 'remarkable change' that occurs in the member of civil society characterizes only one side of his existence, his membership in the political community. As a member of the Sovereign he shares in the legislative power whose lawful acts he is under as a member of the State, as a subject. But alongside this 'manner of existence' the earlier manner of existence embodied in the state of nature is not abolished:

In fact, each individual as a man, may have a particular will contrary or dissimilar to the general will which he has as citizen. His particular interest may speak to him quite differently from the common interest; his absolute and naturally independent existence may make him look upon what he owes to the common cause as a gratuitous contribution ... and regarding the moral person which constitutes the State as a *persona ficta*, because not a man, he may wish to enjoy the rights of citizenship without being ready to fulfill the duties of a subject ... [This] could not but prove the undoing of the body politic. (*SC* 15).

The citizen-subject must therefore, as a man, be forced to obey his own law; he must be 'forced to be free' (*SC* 15). His existence as a citizen is thus predicated upon the force of a governmental power standing outside and over the realm of particular wills. Just as the liberty of the state of nature is exchanged for an equivalent in civil liberty, the mortal danger within the state of nature is likewise transferred to political society. Behind civil liberty there is not only rational devotion to a duty that raises the ego out of subjection to the realm of the passions but the most 'base' of the passions and that which previously grounded all relations of master and slave – the fear of a violent death. In this respect it matters little whether the force expended ultimately issues from the Sovereign or from a Prince who has to some extent encroached upon the Sovereign. What matters is that Rousseau has placed beyond the range of normal possibility any relation between State and Sovereign, or between civil society and the state, that is not antagonistic and reactive. Although this arrangement might remain stable for a lengthy period, it is none the less predicated upon an implicit acceptance of the conditions of civil society. There is no higher unity, but only perpetual strife. Assuming that the particular will of the member of the State is by and large the will of a member of the system of needs, there is no other way in which the general will can maintain itself. Far from demanding that the split between civil society and the state can be overcome,[20] the continued proper relation of State and Sovereign is dependent upon the mediation of the Prince. The Prince enforces as well as administers the law, and it is this threat of force, the 'key to the workings of the political machine,' that 'alone legitimizes civil undertakings' (*SC* 15).

By extending the legitimacy of will as he found it in earlier theories of natural right, Rousseau extends the meaning of citizenship to the point where it paradoxically becomes a reflection of the ancient concept. To renounce one's will becomes tantamount to enslavement. Not to renounce one's will means to participate actively in the formation of

20 See Colletti, *From Rousseau to Lenin*, 182-5.
21 See also *E* 427; there Rousseau reasserts that Sovereign, Subject, and Prince are all *necessary* organs of political society: 'None of these three terms can be varied without at once destroying this proportion. If the sovereign tries to govern, and if the prince wants to make the laws, or if the subject refuses to obey them, disorder takes the place of order, and the state falls to pieces under despotism or anarchy.'

a sovereign will, which, when the equality of absolute wills is accepted as a premise, means the formulation of a general will. Citizens are related by law rather than by privilege or status, but the general will cannot exist without the creation of a state power that overcomes the resistance of the obstacles preventing the continuance of the system of needs.[22] The general will and the sphere of particular wills are exact correlatives. The existence of each is dialectically dependent on the other. There is no thoroughgoing transformation but only, first, an illusory or ideal exchange that maintains the state of nature and, second, enough of a *real* transformation so that the state of nature persisting within the society of the *Social Contract* need not mean the extermination of the human race. The general will exists only by virtue of the particular wills of individuals and exists in order that the sphere of particular wills does not degenerate into 'personal dependence.' The doubling of human existence that takes place is the only form in which civil society can constitute itself as a political community. And the only way the community can maintain the general will in which it realizes political liberty is by creating an intermediary that must keep the two spheres apart in order to maintain its purity.

This is why 'democracy' in Rousseau's sense becomes impossible. It would threaten the purity of the Sovereign were 'the body of the people to turn its attention away from a general standpoint and devote it to particular objects' (*SC* 55). So long as men are as they are – that is, so long as they are constituted in the relations of civil society – the state (that is, the monopoly of force delegated to the Prince) must stand between man and citizen. The violent interlocutor, after all, needs the guarantee of the violence of the state in order to assure himself that others will go on observing the rules of the game as long as he does.

That the system of needs, or civil society, persists substantially unchanged as the inverse of the artificial body of the political state and poses a constant threat to it is also evident in the status of private property under the general will. Although the alienation that constitutes the Sovereign is total and includes goods in the possession of the contractors, the political community is not the proprietor of its collective goods: 'The peculiar fact about this alienation is that, in taking over the goods of the individuals, the community, so far from despoiling them, only assures them legitimate possession, and changes usurpation into a true right

---

22 Cf Marx, *The German Ideology*, in *Reader*, 125: 'the practical struggle of these particular interests, which constantly run counter to the communal and illusory communal interests, makes practical intervention and control necessary through the illusory 'general' interest in the form of the state.'

and enjoyment into proprietorship' (SC 18).[23] Private property undergoes just that sort of 'remarkable change' that takes place in the member of civil society upon his becoming a citizen. On one level, the ideal, 'the right which each individual has to his own estate is always subordinate to the right which the community has over all' (SC 18), but on another level, the reflective, this emancipation from the rule of private property is as ideal as the community is to begin with. In the second *Discourse* private property as the lynchpin of the system of needs was conceived of as the source of all the 'horrors and misfortunes' men suffer in civil society. In the community created by the contract, private property is only formally subordinated once again to the community: 'instead of destroying natural inequality, the fundamental compact substitutes, for such physical inequality as nature may have set up between men, an equality that is moral and legitimate, and ... men, who may be unequal in strength or intelligence, become every one equal by convention and legal right' (SC 19). In place of a *natural* inequality a *moral* equality is substituted – that is, an artificial equality expressed in terms of legal rights. But the *artificial* or *moral inequality* that Rousseau had in the second *Discourse* seen as issuing inevitably from the system of private property is retained. What takes place is what Marx will later call 'the political annulment of private property,'[24] in which distinctions based upon private property are abolished from the state but persist in private life, which in turn has its own effects upon the state.

The right that the community has over all is asserted, but only to set limits to the unequal distribution of property.[25] And even these limits are not included in the fundamental compact itself but are matters of prudent policy. Too great an artificial inequality of wealth threatens

23 For different views of Rousseau's doctrines in relation to property see C.B. Macpherson, *Life and Times*, 16-17; J. MacAdam, 'Rousseau: The Moral Dimensions of Property,'; N.O. Keohane, 'Rousseau on Life, Liberty and Property: A Comment on MacAdam.'
24 Marx, *On the Jewish Question*, in *Early Writings*, 219: 'the political annulment of private property does not mean the abolition of private property; on the contrary, it even presupposes it. The state in its own way abolishes distinctions based on birth, rank, education and occupation when it declares birth, rank, education and occupation to be non-political distinctions, when it proclaims that every member of the people is an equal participant in popular sovereignty regardless of these distinctions, when it treats all those elements which go to make up the actual life of the people from the standpoint of the state. Nevertheless the state allows private property, education and occupation to act and assert their particular nature in their own way, i.e. as private property, as education and as occupation. Far from abolishing these factual distinctions, the state presupposes them in order to exist; it only experiences itself as political state and asserts its universality in opposition to these elements.'
25 See, eg, Rousseau, SC 18-19, 42, 42 n 1.

the health of the body politic, threatens the conditions necessary for the formulation of a general will, but there is nothing in the terms of the contract itself that demands the abolition of the real system of private property.

In the contract the members abstract from all their particular determinations, only to have these particular determinations handed back to them later. The Sovereign should be able to come into existence as the conscious act of will of rational individuals: 'the conditions of the society ought to be regulated solely by those who come together to form it.' Yet this turns out not to be possible. The intervention of a Legislator is necessary to make a 'blind multitude ... see the good they reject' (SC 31). Thus what is at first forgotten in the abstraction from all particular determinations, civil society as an aggregate of rational wills that, as a whole, is irrational, returns in the need for a Legislator. The Legislator, as the personification of a higher rationality, has the task of bringing into existence an articulated whole out of an aggregate of men in an established set of relations with a mass of natural conditions. The society of the contract is the creation of a community not simply out of an aggregate of men but also, since social institutions are dependent upon their relationship to nature, out of an aggregate of contingent, natural conditions: topography, climate, demography, resources, geopolitical factors. The Legislator, taking account of its previous history, must pre-adapt the society's constitution to its natural environment. These given conditions are natural forces that, by forming and conditioning the customs, culture, and public opinion of a society, 'lend force to the laws.'[26] The effects of these given conditions on the people occur in the manner of the relations among things. It is this sphere of thing-like relations among men that the Legislator must take into account and control so that a transformation may take place in their 'manner of existence.'

Yet the Legislator, according to Rousseau, is 'an intelligence ... wholly unrelated to our nature, while knowing it through and through'; moreover, while 'great princes are rare, how much more so are great legislators.' Finally, he adds, it 'would take gods to give men laws' (SC 32). The semi-divine, mythical status of the Legislator stands for the very absence of that higher rationality that would deliver human relations from the sphere of relations among things. The cultural pre-conditions of the moral and collective body constituted in the contract are beyond the ken of the abstract and rational agencies from whom the contract must issue. The cultural pre-conditions of a polity directed by the general will are

26 See, eg, ibid. 35-45; also LA 66-7.

not included in the competence of the members of civil society. If in civil society, in the sphere in which individuals stand to each other as competitive property owners, each makes of the other a thing, an instrument for the satisfaction of his own need, then these relations also belong to the sphere of nature as opposed to moral agency. In the absence of a Legislator, in the absence of a cultural milieu that is the opposite of the culture that can grow out of the relations of civil society, the sphere of citizenship – where the individuals stand in a relation of mutual recognition, a kingdom of ends – is frustrated by its own cultural conditions; it is perpetually denied.

Thus the Legislator must aim at 'changing human nature' (SC 32).[27] Just as the Legislator points to the return of nature that has merely been abstracted from and not abolished, he simultaneously represents the unfulfilled need for the return of something similar to ancient virtue. He must aim at 'transforming each individual, who is by himself a complete and solitary whole, into a part of a greater whole, from which he in a manner receives his life and being.' (SWC 32). A simulacrum of ancient virtue must return behind the back of the bourgeois because in the end the individual rational will is insufficient as a foundation for society. He must perceive himself as part of an organic whole in his capacity as citizen, and he cannot. The Legislator must accordingly 'persuade without convincing' and 'constrain without violence' (SC 34). He must appeal to a higher, divine nature because instrumental reason, the rationality of the abstract individual, cannot comprehend the existence of a communal being. It is therefore necessary for the Legislator to rely on patriotic-national feeling and coercive institutions like censorship and the civil religion.

Hegel took Rousseau to be the quintessential spokesman of the principle of absolute liberty. Man's essence was an inalienable will, not, however, a particular will but the general will. Freedom amounted to the rediscovery on the part of each individual of his identity with the general will. In Hegel's version of the *Social Contract*, which is assimilated to his critique of the French Revolution, this abstract state forgets the essentially private individual and postulates an immediate identity between man and citizen. By contrast Hegel proposes an organic constitution of society that mediates between the two. An immediate identity between man and citizen is possible in the polis but not in the modern

---

27 This is, of course, why Rousseau is so staunchly illiberal as a democrat: the realization that civil society may organize itself ideally and formally as a community of equals, while its reality defeats its ideal, both as an ideal and a practical goal.

world. The absence of such mediation requires the coercive control of individuals in order to create the reign of virtue on earth.[28] In reality, what Rousseau seeks to demonstrate is that, given civil society as a starting point, there is no sufficient reason for such mediation to arise. The state remains a sphere of formal recognition among legally equal subjects, while the substance of social life, though hidden, continues untransformed. Even the continued ideal existence of a communal life depends in turn on the coercive constraint of the life of the particulars. It is necessary that the Legislator 'in a sense mutilate man's constitution in order to strengthen it' (GMS 180). Far from postulating an immediate identity between man and citizen, such as existed in the polis, Rousseau is demonstrating that in the absence of mediation, and the groups formed in civil society are not fit mediations, the co-ordination of these two spheres can only be maintained through coercion.

Hegel saw the roots of the Terror in the immediate identity that Rousseau supposedly postulated between the member of civil society and the member of the Sovereign. But Rousseau was not laying the foundations of the Terror; rather, he was pointing to these foundations as they already existed in modern social life. Liberty, for Rousseau, under modern social conditions could be nothing but an immense burden that must be continually born:

Proud, sacred liberty! If they but knew her ... if they but understood the price at which she is won and held; if they but realized that her laws are stern as the tyrant's yoke is never hard, their sickly souls, the slaves of passions that would have to be hauled out by the roots, would fear liberty a hundred times as much as they fear servitude. They would flee her in terror as they would a burden about to crush them. (GP 29–30)

Marx shared this understanding of the modern state with Rousseau, seeing the Terror not as the result of an absence of mediation that was its imperfection but as a result of its 'self-confidence': 'At those times when it is particularly self-confident, political life attempts to suppress its presuppositions, civil society and its elements, and to constitute itself as the real, harmonious species life of man. But it only manages to do this in *violent* contradiction to the conditions of its own existence.'[29] The reign of virtue that could be established on the basis of modern

---

28 See Hegel, *Phenomenology of Mind*, 355–63; see also Jean Hyppolite, *Studies on Marx and Hegel*, 54–62.
29 Marx, *On the Jewish Question*, in *Early Writings*, 232

social conditions presupposes, for Rousseau, the separation of state and civil society and the intervention of a superior rationality that will manipulate the forces governing the particulars so that they might be brought into proximate agreement with their interests 'bien entendu.'

The need for the Legislator, along with the need for a civil religion, is an admission of the unreality of the contract. These needs are the strongest expressions of the reflective level of the *Social Contract*. The Legislator mediates between the abstract civic life of the members of the Sovereign and their natural, given social conditions. This the citizens cannot do for themselves. The need for him, equivalent to his absence when taken along with his status as mere desideratum, signals the return of the repressed particularity and historicity abstracted from in the contract. A part of this particularity is the existence of myriad groups standing between the abstract individual and his artificial, moral existence in the state. The absence of the higher rationality of the Legislator can only mean that real power will be left in the hands of those groups, whose life constitutes the real substance of social existence under the contract. The hidden substance of social life, the sphere of particular wills, contains the seeds for the demise of the moral and collective body established through the contract. Civil society, denied and defended against in the political state, not transformed but maintained through the Sovereign, prepares the destruction of the Sovereign in several ways.

In the first place, under the strict terms of the contract itself, equality may remain purely formal, merely an appearance or veil for a substantive inequality of condition. The formal equality of political citizenship may hide the untransformed, substantive inequality of a society divided into economic classes: 'Under bad governments, this equality is only apparent and illusory; it serves only to keep the pauper in his poverty and the rich man in the position he has usurped. In fact, laws are always of use to those who possess and harmful to those who have nothing; from which it follows that the social state is advantageous to men only when all have something and none too much' (*SC* 19). It might be objected that equality will remain apparent under bad governments only. And certainly Rousseau maintains that a near equality of wealth is necessary to the preservation of liberty. The main aims of every system of legislation are 'liberty and equality – liberty, because all particular dependence means so much force taken from the body of the State, and equality, because liberty cannot exist without it' (*SC* 42). Civic or political equality requires some moderation of economic inequality. Yet it is noteworthy that here the aim of economic equality is strictly subordinated to the greater and essential aim of political liberty. Nor is this surprising, since equality of property, although a desirable aim of legislation, is not given within the terms of the contract itself. It is consistent with the contract but not required of it. In so far as productive resources are concerned, the citizens may 'share it out among themselves, either equally or according to a scale fixed by the Sovereign' (SC 18). That the institution of economic equality is left up to the activity of the Legislator further suggests that as a realistic possibility it remains a matter of contingent circumstances. Thus these 'general objects ... need modifying in every country in accordance with the local situation and the temper of the inhabitants' (SC 42). Although a 'one-class society of working proprietors'[30] would be consonant with civil liberty, it is not a strict requirement of a 'legitimate rule of administration' following necessity from the nature of the Sovereign, such as indivisibility or inalienability.

Thus when Rousseau makes a plea in the *Discourse on Political Economy* for 'securing the citizens from becoming poor' (PE 250) or in the *Social Contract* that 'no citizen shall ever be wealthy enough to buy another, and none poor enough to be forced to sell himself' (SC 42), it is not a prohibition of wage labour that he has in mind but a guarding of the 'people' against 'corruption.' The principal fear is that with the natural operation of the system of needs there is a constant tendency towards the production not simply of a class of wage labourers but of a mob on the one hand and a set of grandees on the other, between whom the Sovereign will be put up for sale: 'These two estates, which are naturally inseparable, are equally fatal to the common good; from the one come the friends of tyranny, and from the other tyrants' (SC 42 n 1). Rousseau fully expects men to be guided in the society of the *Social Contract* by group interests; otherwise, why exclude 'democracy' as a possibility? But he also knows that these interests need not completely overwhelm and abolish the sphere of political liberty. Although the contract would work best in a small, economically backward, parochial, and culturally unified society, its fundamental principles are of such generality that they are applicable in some form to the entire range of bourgeois social formations.

Even in the most favourable case imaginable, which would be the predominance of a 'middle estate' of petit-bourgeois producers, Rousseau does not expect liberty to be maintained without a constant vigilance on the part of the Sovereign over the workings of the State: 'It is precisely because the force of circumstances tends continually to destroy equality that the force of legislation should always tend to its maintenance' (SC

---

30 Macpherson, *Life and Times*, 17

42). But what are the circumstances that continually challenge and undermine equality if not the operations of the market as they were presented in the second *Discourse*? Thus, even in the best case imaginable within the frame of reference supplied by the *Social Contract*, the sphere of liberty and equality would remain rooted in its opposite. The individual would still live two lives – the life of strife in the system of needs as a member of the State and the life of duty and virtue as a member of the Sovereign. In even the most favourable case the state would remain an alienated form of communal life.

Although the community has the power to redistribute private property (SC 24), there is never any guarantee that this will be accomplished when it is vital to the health of the state. Indeed, we would be foolish if we did not expect the opposite.[31] At times Rousseau even seems to despair of political life altogether. In *Emile*, for example, there is the following singular passage:

Since it is impossible in the state of nature that the difference between man and man should be great enough to make one dependent on another, there is in fact in this state of nature an actual and indestructible equality. In the civil state there is a vain and chimerical equality of right; the means intended for its maintenance, themselves serve to destroy it; and the power of the community added to the power of the strongest for the suppression of the weak, disturbs the sort of equilibrium which nature has established between them. From this contradiction spring all the other contradictions between the real and the apparent, which are to be found in the civil order. The many will always be sacrificed to the few, the common weal to the private interest; those specious words – justice and subordination – will always serve as the tools of violence and the weapons of injustice. (E 197-8)

Although the formation of the general will may appear to be best served by the suppression of partial associations, we have seen that particular wills cannot be suppressed. The next best alternative would be to multiply them and make them as equal as possible (SC 23). This development in the direction of pluralism would not, however, serve to strengthen the general will. It would tend only to replace it with a more or less tenuous 'will of all,' depending upon how acute and intense conflicts of interest were between particular groups. Finally, there is one association within the society that, especially within large commercial

---

31 See Rousseau, PE 263, 268-9.

or industrial nations, would tend to overshadow all the others. This is the state itself. And Rousseau fully expects that the 'Prince must inevitably suppress the Sovereign and break the social treaty' (SC 70).

The problem that Rousseau faces in the *Social Contract* is the legitimate integration and stabilization of a society of atomized, acquisitive agents constituted within the relations of a market society. The particular wills that are the basis of the contract and that are retained within the polity established upon it are not particular wills as such but the wills of rational maximizers of their own utility. Although the *Contract* is abstracted from a larger historical process, it is not a pure inquiry into timeless principles of Right. All the same, Right is not irrelevant to either the problem or its solution. In order to be stable, the rule of administration that Rousseau proposes must also be legitimate. And the foundations of its legitimacy are to be found in the same source whence the problem itself issues – that is, in will. Rousseau is not satisfied with the Hobbesian solution, which, although it might appear sufficiently stable, is unaware of the possibility of founding a Sovereign power upon a principle of reciprocity that is also grounded in existing social relations. The extension of the sovereignty of the individual will that Rousseau proposes, by making it not only the source of sovereign political power but also an integral part of that power, supplies the legitimate basis of authority that so many thought to be lacking in Hobbes.

But in order to be legitimate, this solution must also be stable. The sovereign power is only legitimate so long as it is informed and guided by a general will, the principle of which is grounded in the relations of instrumental reciprocity constituting the system of needs, or the 'state of nature' from which the *Contract* begins. The member of the Sovereign will perceive the general will to be legitimate in so far as it is an extension of the 'preference each man gives to himself.' He may go so far as to recognize in civil liberty, in 'obedience to a law which we prescribe to ourselves,' a form of freedom better than the perilous independence of the state of nature. But he will equally perceive that the existence of a general will does not abolish the sphere of particularity, of the clash and conflict of particular wills in the State. If he is clever and circumspect, or ruthless and spirited like the violent interlocutor, he will only consider such a contract upon the condition that Sovereign and State are always separated and joined by a Prince. The fragmented and agitated society of the state of nature thus finds its salvation in a formal community of equal legislators. The substance of community turns out to be legislation, and legislation can exist only in so far as State and Sovereign are kept separate and apart. But in the Legislator it turns out that the legislation that is to be the substance of community is itself already a function of community. A whole range of prior conditions, a whole host of circumstances belonging not to the province of Right but to political sociology, as we would now call it, must exist in order to allow 'a blind multitude' to legislate as a people. But even were such conditions to exist, the separation of State and Sovereign would still persist. For under this scheme 'democracy' is conceived of as a limit situation, as a conceptual possibility defining the limits of what can be realized. Yet it seems 'impossible to have a better constitution' than democracy. And if the reader remembers the discussion of primitive society, it will be evident that, although in the *Social Contract*, democracy is described as fit only for gods, Rousseau is well aware that among certain men it has been and is being practised. It is only a certain terminology that would deny to the primitive a political life, but Rousseau realized that what appears to be a non-political form of association was in actuality one in which the governing and governed bodies had not yet been separated (see above, pages 91ff).

Many readers of Rousseau, at least among those who do not tend to read the *Contract* as a manifesto for a collectivism aimed at crushing all individuality, value the ideal of the general will as foreshadowing the later ideals of German idealism and of Marx. Taking the notion of a particular will as designating not the will as structured within the system of needs but as the particularity of any 'natural' individual, they see in the general will and willing obedience to it an ideal synthesis of the particular and the universal, the individual and the social. They see in it the *Rechstaat* or the free association of producers and the reintegration of civil society and the state. And it would be difficult to assert that both of these ideals cannot be found within the *Social Contract*. But both of them are found within the *Social Contract as* ideals, and not as timeless ideals but as the ideals that follow from the peculiar circumstances of a definite set of social circumstances, albeit at a high level of abstraction.

While ideals are present in the *Social Contract*, there is also a ruthless laying bare of the conditions that defeat the ideals in practice. And these are the same conditions from which the ideals themselves grow. As far as the free association of producers that reintegrates state and civil society is concerned, Rousseau is clear in rejecting this in his denial of the possibility of democracy. With democracy excluded, what is left over in the range of possibility are polities all of which represent alienated forms of communal life. Concerning these Rousseau is less than optimistic much of the time. They are forms of unstable compromise that tend to degenerate from causes inseparable from their existence:

According to my old ideas, the great problem of politics, which I compare to the squaring of the circle in geometry ... is to find a form of government which puts the law above the individual ... If such a form is unhappily beyond our power to find - and I frankly admit that in my belief it is - then my conviction is that we must fly to the opposite extreme, set the individual at one bound as high as possible above the law, and establish arbitrary despotism - the most arbitrary that can be devised. I should wish the despot to be a God. In a word, I see no possible mean between the austerest democracy and the most complete Hobbism. For of all conditions, the conflict between the individual and the law, which plunges the state into ceaseless civil war, is the very worst. - But Caligula, Nero, Tiberius! Good God! I roll myself in the dust and groan to think I am a man.[32]

To Rousseau the wrong in the ideal of the *Rechstaat* is clearly evident. It is the persistence of the duality of social individuality within the framework of the sovereignty of law. The ceaseless civil war of which he speaks is not only the conflict between the actualized will of the Sovereign in the Prince over against the State but an internalized conflict of the individual with himself.

It will be objected that although Rousseau may have at times despaired of its actualization, surely he was satisfied with his ideal of 'an austere democracy' as a standard by which political practice could be judged and as a goal by which it could be oriented. This question, though, cannot be answered satisfactorily until *Emile* is examined. For it hinges on the qualification 'austere.' In the *Social Contract* democracy is presented as a limit situation largely because of the austerity, the 'self-denial' it demands. It is in the nature of the bourgeois individual, of the self as structured within the system of needs, to create the burden of this need for austerity. As long as Rousseau is limiting himself to considering 'men as they are,' the demands of virtue required of the members of an austere democracy are themselves too great for Rousseau to be satisfied with it as an ideal. It is only necessary to remember the case of Julie or to dwell for a moment on the requirements of ancient virtue to realize this.

In the end, then, what can be said of the status of the solution Rousseau offers to his problem? This status is, as long as it is remembered that

32 Rousseau, 'Letter to Mirabeau,' 26 July 1767, quoted in Vaughan, *Writings*, 1.116

the solution is the alienation of communal life in the state, at best ambivalent. Perhaps Rousseau could have said along with Marx that 'political emancipation is certainly a big step forward. It may not be the last form of general human emancipation, but it is the last form of human emancipation within the prevailing scheme of things.'[33] Leo Strauss has suggested that in the *Social Contract* Rousseau, basing himself upon the materialistic and historical outlook developed in the second *Discourse*, proclaimed that men had arrived at a 'privileged historical moment' where they could assume control over a history previously subjected to blind and mechanical lawfulness.[34] But is is precisely because Rousseau was a better materialist and more of a historical thinker than Strauss imagined that in the *Social Contract* he both raises the demand and demonstrates that it was, under contemporary conditions, conditions whose end he could not foresee, something that men might still only pretend to. Yet the claim might die if the pretence were not maintained.

For the *Social Contract* is *the* founding document of the notion of political emancipation. In it the form of the early liberal state is definitely transcended in the theory of popular sovereignty. By working through premises common among modern theorists of natural law to a conception of the perfected political state, both the limited government of Locke and enlightened despotism – both of which were, curiously, favoured by the Enlightenment – meet a challenge that they have never fully overcome. Yet the founding document of political emancipation, especially when taken together with Rousseau's other writings, in its careful delimitation of the grounds, conditions, and limits of the sovereignty of a general will, already supplies the elements of a critique of the notion of political emancipation as a full emancipation of social individuality. Although in the *Social Contract* the will is returned from the possession of a master, it is not returned to itself. The question is, then, did Rousseau see beyond 'the prevailing scheme of things' or did he in the end succumb to the failing for which he constantly berated his greatest predecessors – that they ontologized the actual and mistook the social individual for the member of the system of needs? Rousseau could not in his day relinquish the *Social Contract*, since it represented the best attainable within the prevailing scheme of things. Also, he could not relinquish it because it pointed, as an ideal, beyond the prevailing scheme. But Rousseau did not simply go on in *Corsica* and *Poland* to try to approximate his austere and regressive democracy. He also wrote *Emile*.

33 Marx, *Jewish Question*, in *Early Writings*, 221
34 *Natural Right*, 271-3

CHAPTER EIGHT

Emile: The Reconciliation of Art and Nature

> A man cannot become a child again, or he becomes childish.
> But does he not find joy in the child's naïveté, and must
> he himself not strive to reproduce its truth at a higher stage?
> Does not the true character of each epoch come alive
> in the nature of its children?
> Marx, *Grundrisse*

The Problem of *Emile*

If the *Social Contract* does not represent a synthesis of society and the individual, nature and history, reason and the human heart, the question inevitably arises as to whether Rousseau ever did theorize a possible transcendence of the alienation that, in various forms and with increasing intensity, has characterized humanity since its beginnings. For the origin of humanity coincides, according to the *Discourse on the Origins of Inequality*, with alienation from nature. The original 'natural man,' while he did not live in a state of alienation, was not yet human. This alienation may not have been at first very intense in the primitive community, since self and society were still directly joined, but it was none the less present. It might, however, be reasonable to represent the *Social Contract* as setting the limits to the possibility of a synthesis in history. There would still be alienation, but this alienation would be based on a greater degree of equality and justice – at least under 'good' governments. The view of Rousseau as a historical fatalist, and therefore as one who was unable to conceive of social relations as not being inherently bourgeois, might still stand. If there were to be transcendence for *this* Rousseau, it would take place in areas that sought for reconciliation outside history and society – in religion, mystical experience, and art.

Rousseau himself seems to lend support to this conclusion when, in the second *Discourse*, he poses the alternative facing men as one between a regression behind culture and a continuous but doomed effort to improve political life in the state:

What, then is to be done? Must societies be totally annihilated, and must we return again to the forests to live among bears? This is a deduction in the manner of my adversaries, which I would as soon anticipate as let them have the shame of drawing. O you, who have never heard the voice of heaven, who think man destined only to live this little life and die in peace; you, who can resign in the midst of populous cities your fatal acquisitions, your restless spirits, your corrupt hearts and endless desires; resume, since it depends entirely on yourselves, your ancient and primitive innocence: retire to the woods, there to lose the sight and remembrance of the crimes of your contemporaries; and be not apprehensive of degrading your species, by renouncing its advances in order to renounce its vices. As for men like me, whose passions have destroyed their original simplicity, who can no longer ... live without laws and magistrates ... those, in short, who are persuaded that the Divine Being has called all mankind to be partakers in the happiness and perfection of celestial intelligences, all these will endeavour to merit the eternal prize they are to expect from the practice of those virtues, which they make themselves follow in learning to know them. They will respect the sacred bonds of their respective communities; they will love their fellow-citizens, and serve them with all their might; they will scrupulously obey the laws, and all those who make or administer them; they will particularly honour those wise and good princes, who find means of preventing, curing or even palliating all these evils and abuses, by which we are constantly threatened ... *But they will not therefore have less contempt for a constitution that cannot support itself without the aid of so many splendid characters, much oftener wished for than found; and from which, notwithstanding all their pains and solicitude, there always arise more real calamities than even apparent advantages.* (DOI 228-9; emphasis added)

These are the only alternatives left open. But neither alternative is sufficient, and each is met by Rousseau himself with a large degree of scepticism. He who goes on to engage in public life has no less contempt for the very civilization whose ills he will attempt to palliate than he who seeks impossibly to regress behind civilization itself. The person who hears the call to a life of public virtue is drawn to it not out of conviction that his acts have a reasonable hope of success but from a hope of meriting the 'eternal prize' at the hands of the Divine Being. But he who opts for solitude and innocence will bear the 'restless spirits' and 'corrupt hearts and endless desires' out of social life into his illusory sylvan paradise.

The *Discourse on the Origins of Inequality* ends in an impasse rather than in a choice of satisfactory alternatives. But this impasse results largely from the fact that inside the second *Discourse* Rousseau had not sufficiently disentangled the effects of the two major forms of alienation. The conclusions drawn from the *Discourse* are largely negative because of Rousseau's own ambivalence. At times it seems to him that the evils of social life are rooted primarily in social existence as such; that, since *amour-propre* is inseparable from self-consciousness, social life itself bears the seeds of inevitable domination:

always asking others what we are, and never daring to ask ourselves, in the midst of so much philosophy, humanity and civilization, and of such sublime codes of morality, we have nothing to show for ourselves but a frivolous and deceitful appearance, honour without virtue, reason without wisdom, and pleasure without happiness. *It is sufficient that I have proved that this is not by any means the original state of man, but that it is merely the spirit of society, and the inequality which society produces, that thus transform and alter our natural inclinations.* (*DOI* 221; emphasis added)

At other times, however, it is not *amour-propre* as such which is a necessary and sufficient condition of inequality and its attendant evils. Present inequality, rather, 'becomes at last permanent and legitimate by the establishment of property and laws' (*DOI* 221). This is especially the case if we remember that in primitive society *amour-propre* was relatively harmless and did not interfere with the communal realization of individual ends.

The second *Discourse* came to a disappointing conclusion because in it Rousseau had not yet squarely faced the question of whether historical-social existence as such was the irremediable root of the various forms of alienation he had begun to trace or whether alienation was a function of specific social and historical circumstances. The second *Discourse* describes two forms of alienation: alienation from nature, which is coextensive with a human and social existence, and a historically rooted alienation linked to specific social systems. But these two forms of alienation tend most of the time to be confounded. In the second *Discourse* Rousseau makes objectification, or alienation from nature – the necessity the human species faces and the need it acquires to develop its powers in continual interaction with objective nature – both a form of and a *source* of alienation. In that work there is no attempt, or little attempt, if we consider his qualified approval of primitive society, to separate and evaluate the relative weights of these two forms of alienation as constituting the fundamental flaw in human existence.

The Kantian interpretation of Rousseau stresses his abandonment of original sin. In this view he was the first to possess the consciousness of the responsibility or 'imputability' of society for evil. The subject of responsibility for evil was no longer the individual but human society, which in itself awakens *amour-propre*. Thus the problem of theodicy is transferred from the realm of metaphysics into that of ethics and politics. It becomes man's business to achieve the justification of God inside his worldly activity. The overcoming of alienation lies in the creation of a form of community 'rooted wholly in common subjection to a law that is inwardly recognized as binding and necessary.'[1] The political community, infused with the ethos of law (understood as a universal and constant norm), is an imitation of the inviolable order of natural law through which God rules the extra-human universe. Moreover, according to the Kantian interpretation, the rejection of original sin does not mean that human life holds the promise of happiness. Rousseau was no eudemonist. For him the meaning and value of human existence are held to lie exclusively in the power of renunciation implicit in the responsiveness of the human conscience to the pure ethos of law.[2]

This interpretation of Rousseau, however, fails to recognize that he considered this route towards the overcoming of alienation to be fundamentally flawed. Ultimately the rule of law was for Rousseau merely a palliative, 'for the flaws which make social institutions [by which, in the present context, Rousseau means the state] necessary are the same as make the abuse of them unavoidable ... for laws as a rule, being weaker than the passions, restrain men without altering them' (*DOI* 215). The attempt to rely on an imitation of God is beyond the capacity of human artifice. And the political community that sets the laws above the passions is subject to an inevitable decline. So the *Social Contract* turns out, after all, not to be the ultimate or the best solution to the problem of alienation posed in the second *Discourse*. The 'political' solution to the problem of alienation, the attempt to return the will to itself in the perfected political state, is flawed not only because it

1 Cassirer, *Question*, 75
2 Ibid., 81

remains unstable (and it remains unstable because in it the civil society that turns incessantly unequal and oppressive is only overcome *ideally*) but because it is inevitably hubristic. Its hubris lies in the very sublimity of its morality – in the need for the Legislator to erect institutions that will in turn help to form manners and morals enforcing a high level of renunciation of the passions inflamed by the very social relations upon which it is erected and which it is designed to preserve. And it is evident from Julie's history that Rousseau does not accept an equation of the value of human life with the power of renunciation. For the power of renunciation is a part of the requirements of social reproduction, and these have historically constituted a tyranny over nature – a tyranny over nature in the interests of domination and inequality.

Once the *Social Contract* and its version of virtue as moral autonomy are seen not as the solution to the problem of alienation but as one of the forms, perhaps the best form, that alienation might take under modern conditions, it might seem that Rousseau's rejection of original sin as a radical depravity of the individual has been replaced with a new version of original sin – the existence of society as such, of culture as such, would constitute a fall quite as serious as that undergone by Adam and transmitted in perpetuity to his offspring.[3]

The texts considered so far leave no avenue even part way out of this impasse. If human perfectibility includes the striving for perfect virtue on the part of the community (the *Contract*), or the individual (Julie), then perfectibility, in so far as it opens up the possibility of such striving, remains what Rousseau in the second *Discourse* feared it to be, a 'distinctive and almost unlimited faculty' that 'is the source of all human misfortunes' (*DOI* 171).

Rousseau, however, could not rest content with this supremely fatalistic view of the human condition. The natural striving after happiness and the very restlessness of the condition of alienation seemed for him always to call up at least the demand that it be overcome: 'Is it not quite unworthy of a man never to be able to be in accord with himself, to have one rule for his actions, another for his feelings, to think as though he were without spirit, and never to appropriate completely for himself, throughout his life, that which he does?' (*LNH* 362)[4] Moreover, the very hypothesis

---

3 Thus Lemos, *Political Philosophy*, 28–30, believes that the original man is already in a condition of original sin that is only made worse in his accession to culture and 'metaphysical freedom.' For Lemos, egoism in Rousseau's sense is not only permanent but analogous to the Christian notion of original sin, and this is what, above all, separates Rousseau from Marxism and makes him more 'realistic' (p 181–3, 185).

4 See also *E* 45: 'The other animals possess only such powers as are required for self-

of human perfectibility, the rootedness of human cultural existence in nature, seemed to promise that 'everything that man has made, man may destroy. Nature's characters alone are ineffaceable' (*E* 15).[5] In *Emile* he attempts to rethink both the necessity of the psychic misery that seemed embedded in social relations as such and also the possibility of social relations based neither upon instrumental reciprocity nor upon the immediate identity of the individual with his social role.

Kant himself was quite correct in seeing in *Emile* the attempt to overcome the conflict between nature and culture:

> the assertions of the celebrated J.J. Rousseau ... are often misinterpreted and do, indeed, have an appearance of inconsistency. In his *On The Influence of the Sciences* and his *On The Inequality of Man* he shows quite correctly that there is an inevitable conflict between culture and the human species, considered as a natural species of which every member ought wholly to attain his natural end. But in his *Emile*, his *Social Contract*, and other writings he tries to solve this much harder problem: how culture was to move forward, in order to bring about such a development of the dispositions of mankind, considered as a *moral* species, as to end the conflict between the natural and the moral species ... in itself and as a natural disposition, impulse serves a good purpose. The real trouble is that, on the one hand, culture progressively interferes with its natural function, by altering the conditions to which it was suited; while on the other hand, natural impulse interferes with culture until such time as art will be strong and perfect enough to become a second nature. This is indeed the ultimate moral end of the human species.[6]

Because he thought in terms of ending the conflict between nature and culture through the perfection of moral virtue, it was natural that Kant should join the *Social Contract* with *Emile* in this way. In the same way nature, or 'impulse,' is perceived as something entirely pre-programmed and almost entirely unmalleable. The perfection of second nature is therefore characterized as a condition where natural impulse no longer *interferes* with culture, where art and second nature *replace* the first.

Rousseau, however, did not think in terms of static drives; the passions for him were, like the intellectual faculties, not givens but results of

---

preservation; man alone has more. Is it not very strange that this superfluity should make him miserable?'
5 Modified translation
6 Immanuel Kant, 'Conjectural Beginning of Human History,' in *On History*, 60-3

dynamic processes continually unfolding. Thus the perfection of art did not mean the substitution of a second nature based upon a renunciation of the first. The reconciliation of nature and culture meant rather the necessity first to liberate desire: 'It is a torrent which breaks down your feeble dikes and carries all before it. Enlarge its bed, and let it flow without obstacle, and it will do no harm' (*LCB* 261). But this reconciliation of nature and culture, upon which any possibility of a transcendence of alienation depends, cannot take place within the social order as it stands. It is no longer, for Rousseau in *Emile*, society as such that imposes the necessity of a conflict between nature and culture. It is rather 'the present defective state of society, in every respect contrary to nature, which nothing can totally suppress; incessantly tyrannizing over her, and forcing her to reclaim her just rights. I traced the consequences of this contradiction, and saw that it alone was sufficient to account for all the vices of individuals, and all the evils of society' (*LCB* 296). *Emile* as a whole is thus the attempt to separate theoretically a historical and social existence from the history of alienation and to separate the necessary denaturation of a cultural and social being from the unnecessary or excessive denaturation attending inequality or class-divided society.

In the second *Discourse* Rousseau had made historical existence as such both a form of alienation and a source of even further alienation. *Amour-propre* was in itself a loss of self inherent in the very social relations out of which a human subject emerged. But it was not at all clear whether a possible mode of the social formation of the individual might avoid much of the pain of the separation from nature, and also what social relations might, in a sense, follow from this. *Emile*, though, does not ask how social relations must change in order that a synthesis of nature and culture might be possible; it does ask whether there is a possible synthesis of nature and culture such that the social relations of civil society might be transcended. This possible synthesis of nature and culture Rousseau finds in a manner of acculturation that does not pay heed to social relations as they have been. Nor is this synthesis an acculturation to society as it is. A resolution of the split between culture and the natural species will mean a process of acculturation that attends strictly to the necessary denaturation of the individual, while eschewing the excess denaturation required by the historical forms of social inequality.

In the second *Discourse* Rousseau removed the stigma of original sin from the abstract individual, from the soul of Christian man inherited by liberalism, only to be unsure as to whether it reappeared in social existence as such. The original amorality and *bonté* of *man* led insensibly but inevitably to the wickedness of *men*. Unlike the *Social Contract*, where he bases his speculations on men as they are and the laws as they might be, Rousseau returns in *Emile* to his original thesis of the 'natural goodness' of man. But having never rejected original sin abstractly as a simple falsehood, he now realizes that it is a matter of explaining original sin: 'Original sin may serve to explain everything but its own principle, and this is the very thing to be explained' (*LCB* 255). In order to break the causal link between *amour-propre* and social evil it must be shown that although this was necessarily true of the past, it need not be true in future: 'man being naturally and originally good, men became wicked. The great object of my book is the means of preventing this. Not that I affirmed that in the present order of things it is absolutely possible; but this I affirmed, and do still, that there are no other means of effecting it, but those I have pointed out' (*LCB* 252).[7] Social relations as such contain in themselves the occasion for the development of the spirit of social domination, but social relations vary over history; each system develops *amour-propre* in different directions, and 'we should be like the Laplanders, who fix the natural stature of man at four foot, if we should circumscribe the human mind with the standard of those little souls which we see around us' (*LCB* 327).[8]

The formation of Emile, although manifestly not conclusive proof of the break in the causal link, is the only way Rousseau has of theorizing the possibility. Because there have been and are no cultures that do not in some way or in some degree tyrannize over nature, reason in this case must embrace imagination to produce a figure embodying the theoretical possibility of a synthesis between nature and culture. To imagine, to produce theoretically a man who, although social, retains his original goodness, would be to falsify the equation between historical existence and social alienation. *Emile* is not primarily a practical program for the education of the natural man but a test of the hypothesis left unformulated in the second *Discourse*, that social existence as such does not inevitably generate the alienation of civil society and that the apparent fatality of the descent from nature into the historical forms of alienation is a false product of retrospection:

You say quite rightly that it is impossible to make an Emile. But I cannot believe that you take this book to be a real treatise on education. It is a philosophical enough work on that principle advanced by the author in other writings, that man is naturally good. In order to bring this principle into accord with that

7 Modified translation
8 Modified translation

other no less certain truth that men are wicked, it was necessary to show, in the history of the human heart, the origin of all its defects. That is what I have done in this book, often with justice and sometimes with sagacity. (CG 11.339)

To give a genetic explanation of all the vices in an examination of the history of the human heart is *ipso facto* to affirm the possibility that goodness might survive the social formation of the individual. And to affirm this possibility is to establish the further possibility of social forms in which historical alienation is transcended. Rousseau must demonstrate that in society original goodness need not degenerate into 'méchanceté' on the one hand and a hypertrophy of virtue on the other. There is no other way for him to make the distinction between objectification (or, in Starobinski's terms, the 'alienation' of the subject in exterior activity) and alienation properly so called, to create the theoretical possibility of a society in which social alienation does not inevitably follow from the objectification necessary to human existence. To make the distinction between necessary and excess denaturing will establish that not only does original sin not belong to the nature of the individual considered abstractly; it is not inherent in social existence itself.

Emile, however, does not simply bear a negative significance. The thesis that it is not the simple alienation from nature that is the basic and generative flaw has important, even crucial, positive significance. If objectification and alienation are in principle separable, this opens up the possibilty of a historical transcendence of past and present forms of social existence: 'One thus knows or one can know the first point from which each of us departs to arrive at the condition of manhood, but who is it who knows the other extremity? ... We are ignorant of what it is that our nature allows us to be' (*EMF* 62). What nature permits the species to become, what the outlines of a condition transcending the historical forms of alienation would look like, is visible only in the finished figure of Emile. And this finished figure would remain too vague and too remote unless it were comprehended in its development.

The finished figure of Emile (the imaginary person) has as its immediate ground the unique process of acculturation that will be his. But Emile also appears outlined against a more remote background, Rousseau's previous works, which both lend meaning to *Emile* and draw meaning from it in retrospect. Thus in one way *Emile* is self-criticism or revision on Rousseau's part – a correction of his ambivalence over the status of historical existence as such. But if only revision were intended, one might wonder why Rousseau did not simply correct or revise the second *Discourse*. The answer might be that in order to produce the imaginary

Emile, the historical development outlined in the *Discourse* and deepened and developed in various ways in *Julie* and the *Social Contract* was necessary. Although objectification and alienation are separable theoretically, or in principle, they have historically been inseparable. It is only on the basis of this previous development that the consciousness of their separability as a real possibility emerges. Thus the work undertaken in the second *Discourse* still stands – the history of objectification has been the history of alienation. And so it has been amply possible to read Rousseau's refusal of alienation back on to his attitude to human life and civilization as such. But the fact that alienation and objectification have been historically inseparable – the fact that the second *Discourse* is not false – allows Rousseau in *Emile* to advance the even more radical hypothesis that not only might the historical forms of the alienation of man from himself, from his labour, and from his community be overcome but the anguish of the separation from nature itself might be amenable to considerable amelioration. If the figures of the natural man on the one hand and the citizen on the other represented contradictory ideals for Rousseau and if the organization of primitive society is no longer, because of technological and other developments, a realistic alternative, *Emile* may nevertheless represent the real possibility of a synthesis.

Excess Denaturation and Negative Education

If Rousseau established, in the second *Discourse*, that artifice is man's nature, that human nature is inseparable from the history of artifice, that human beings are constituted only within social practice, he nevertheless also affirmed that the history of artifice has from the start been inseparable from a mutilation of nature. Over and above the loss of the peculiar contentment or non-susceptibility to misery that characterizes a being in immediate unity with its surroundings, the second *Discourse* suggests that the historical forms of civilization have enforced an excessive renunciation of nature in the interests of maintaining systems of economic and political subordination. *Emile* begins by placing the onus of responsibility for the lack of a reconciliation between nature and culture squarely upon the shoulders of past cultural practice:

God makes all things good; man meddles with them and they become evil. He forces one soil to yield the products of another, one tree to bear another's fruit. He confuses and confounds his time, place and natural conditions. He mutilates his dog, his horse and his slave. He destroys and defaces all things; he loves all that is deformed and monstrous; he will have nothing as nature made it, not even man himself, who must learn his paces like a saddle-horse, and be shaped to his master's taste like the trees in his garden. (E 5)

It might sound from this passage as though a dichotomy between nature and culture worse than that implicit in the second *Discourse* were being announced. But Rousseau is quick to affirm that 'things would be worse without this education, and mankind cannot be made by halves' (E 5). It is clear from Rousseau's historical reflections that what is suggested beneath the rhetorical hyperbole of this passage is a connection between the cultural project of the domination of nature and the mutilation of human nature. Culture deforms human nature, at the same time that it forms it, to the extent that culture is itself governed by the blind imperative of subordinating external nature. This is why the history of civilization has been a history of increasing alienation and repression, reaching its apogee in the system of needs. In the system of needs the primordial human need for existence is transformed into an unlimited and inexhaustible need to find self-confirmation in possession and consumption. But an inseparable condition of the internalization of the imperatives of the system of needs is the instrumentalization of the self. And this is so contrary to our original but imperishable nature that it requires an elaborate, if not total, control. Thus 'our wisdom is slavish prejudice, our customs consist in control, constraint, compulsion. Civilized man is born and dies a slave. The infant is bound up in swaddling clothes, the corpse is nailed down in his coffin. All his life long man is imprisoned by our institutions' (E 10).

All of this does not mean that there is no solution within a cultural existence: 'when I want to train a natural man, I do not want to make him a savage and to send him back to the woods' (E 217). Such a thing is no longer even possible; biological evolution has progressed with a finality that does not allow humanity to retreat behind culture in fact: 'When man for the first time encroaches upon the care nature takes, she abandons the work and leaves everything to human art ... We can no longer dispense with the institutions that make our unhappiness. The man of nature has disappeared, never to reappear, and he who withdraws most from nature is he whom art most neglects. He has no other education but that of the world, the worst one can have' (*EMF* 57). In a sense Emile will receive an education modelled on that which would have been most likely in and suitable to primitive society. For the primitive, being furthest removed from the compulsory productivity and self-instrumentalization of the system of needs, is that condition in which art neglects man the least. The most civilized is the least artful, because in civilization art is most compelled to neglect, subordinate, mutilate the unique and infinitely valuable potential belonging to the perfectible being.[9] Emile is not to receive the education of a man of Rousseau's world; he is not to be formed within or for the bourgeois world. For such a man is 'ever at war with himself, hesitating between his wishes and his duties, he will be neither a man nor a citizen. He will be of no use to himself nor to others. He will be a man of our day, a Frenchman, an Englishman, one of the great middle class' (*E* 8). Nor will Emile be educated in the ancient mode; he will not receive the public education dreamed of by Plato or the one instituted by Lycurgus. For although Emile is a figure of the social individual, his individuality is not the immediate expression of communal life:

The natural man lives for himself; he is the unit, the whole, dependent only on himself and on his like. The citizen is but the numerator of a fraction, whose value depends on the community. Good social institutions are those best fitted to make a man unnatural, to exchange his independence for dependence, to merge the unit in the group, so that he no longer regards himself as one but as part of the whole, and is only conscious of the common life. (*E* 7)

Both the citizen and the bourgeois are at war with themselves; both are the products of contradictory forces: 'Our inner conflicts are caused by these contradictions. Drawn this way by nature and that way by man, compelled to yield to both forces, we make a compromise and reach neither goal. We go through life, struggling and hesitating, and die before we have found peace, useless alike to ourselves and to others' (*E* 9). Emile, however, will be raised for no social order that requires a tyranny over nature, but rather for himself alone: 'It would be curious to examine a man raised for himself and to see what he would become for others' (*EMF* 59). To educate a man for himself alone will require that excess denaturation should be absent in his upbringing. We shall see *how* Rousseau proposes to accomplish this.

But will this new version of the natural man, since he is raised, in a sense, outside the demands of society, be suited to a social existence? Is Rousseau not simply proposing a regression, and an impossible one at that, to a cultural existence that is no longer social? Is this merely another of Rousseau's famous paradoxes? It is precisely because he distinguishes between excess denaturation and that which is necessary

---

9 For a similar view from a modern anthropologist, cf Dorothy Lee, *Freedom and Culture*.

to a human and social existence[10] that the proposition is paradoxical: 'there are so many contradictions between the rights of nature and the laws of society that to conciliate them we must continually contradict ourselves. Much art is required to prevent man in society from being altogether artificial' (E 282). The natural man who lives with others, the truly social *individual*, is not the blind product of nature but the product of the most highly developed art. This art has, however, relinquished the project of dominating nature; it has cut its ties with the system of needs and thus no longer need tyrannize over internal nature. Instead it may devote itself to establishing a harmony between the demands of nature and the demands of human society:

Everything should therefore be brought into harmony with these natural tendencies, and that might well be if our three modes of education merely differed from one another; *but what can be done if they conflict, when instead of training man for himself you try to train him for others? Harmony becomes impossible.* Forced to combat either nature or society, you must make your choice between the man and the citizen, you cannot train them both. (E 7; emphasis added)

The choice between man and citizen, and therefore the conflict and inevitable disharmony between them, arises only when a man is not trained for himself alone. The conflict between man and citizen arises within the social process of excess denaturation, a process that, if begun in childhood, continues throughout life. Excess denaturation does not issue from an eternal tension between individual and social existence.

[But] how will a man live with others if he is educated for himself alone? If the twofold aims could be resolved into one *by removing the man's self-contradictions*, one great obstacle to his happiness would be gone. To judge of this you must see the man full-grown, you must have noted his inclinations, watched his progress, followed his steps; in a word you must really know a natural man. When you have read this work, I think you will have made some progress in this inquiry. (E 9; emphasis added)

'Self-contradictions' are, however, not the same as the 'inner conflicts' produced by a society that contradicts nature by excessive denaturation (see page 213). It is rather that self-contradictions, as was the case with Julie, become the occasion for the development of inner conflicts. *Self-contradiction emerges together with alienation from mere nature.* It is

---

10 Burgelin calls it a 'dénaturation naturelle' in *Existence*, 484.

a potential inherent in a being that must integrate desire into particular modes of cultural activity, and in a being the expression of whose naturally given drives requires thought and rational objectifying activity.

To be human, for Rousseau, is not simply to be a composite, in the sense of a coexistence of self-contained levels. The very being of the human individual as an individual is a result of the dynamic interaction of nature (in the sense of the inner drive) and an external necessity *mediated by other men* (EMF 57). For Rousseau all existing and previous forms of society, excepting perhaps the very primitive, subordinate inner nature to the rationality of domination, and do so via the mechanism of self-esteem regulation. The need for self-esteem arises out of man's very nature, coinciding with the development of both the species and the individual. *Amour-propre*, arising necessarily in both phylogenesis and ontogenesis, eventually becomes a crucial aspect of the reproduction of civil societies. The individual has been constituted in excessive denaturation because societies have heretofore both aroused an exaggerated need for self-esteem and supplied ways of gratifying that need that involved a tyranny over nature – alienated labour and hypertrophied 'virtue.' The unfolding of Emile's character therefore essentially involves two intimately interrelated processes: the prevention, in so far as it is possible, of the self-contradiction or ambivalence that attends the emergence of *amour-propre*, and the transcendence of *amour-propre* in the pleasurable sublimation of desire, the full cultural integration of *amour-de-soi*.

The men produced by and for civil societies are, in Rousseau's eyes, for the most part cases of artificially arrested development. Those who seem most highly developed, the paragons of virtue like Julie and Wolmar, are in reality defending against conflicts of which they are no longer aware: 'We were meant to be men, laws and customs thrust us back into infancy' (E 49). What appears to be sublime is in reality denial or reaction-formation.

Excessive denaturation thus has an ironic structure. Adults who are thrust back into infancy have been infants who were treated as though they were adults: 'Parents who live in the civil state transport their child there prematurely; in giving him greater needs than he would otherwise have, they do not alleviate his weakness; they augment it. They augment it even more in exacting from him what nature would not demand, in subordinating to their wills the little power he has to serve his own needs, in changing on all sides into slavery the reciprocal dependence in which his weakness holds him and their affection holds them' (EMF 88). Excessive denaturation is imposed by relying on the child's dependence and weakness to exact from it behaviour that offends against nature,

Emile / 221

in the sense that it does not follow from any inner need of the child itself and the child is not yet fully capable of performing it. These demands only increase the child's weakness and, along with that, his dependence. The demand and expectation that he be an adult in minature give rise to the need on his part to live up to the demands of adult society, since 'nature has made children helpless and in need of affection' (E 52). Now, however, the child is pulled in one way by nature and in another way by men. If it is not yet capable of performing what is demanded, this conflict can only add to its frustration. Frustration in turn adds to weakness and weakness to dependence. Out of an exaggerated dependence comes a further susceptibility to identifying its own 'sense of existence' with the accomplishment of what its parents, its source of support and affection, demand. Thus the child eventually makes itself into the model of what its parents wish it to be. But in so doing it has, in cultures based on inequality, learned to instrumentalize itself: 'you accustom him to allow himself always to be led, to be nothing but an apparatus in the hands of another. Should you wish him to be submissive when he is small, prepare yourself to see him credulous and gullible when grown up' (EMF 182).

Excessive denaturation thus consists in the imposition of a demand that is not required by nature *before* that demand can be met without the child's cutting itself off from its own urges. When the child succeeds in replacing what nature urges with what its parents command, nature is not abolished or even transformed but repressed – one is tempted to say 'replaced' with second nature:

> But that art that is capable of disguising, bending, even smothering nature, cannot change it completely. It more often obliterates the source of our passions than it gives them a direction as contrary as it would take to render us truly civil ... here we are so enchained, so oppressed, so weighted down by social institutions, that we are left without anything free anymore but thought; thought itself is in bondage to opinion, and if it were possible that a man conserved his primitive manner of seeing and feeling in the midst of so many prejudices, he would be forced out of prudence to be deceitful in order not to be treated at the very least as a madman. (EMF 56)

In such a situation the primitive way of feeling and seeing, the childish, dependent, and ambivalent mentality, is preserved beneath the 'social spirit' that is the external appearance (EMF 57). Nature and culture can then never approach a reconciliation until this repression is lifted, until reality and appearance coincide. But when nature is recognized, or recognized, as it were, avenues towards a genuine reconciliation are opened: 'Whoever has the courage to appear always as he is, sooner or later becomes what he ought to be' (*CG* 3.101). In Julie's therapy the courage of this recognition was manifestly lacking, since her 'cure' constituted a threat to the social order. Thus, when the claims of nature and their conflicts with culture are not recognized, the outcome is neurotic conflict.

Rousseau therefore believes that the defects and flaws that society introduces into human existence in childhood can be reduced ultimately to a single formula: 'Their defects of body and mind may all be traced to the same source, the desire to make men of them before their time' (*E* 9). But the mode of acculturation that he envisions for Emile does not consist of simply allowing nature to take its course. Human ontogenesis, like human phylogenesis as it was described in the second *Discourse*, can only take place within an experience constructed intersubjectively in relations of social action: 'Everything is instruction for active and feeling beings' (*EMF* 63). The human race is the product of an education imposed upon it by the prolonged dependence and helplessness of the infant (*E* 6, 393). Humanity civilizes itself and, to reiterate, 'Nature has, so to speak, abandoned its functions as soon as we usurped them' (*OCI* 327). There is no alternative to asserting social control over nature. The child born into a condition of prolonged dependence cannot help but develop in response to a given situation: 'Is not this poor child, without knowledge, strength or wisdom entirely at your mercy? Are you not master of his whole environment so far as it affects him? Cannot you make of him what you please?' (*E* 84-5) The method Rousseau proposes differs essentially from previous notions of education in the way it attempts to match psychic development with physical maturation. The demands made on the child will not exceed his ability at any point to respond effectively to his physical and social environment (*E* 6, 44, 49, 129, 279).

This non-excessively denaturing mode of acculturation Rousseau calls a 'negative education':

I call positive education that which tends to form the understanding before the proper time, and to give a child prematurely the knowledge of the duties of a man. I call that negative education, which tends to perfect the corporeal organs, the instrument of our knowledge, and which prepares us for reasoning by exercising our senses. (*LCB* 263)

The education of the earliest years should be merely negative. It consists not in teaching virtue or truth, but in preserving the heart from vice and from the spirit of error. (*E* 57)

Rousseau distinguishes three sources that contribute to the formation of the individual. The first is nature, 'the inner growth of our organs and faculties'; the second is that which comes from men, and the third is the 'education of things' (*E* 6). In order for the individual to be at peace with himself these three 'masters' must not conflict. But since only the second is largely within human control, it must be brought into agreement with the other two. To the extent that the experience of the physical environment, the education of things, is within human control, it must also be brought into agreement with nature. Thus a negative education is that which co-ordinates experience (of things and of men) to assist the process of maturation, which is in itself, Rousseau assumes, by this point in the biological development of the species, to some extent predisposed to the acquisition of a cultural and social mode of existence. Yet this co-ordination, to prevent the neurotogenic consequences of excessive denaturation, is limited in what it can demand of nature and in how these demands are posed.

Rousseau accuses civilization of having heretofore tyrannized over and deformed nature. The tyranny consist largely in the instrumentalization of the child's bodily organic drives, leading to its own self-instrumentalization in the interest of satisfying an exaggerated need for self-esteem. This process is most acutely revealed, Rousseau contends, in the cultural attitude towards time imposed upon and eventually internalized by the child. The original proto-human lived in the eternal present. The human species, however, emerged from the permanent here and now of its animal forebears within a process of social labour. The necessity of labour and its instrumentality create, as it were, the flow of human time in which the present is continually pushed into the past by a future with a constant horizon, a horizon that never approaches:

Prudence! Prudence which is ever bidding us look forward into the future, a future which in many cases we shall never reach; here is the real source of all our troubles! How mad it is for so short-lived a creature as man to look forward into a future to which he rarely attains, while he neglects the present which is his? this madness is all the more fatal since it increases with years, and the old, always timid, prudent and miserly, prefer to do without necessaries today that they may have luxuries at a hundred. Thus we grasp everything, we cling to everything; we are anxious about time, place, people, things, all that is and will be; we ourselves are but the least part of ourselves. We spread ourselves, so to speak, over the whole world, and all this vast expanse becomes sensitive. (*E* 46)[11]

11 See also *EMF* 86.

In the primitive community there is still time for play, for singing and dancing; there *amour-propre* takes the form of display. But inside the system of needs, prudence becomes permanent and compulsive, since inside it a man cannot even remain where he is without constantly endeavouring to increase his power.

The progress of civilization, in so far as it means the increase of 'prévoyance,' coincides with the permanent flight of time into a receding past and unattainable future: 'How many voices are going to be raised against me. I already hear the clamour of that false wisdom that throws us ceaselessly out of ourselves, that always counts the present for nothing and, searching for a future that flees in proportion to one's approach, transports us continually where we are not, and where we will never really be, in such a way that death always surprises us in our preparations to enjoy life' (*EMF* 82).[12] Even the fear of death, for Rousseau, is a result of the way in which human societies have structured time:

Human institutions are one mass of folly and contradiction. As our life loses its value we set a higher price upon it. The old regret life more than the young; they do not want to lose all they have spent in preparing for its enjoyment. At sixty it is cruel to die when one has not begun to live. Man is credited with a strong desire for self-preservation, and this desire exists; but we fail to perceive that this desire, as felt by us, is largely the work of man. (*E* 46)

When applied to education this cultural structuring of time leads to the instrumentalization of the child's drives, to arresting a process of development that would necessarily take place in the course of maturation and experience but might take place in a qualitatively different manner. Because to be a man has meant to be rational and rationality has come to mean above all 'prévoyance,' prudence or foresight, children must become men before their time; their time must not be wasted on childhood. In order, however, not to waste time, society must impose those inner conflicts in such a way that the self-contradictions attendant upon the emergence from mere nature cannot be overcome. Therefore Rousseau's fundamental maxim in regard to the education of Emile will be the reverse of that inherent in the system of needs:

May I venture at this point to state the greatest, the most important, the most useful rule of education? It is: do not save time, but lose it. (*E* 57)

---

12 See also *E* 43.

When we are in no hurry to teach there is no hurry to demand, and we can take our time, so as to demand nothing except under fitting conditions. Then the child is training himself. (*E* 67)

The only way to avoid the inner conflicts that have attended civilization is to refrain from interposing excessively denaturing cultural demands between the child's emerging self-consciousness and its own nature.

Do you wish to establish law and order among the rising passions, prolong the period of their development, so that they may have time to find their proper place as they arise. Then they are controlled by nature itself, not by man; your task is merely to leave it in her hands. (*E* 180)

Respect childhood, and do not be in any hurry to judge it for good or ill. Leave exceptions to show themselves, let their qualities be tested and confirmed, before particular methods are adopted. Give nature time to work before you take over her business, lest you contradict her operations. (*E* 71)[13]

Although Rousseau calls his method a negative education, it is not entirely so. It is largely negative because it refrains from the imposition of excessively denaturing cultural demands that are characteristically imposed in the form of a certain temporal regimen. What the demands are seems to be inseparable from how they are imposed, and how they are imposed seems to depend in turn on when they are imposed. It would nevertheless be mistaken to think of Rousseau as wishing to impose the same demands as does the civilization he condemns, only in a different order or with a different rhythm. Time is not the external form for an unvarying content. The consequences of this negative education for the social order only become visible in the finished figure of Emile. But Emile's education necessarily has a positive side, inseparable from a being whose nature is artifice. Emile cannot develop on his own. For although he is a natural man, he is not a creature of instinct and must learn the mediation of his desires in activity and in relations with others.

Necessary Denaturation: The Education of Emile

Emile's development passes through two major stages, each composed of many minor ones. I will not be able in a reasonably brief space to present that development in its richness of detail and incident. Rousseau

---

13 Modified translation

himself tells us, however, that 'my method does not depend on my examples; it depends on the amount of a man's powers at different ages, and the choice of occupations adapted to those powers' (*E* 155).[14] I am concerned here most of all with Rousseau's method and what that method explicitly and implicitly reveals concerning 'the human condition,' which Rousseau considers 'our true study' in Emile.[15]

The first of the major developmental stages comprises the differentiation of an ego out of a primary unity, and also the beginnings of relations with human others in response to the requirements of objective reality. The second, which overlaps to a certain extent with the later phases of the first, comprises the onset of adult sexuality and its partial transformation into love and social feeling in conjunction with the acquisition of conscience and virtue. The undisturbed progress of the second phase depends on the successful resolution of the conflicts in the first: 'The most dangerous period in human life lies between birth and the age of twelve' (*E* 57).[16] Emile's capacity to acquire a virtue that is not the expression of neurotic misery is based on a positive development of *bonté*, which in turn follows, at least partially, from the relative lack of the conflicts that ordinarily arise from the development of *amour-propre*.

Rousseau realizes that the child is not born as an adult in miniature. He is rather totally dependent on the adults who nurture him, and this dependence is rooted in his almost complete lack of ego capacities. Corresponding to that lack is the lack in the new-born infant of any sense of distinction from external entities:

We are born capable of learning, but knowing nothing. The mind, bound up with imperfect and half-grown organs, is not even aware of its own existence. The movements and cries of the new born child are purely reflex, without knowledge or will ... The child's first mental experiences are purely affective, he is only aware of pleasure and pain; it takes him a long time to acquire the definite sensations which show him things outside himself, but before these things present and withdraw themselves, so to speak, from his sight ... the recurrence of emotional experience is beginning to subject the child to the rule of habit. (*E* 28)

---

14 See also *EMF* 198; cf Bloom, 'Education,' 135-53, who wishes to see much greater significance in the stories.
15 Rousseau, *EMF* 252
16 See also ibid., 98.

Although the child lacks all consciousness of self and other, he is not without definite attachments, the quality of which go a long way towards determining his capacity to form later sublimations and social attachments: 'But the first affections are the source of all compassion. He who begins life loving nothing will love nothing the rest of his life ... here we are outside of nature from the first step' (*EMF* 67). At first his capacities are so rudimentary that there is no alternative to ministering to his wishes as much as possible. And because the affective tone of this earliest period of complete narcissism, parallel to the undifferentiated sense of existence experienced by the savage proto-man, is crucial to the development of later relationships, Rousseau insists on intensive mothering as long as this is the case.

In time, however, this becomes less necessary, as physical maturation allows the child to develop the abilities needed to procure his own satisfactions through activity within the world of objects. He begins to gain a sense of reality, an idea of his distinction from the objects of his needs, only with the exercise and maturation of his 'organs' and with the experience of frustration. But the inevitable frustrations that are also necessary to develop a sense of reality, a sense of the independent existence of objects and other wills, and the abilities to engage reality effectively, constitute a series of crises: 'These tears, which you think so little worthy of your attention, give rise to the first relation between man and his environment; here is forged the first link in the long chain of social order' (*E* 32).

Tears are a sign of distress, of an unsatisfied need, and give way either to satisfaction or to frustration. As soon as frustration is experienced as issuing from another person, especially from another who was previously experienced as the source of satisfaction, it gives way to submission or rage. For the human infant, who is born into a condition of prolonged dependence and who must necessarily learn the distinction between self and other within a series of frustrations administered by the external world, ambivalence is a constant possibility. Consider the following passage:

Self-love [amour-de-soi] is always good, always in accordance with the order of nature. The preservation of our own life is specially entrusted to each one of us, and our first care is, and must be, to watch over our own life ... Self-preservation requires, therefore, that we shall love ourselves; we must love ourselves above everything else, and it follows directly from this that we love what contributes to our preservation. Every child becomes fond of its nurse; Romulus must have loved the she-wolf who suckled him. At first this attachment is quite unconscious;

the individual is attracted to that which contributes to his welfare and repelled by that which is harmful; this is merely blind instinct. What transforms this instinct into feeling, the liking into love, the aversion into hatred, is the evident intention of helping or hurting us. We do not become passionately attached to objects without feeling ... but those from which we expect benefit or injury from their internal disposition, from their will ... inspire us with like feelings to those they exhibit towards us. Something does us good, we seek after it; but we love the person who does us good; something harms us and we shrink from it, but we hate the person who tries to hurt us.

The child's first sentiment is self-love, his second, which is derived from it, is love of those about him; for in his present state of weakness he is only aware of people through the help and attention received from them ...

So a child is naturally disposed to kindly feeling because he sees that everyone about him is inclined to help him, and from this experience he gets the habit of a kindly feeling toward his species; but with the expansion of his relations, his needs, his dependence, active or passive, the consciousness of his relations to others is awakened, and leads to the sense of duties and preferences. Then the child becomes masterful, jealous, deceitful and vindictive. If he is not compelled to obedience, when he does not see the usefulness of what he is told to do, he attributes it to caprice, to an intention of tormenting him, and he rebels ... Self-love, which concerns itself only with ourselves, is content to satisfy our needs; but selfishness [amour-propre], which is always comparing self with others, is never satisfied and never can be; for this feeling, which prefers ourselves to others, requires that they should prefer us to themselves, which is impossible. Thus the tender and gentle passions spring from self-love, while the hateful and angry passions spring from selfishness. (E 174-5)

The primary condition is one of absence of separation between self and other. In this condition the child experiences either pleasure or pain, but has no awareness that action and all that it entails are necessary to gain pleasure and avoid pain. When in pain the child automatically gives a signal of distress, although of course it is not conscious of its crying as a sign. Since it is cared for by adults who minister to all its needs, it tends to experience its dependence as omnipotence. The wish is at first equivalent to the deed. In the course of maturation and experience it gradually begins to differentiate objects and learns that these persons are the source both of its pleasure and of its frustrations. The non-differentiated state of pleasure and pain gives way to a condition in which ambivalence must characterize its relations with others. The persons whom it has come gradually to love as separate objects are also hated. At the same time that it becomes aware of its dependence upon them, it becomes dependent upon their affection. Its 'sense of existence,' its substitutes for the original condition of unity, are conditional upon the perceived attitude of the objects upon which it is dependent. But not having yet developed a sufficient sense of reality and still being dependent not only on the affection of others but on their real intervention to secure its needs, the child experiences the demands imposed upon it as a 'desire to torment it.' Its own frustrations and anger become the evident anger and desire to frustrate of the other. Thus love and hate are in their origins inseparable.

The real problem is, however, that the earliest condition cannot be spontaneously relinquished. The child clings to that omnipotence in thought that was identical to its state of complete dependence. At first frustration can therefore be met only by an attitude of either mastery or slavery: 'There is no middle course; he must rule or obey. Thus his earliest ideas are those of the tyrant or the slave. He commands before he can speak, he obeys before he can act, and sometimes he is punished for faults before he is aware of them, or rather before they are committed. Thus early are the seeds of evil passions sown in his young heart. At a later day these are attributed to nature, and when we have taken pains to make him bad we lament his badness' (*E* 15-16). The control that he wishes to exert over the world and over others is magical: 'it does not need much experience to realize how pleasant it is to set others to work and to move the world by a word' (*E* 34). The child's mind, dominated by fantasies of omnipotence, animates the world around him: 'as soon as anything opposes him he regards it as rebellion, as a determination to resist him; he beats the chair or table for disobeying him' (*E* 174). And the extent to which he is made to rely upon imaginary satisfactions, upon fantasies, will correspondingly retard or fixate his development in the acquisition of real control over both the external world and his own desires. Thus the fantastic ambitions associated with the development of *amour-propre* will become ever harder to relinquish, since 'the real world has its limits; the imaginary world is infinite' (*EMF* 84).

In a condition of excessive denaturation, unrealistic demands, demands that cannot be met by the child except at the cost of cutting himself off from his own desire, will give rise to high levels of frustration, frustration that leads to anger. But since this anger is directed against someone who loves the child, it will not be accepted as such. Instead he will attribute his anger to the other's desire to hurt him and will react by asserting his own omnipotence in the realm of fantasy: 'It is in this disproportion between desire and power that the monsters of the imagination are formed' (*EMF* 231). At the same time, since the birth of *amour-propre* coincides with the beginnings of the need for self-esteem mediated by the other, he will repress the desires that he perceives are unwelcome to the adult world, and also the aggression associated with them. He will seek his sense of existence at first in the esteem of his parents and later on in the recognition of his conscience. Thus self-contradictions give way to inner conflicts, and these inner conflicts are maintained at the cost of the imposition of a hiatus between desire and the sense of self. One can only be oneself when behaving in such a way as to satisfy the demands of the (eventually internalized) other; but as long as one pursues oneself in this manner, a large part of the self (repressed desire) remains outside the self: 'The combination of weakness and domination engenders nothing but madness and misery' (*EMF* 92).

The period of immediate unity thus necessarily gives way to a period of ambivalence. When excessive denaturation is imposed, ambivalence is heightened and deepened, simultaneously generating submission to the dictates of society and fantasies of omnipotence. Submission takes the form of cutting off from the self the desire that gave rise to the frustration (administered by those upon whom one is dependent) and the threat of affection withdrawn. Since children are not rational and since, during this period, self and other, subject and object, are only imperfectly distinguished from each other, the child, whose life is largely governed by fantasy, imagines that because he hates (since he is frustrated), he is hated. But since he has begun to separate self and other, he now lives within a relation. He has ideas without thinking abstractly, and his idea of self is largely composed of the idea he has of the reception of this self by the others. *Amour-propre* becomes fused, as it were, with the project of domination.

The separation of self and other and the ability to act and to reason Rousseau recognizes as following only from frustration. But this does not mean that frustration *must* give rise to a level of ambivalence that enforces denaturation and that fixes *amour-propre* to domination. Frustration need not be imposed in such a way as to leave the child no other recourse but the self-contradiction of ambivalence and the inner but eminently social conflicts to which ambivalence makes the child susceptible. The most important task of education is the development of the child's sense of reality: 'it is to make him feel ... the heavy yoke of necessity that nature imposes on man' (*LNH* 571). He will only develop such a sense (which is *impaired* by excess denaturation) and forego or relinquish his fantasies of omnipotence gradually. He will develop relatively free of conflict, but not through submission to the arbitrary demands of the adult world. Only to the extent that he matures naturally will he be able to find suitable substitutes in the cultural world for his immature modes of satisfaction: 'The child is only naughty because he is weak; make him strong and he will be good; if we could do everything we should never do wrong' (*E* 33).

Ambivalence is made unmanageable by the interposition of a threatening and caressing will between the child's emerging self and external necessity, the necessity he must overcome to satisfy his desire and the desire that he must inhibit, delay, and transform in order to overcome necessity. These things Rousseau believes he will learn to do in the course of time if he is simultaneously shielded from the demands of excessive denaturation and presented with suitable experiential opportunities. The tutor's remedy will therefore be to seem to leave Emile as much as possible to his own resources, in order to allow his maturing capacities time to overcome frustration in ways that do not require a repression of his desires: 'Arrange it that everywhere around him he perceives nothing but the physical world. Otherwise you may be sure that he will make of the moral world about which you speak to him imaginary and fantastic notions that you will never destroy' (*EMF* 94). The tutor will comply with every wish for which Emile objectively requires his assistance, except the desire for power. To the latter he will remain indifferent (*E* 35, 53, 85ff). Thus Emile, in the process of learning the separation of self and other, in learning to integrate his drives with his activity in accordance with the fundamental requirements of a cultural existence, will experience the restraints imposed upon him as issuing not so much from the will of the tutor, in the form of a threatened withdrawal of affection, as from natural necessity. The necessary constraints upon and deflections of desire inseparable from the formation of an ego may proceed relatively untroubled by the premature formation of a moral world with its heightened ambivalence and incomprehensible and thus unjustifiable demands. It is the will of the other that calls up the old reliance upon imaginary omnipotence. Emile, unencumbered by the recalcitrant will of those upon whom he depends, will discover that when the world yields to his desire, it does so only to the extent that he acts realistically within it, and that when he is unable to fulfil his desire, he is constrained by his own weakness, not by the will of another; and 'we do not rebel against necessity when once we have perceived it' (*E* 125).

When Rousseau wants to rely on the developing strength of the child in order to avoid the sorts of frustrations that nourish ambivalence, this should not be taken to mean that the child should be urged or commanded to achieve feats of self-control beyond the capacities of its developing nature. Strength for Rousseau is a relative term. One is strong to the extent that one's power is adequate to one's needs. Strength is a measure of equilibrium. The happiness of the original man was a function of the spontaneous equilibrium between his capacities and his needs. With the development of human perfectibility, however, this static equilibrium was upset and replaced with a dynamic disequilibrium. What was gained in the development of human capacities was lost, in terms of happiness, by the development of needs that became impossible to satisfy. *Amour-propre* is inherently unsatisfiable (*E* 44-5).[17] *This* phylogenetic process is repeated in each ontogenesis. Static equilibrium is experienced by the child before he experiences himself as separate, because all his wishes are fulfilled seemingly without effort by those upon whom he is dependent. But in order to become human he must learn to rely upon his own mediation of the external world and hence of his drives. Since he remains dependent throughout this process it is possible for him to mistake the care of others for his own power. He will strive to maintain this power over others, at the expense of developing his own capacities.

Rousseau is proposing, by contrast, that necessary denaturation proceed as a dynamic equilibrium. Under the force of the unavoidable constraint imposed by nature, the child will develop its capacities. As these develop, the child will become less dependent and less weak. It is not desire that must be constrained. Desires are themselves necessary to the development of all the human capacities: 'Our passions are the chief means of self-preservation; to destroy them is therefore as absurd as it is useless; this would be to overthrow nature, to reshape God's handiwork. If God bade man annihilate the passions he has given him, God would bid him be and not be; He would contradict himself. He has never given such a foolish commandment' (*E* 173). The development of strength therefore does not simply mean denaturation, for the human capacities only develop in response to a reserve of natural passions not blocked from attaining avenues of expression:

What then is human wisdom? Where is the path of true happiness? the mere limitation of our desires is not enough, for if they were less than our powers, part of our faculties would be idle, and we should not enjoy our whole being; neither is the mere extension of our powers enough, for if our desires were also

17 See also, eg, *RJ* 196: 'Sitot que cet amour absolu dégénère en amour-propre et comparatif, il produit la sensibilité négative, parce qu'aussitot qu'on prend l'habitude de se mesurer avec d'autres et de se transporter hors de soi, pour s'assigner la première et meilleure place, il est impossible de ne pas prendre en aversion tout ce qui nous surpasse, tout ce qui nous rabaisse, tout ce qui nous comprime, tout ce qui étant quelque chose, nous empêche d'etre tout.'

increased we should only be the more miserable. True happiness consists in decreasing the difference between our desires and our powers, in establishing a perfect equilibrium between the power and the will. Then only, *when all its forces are employed, will the soul be at rest and man will find himself in this true position.* (*E* 44; emphasis added)

Emile's equilibrium will be maintained not through premature denaturation imposed in the interests of social performance and also not through the mechanisms supplied by a heightened *amour-propre*. In Rousseau's eyes the necessary denaturation will take place within the process of the child's separation from nature. Needs that do not spring from the regressive wish for omnipotence the child will learn to satisfy as his capacities mature along with its experience:

Nature provides for the child's growth in her own fashion, and this should never be thwarted ... If we did not spoil our children's wills by our blunders their desires would be free from caprice ... All their own activities are instincts of the body for its growth in strength; but you should regard with suspicion those wishes which they cannot carry out for themselves, those which others must carry out for them. Then you must distinguish carefully between natural and artificial needs, between the needs of budding caprice and the needs that spring from the overflowing life just described. (*E* 50)

It is by allowing nature and experience time to interact that the child will become capable of finding his own routes to integrating nature and culture. If the wish for omnipotence were not heightened through excess denaturation, it would be relinquished naturally as the child is offererd and becomes capable of realistic modes of satisfaction: 'Now I consider those who would prevent the birth of the passions almost as foolish as those who would destroy them, and those who think this has been my object hitherto are greatly mistaken' (*E* 173).

A child who is allowed to develop in this way will also not experience the need to relinquish desires before he is capable of doing so. Thus the child need not cut himself off from his own desires. When he *does* suppress desire, he will do so for the sake of gaining a real versus an imagined satisfaction. This the child can accomplish when he relinquishes, or better, transforms that desire, not via the demand of those upon whom he depends but when it becomes evident that the real satisfaction, although not immediate or total, offers a real relation with the world and hence is better:

Let us lay it down as incontrovertible rule that the first impulses of human nature are always right; there is no original sin in the human heart, the how and why of the entrance of every vice can be traced. The only natural passion is self-love or selfishness taken in a wider sense. This selfishness is good in itself and in relation to ourselves ... his self-love only becomes good or bad by the use made of it and the relations established by its means. Until the time is ripe for the appearance of reason, that guide of selfishness, the main thing is that the child shall do nothing because you are watching him or listening to him; in a word, nothing because of other people, but only what nature asks of him; then he will never do wrong. (E 56–7)

In a sense he will remain transparent to himself and to others, that transparency signalling the absence of the need to defend against the suspect desire's reaching consciousness: 'Thus not seeing you at all eager to thwart him without end ... having nothing to hide from you ... he will show himself such as he is without fear' (EMF 122).[18] The child who, by contrast, is exposed to excessive denaturation is given cause to repress his own nature: he 'fears himself and he flees from himself; he errs in rushing outside of himself' (PF 251). The repressed desire is not abolished but impels a flight into unsatisfying activity motivated primarily by the need to defend against the repressed desire itself. Excess denaturation thus weakens, although the weakness may be hidden by a rigid and brittle show of strength. To reiterate,

Parents who live in the civil state transport their child there prematurely. In giving him greater needs than he would otherwise have, they do not alleviate his weakness; they augment it. They augment it even more in exacting from him what nature would not demand, in subordinating to their wills the little power he has to serve his own needs, in changing on all sides into slavery the reciprocal dependence in which his weakness holds him and their affection holds them.[19]

The reserves of strength that he possesses – that is, whatever abilities he has gained to transform his drives in learning to act in the world of objects – are thus subordinated to an extraneous need and diverted

18 See also 160; cf E 283–4.
19 See chap. 8, n 15, and EMF 89; also E 395–6: 'Most of the habits you have instilled into young people are not really habits at all; they have only been acquired under compulsion, and being following reluctantly they will be cast off at the first opportunity. However long you remain in prison you never get a taste for prison life; so aversion is increased rather than diminshed by habit.'

from possible sublimations towards defence. This occurs, moreover, not because the child is impelled by nature towards what is inherently bad but because the civil state requires excess denaturation: 'There are acts that are only bad because they are forbidden; take away the prohibition, and there is no more harm in doing them' (EMF 232).

The tutor's role, therefore, is not to instruct a passive pupil while restraining an impetuous and disorderly nature but, carefully choosing opportune moments in accordance with his pupil's physical and cognitive maturation, to offer pathways for the sublimation of the pupil's developing desires:

By bringing before him what he needs to know, we enable him to develop his own tastes, his own talents, to take the first step towards the object which appeals to his individuality and to show us the road we must open up to aid the work of nature. (E 155)[20]

First of all bear it well in mind that it is rarely for you to propose what he ought to learn; it is for him to desire it, to seek it, to find it; your cares ought to be limited to giving birth to this desire indirectly and to giving him the means to satisfy it. (EMF 184)

The tutor's control is extended only so far as to construct the situation in which Emile is able to learn to substitute realistic satisfactions for the fantastic ones of a childish imagination.

Emile is divided into five books. Books 1 to 3 concern the education of the earliest years, up to the age of twelve. These years correspond to, or parallel, the asocial state of nature of the second *Discourse*. Excessive denaturation is avoided through a preservation of an analogue to the asocial state. Or course Emile is not in reality an asocial being, even at this age. But he is kept shielded from the full intensity of even non-excessively denaturing demands in order that nature's capacity to find modes of expression adequate to the demands of culture and physical necessity might be preserved in him, without the establishment of the gap between desire and consciousness that characterizes the 'normal' civilized individual. Emile has had to repress his own nature to some extent; he has had to forgo the infantile striving after immediate, magical, and total gratification. Unlike the normal child, he no longer harbours fantasies of omnipotence and is therefore not tied via *amour-propre* to 'opinion.' Were he not to mature any further, he would thus remain a

[20] See also 84-5, 95.

savage, enclosed within himself because of his relative strength. In fact Emile is, although relatively strong, absolutely weak. In no sense can he remain the isolated atom he seems to be because of his relative independence. For Emile is and will remain dependent on human society for even his most rudimentary needs.[21] But beyond his physical dependence upon society and its division of labour, he would, if left in this state, remain impoverished in a different way: 'He who, by reason of being concentrated within himself, finally comes to love only himself ... no longer enjoys anything; the unfortunate no longer feels, no longer lives; he is already dead.' The effort expended to prolong the state of nature is undertaken in order that the transition to the social state might be achieved without the disturbance of inner conflicts that arise from unresolvable self-contradictions. In order, however, to enter society fully, Emile, who has previously not acquired any idea of duty, must acquire 'virtue': 'I have restrained him so far through his ignorance; henceforward his restraint must be his own knowledge' (E 282). Books 4 and 5 describe this process as a succession of transformations of sexuality.

The negative education of the earliest years does not have merely negative results. Rousseau expects that if excess denaturation is avoided, the worst excesses of *amour-propre* will be avoided, since *amour-propre* is only the outgrowth of the profound ambivalence that characterizes the person fixated at the stage of dependence upon the will of others. It is this simultaneity of dependence and capricious will that weakens the sense of reality, thus blocking the possibility of sublimation and increasing the hold of magical thinking. The normal individual, dependent upon others, is cut off from his nature and therefore cannot integrate it into the cultural order. At the same time the nature of his repressed desires has been changed, as it were, because they are now linked to the infantile project of omnipotence.

With the onset of adult sexuality there is a recurrence of the crisis of the first stage. Up to that point Emile has managed to develop a 'natural' *bonté*, or kindness, corresponding to his relative independence from others. But he is not virtuous, nor does he require virtue. He is neither servile nor imperious but is acquainted with both compliance and refusal, and

---

21 Rousseau, E 156: 'According to this principle, anyone who wanted to consider himself as an isolated individual, self-sufficing and independent of others, could only be utterly wretched. He could not even continue to exist, for finding the whole earth appropriated by others while he had only himself, how could he get the means of subsistence? When we leave the state of nature we compel others to do the same; no one can remain in a state of nature in spite of his fellow creatures, and to try to remain in it when it is no longer practicable, would really be to leave it, for self-preservation is nature's first law.'

'his progress has not been bought at the price of his happiness, he has gained both' (E 124-6). With the emergence of the biologically powerful sex-drive Emile is once again thrust into a situation of potential dependence that would threaten his 'inner harmony.' Yet at the same time this drive is the means by which will be forged the 'ties that united him to his species' (E 194).

In Emile *amour-de-soi* survives the crises of ego-development and becomes the foundation of positive social feeling. It becomes the basis of compassion. A sort of narcissism is always the basis of relations with others (EMF 56). But in Emile it is no longer the first narcissism that does not recognize the existence of the distinction between self and other; nor is it the slavish-tyrannical narcissism that attempts to reduce the other to a condition of self-aggrandizement or takes refuge in submission to the other. In Emile the reservoir of self-love becomes the basis of erotic ties binding him to his fellows.

I would try to show how the first impulses of the heart give rise to the first stirrings of conscience, and how from the feelings of love and hatred spring the first notions of good and evil. I would show that justice and kindness are no mere abstract terms, no mere moral conceptions framed by the understanding, but true affections of the heart enlightened by reason, the natural outcome of our primitive affections; that by reason alone, unaided by conscience, we cannot establish any natural law, and that all natural right is a vain dream if it does not rest upon some instinctive need of the human heart. (E 196)

Extend self-love [amour-de-soi] to others and it is transformed to a virtue, a virtue which has its roots in the heart of every one of us. (E 216)

Social feeling or compassion can be derived from the narcissistic reservoir of *amoir-de-soi* by way of imaginative identification with others as fellow sufferers. In this way even *amour-propre*, to the extent that it is present, can be fused with compassion. According to Rousseau we feel compassion only on the basis of a favourable comparison of our own condition with that of those who are suffering. Thus, when *amour-propre* has not become transformed into the striving for domination, it serves as a means of facilitating the identification that is at the basis of human compassion. In being fused with compassion, it is turned into its opposite.[22]

22 On the development of compassion see Rousseau, E 182-6; contrast this with Bloom's derivation of compassion and sociability not primarily from *amour-de-soi* but from *amour-propre* in 'Education,' 184; see also LCB 936: 'J'ai fait voir que l'unique passion qui naisse avec l'homme, savoir l'amour-propre, est une passion indifférente en elle-même

Given Emile's previous education, the partial transformation of sexual desire into compassion is a relatively simple and smooth affair. When it comes to love, however, the dangers are greater, since Emile will be all the more dependent on the object of his desire. In order to prevent the re-emergence of *amour-propre* given over to domination, the tutor must, for the first time, instil in Emile a fear of his own desire. Yet this fear will be a fully conscious and rational fear. The excessive denaturation that separates self and desire is also based on a fear of desire, but this fear is an outcome of the internalization of an external threat. In excessive denaturation what is feared is abandonment by the other upon whom one is still dependent in the wishful world of fantasized omnipotence. The other side of omnipotence is annihilation. And the virtue that is a reactive fear of desire is not so much a realistic judgment upon that desire as it is a subordination of that desire to an imagined threat of annihilation.

Rousseau, however, wishes that Emile not conceal his desire from himself or from the tutor. The tutor therefore does not wish to establish virtue by means of *amour-propre*. Sexual desire in Emile will not be contained or constrained through the internalization of a punitive agency threatening annihilation from within the self. Virtue is not to be a denial of the passions but a safeguard against their self-destruction. For what passes as virtue in the normal man, the man who is educated for others, is a pitting of passion against passion, not a judgment of reason on the passions. Thus Rousseau, *because* he refuses, as we have seen (page 144 above), the identification of happiness and virtue made by the Stoics, draws none the less on the Stoic ideal to instil in Emile a higher degree of autonomy from his desires. Prior to this stage Emile had been free in the sense that he enjoyed an absence of self-contradiction, since his desires never exceeded his capacities to fulfil them. Now he must learn, without inner conflict, to subject a fully conscious and legitimate desire to the judgment of reason:

But tell me ... *though this passion is pure, is it any less your master? Are you the less its slave?* And if tomorrow it should cease to be innocent, would you strangle it on the spot? ... *it is a mistake to classify the passions as lawful and unlawful, so as to yield to the one and refuse the other. All alike are good if we are their masters; all alike are bad if we abandon ourselves to them ... To feel or not to feel a passion is beyond our control, but we can control ourselves*

---

au bien et au mal; qu'elle ne devient bonne ou mauvaise que par accident et selon les circonstances dans lesquelles elle se développe.'

... Do not expect me to supply you with lengthy precept of morality, I have only one rule to give you which sums up all the rest. Be a man; restrain your heart within the limits of your manhood ... however narrow they may be, we are not unhappy within them; it is only when we wish to go beyond them that we are unhappy, only when, in our mad passions, we try to attain the impossible; we are unhappy when we forget our manhood to make an imaginary world for ourselves, from which we are always slipping back into our own ... Would you live in wisdom and happiness, fix your heart on the beauty that is eternal ... learn to lose what may be taken from you; learn to forsake all things at the command of virtue, to set yourself above the chances of life, to detach your heart before it is torn in pieces ... Then you will be happy in spite of fortune ... You will find a pleasure which cannot be destroyed, even in the possession of the most fragile things; you will possess them, they will not possess you, and you will realize that the man who loses everything, only enjoys what he knows now to resign. (*E* 409-10; emphasis added)

Stoic autarky is, however, not the aim Rousseau has in mind for Emile. His destiny is to be fully engaged in the world. The moment of disengagement, the fixing of his sights on 'the beauty that is eternal,' the emphasis the tutor places on the ephemeral quality of human attachments and existence, are meant finally to detach Emile from the desire for perfect identity. As he approached the age of reason, Emile had been taught essentially the same through the words of the Savoyard vicar, only in the realm of theoretical reason: that knowledge never fully corresponds with its object and that the perfect identity of subject and object is an impossibility (*E* 230ff).[23] Love is not the route for Emile to the philosophic knowledge of eternal truth. Rather, the philosophic detachment that follows from a knowledge of human limitations is the route towards the capacity to love.

It is not possible to follow in detail here the long and complex chain of manoeuvres in which the tutor engages in order to lead Emile towards virtue. It is enough to emphasize that the virtue that the tutor aims at attaining is not in conflict with happiness. As we have seen, it depends on a fully conscious recognition, evaluation, and transformation of desire. Moreover, it may be described as the attainment of the capacity to enjoy the uniquely human pleasure that depends on obstacles to the realization of desire, that recognizes the independence of the object: 'I have brought Emile up neither to desire nor to wait, but to enjoy! and when his desires

---

23 Also, eg, *CG* 10.342: 'La vérité pour nous est couverte d'un voile, mais la paix et l'union sont un bien certain.'

are bent upon the future, their ardour is not so great as to make time seem tedious. He will not only enjoy the delights of longing, but the delights of approaching the object of his desires; and his passions are under such restraint that he lives to a great extent in the present' (*E* 374).

In the end Sophie and Emile are finally united. But Emile's union with the object of his desire is not attained through conquest. Nor is their relationship to be bound by the constraint of duty. Their pleasure in each other is to be won only in full recognition on both parts of the independence of the other: 'Constraint and love do not agree together, and pleasure is not to be had for the asking ... obtain all from love and nothing from duty, and let the slightest favours never be of right but of grace' (*E* 440-1). Emile's tutelage concludes with this final resolution of ambivalence and with the full recognition on his part that happiness and freedom are bound up with the absence of the need to dominate. Yet this final transcendence of the drive to domination is not dependent upon a split between nature and culture or between passion and reason. The attainment by Emile of a human and social existence does not call for an overbearing and punitive social agency within the psyche. Unlike Julie's, Emile's conscience is not overburdened with the results of unresolved ambivalence.

Conclusions: Emile as Metaphor

With Emile's maturity the process of theoretically separating alienation from objectification reaches its end. Emile is a product of the lifting of excess denaturation; he is in Rousseau's eyes a figurative anticipation of what nature would allow the species to become were it historically possible to impose only that denaturation necessary for a human and cultural existence. The abolition of excess denaturation results neither in a regression behind civilization nor in an impossible quest after the perfection of virtue: 'Let us never seek the chimera of perfection, but the best possible, following the nature of man and the nature of society' (*LA* 253). Emile also represents the possibility of the fulfilment of the promise of the *Social Contract* – a democracy that need not be austere.

Emile, the imaginary person, embodies the theoretical possibility of a cultural and political existence in which the alienation that has characterized the historical process in the past has been abolished. Just as Plato asks the reader of the *Republic* to discover the character of the just man in the larger characters of the just city, Rousseau in *Emile*, which is in some ways an attempt to invert and supersede the *Republic*, asks his reader to find the character of the just city in the smaller figure of Emile, who is 'a good man and a lover' (E 292).[24] The possibility of lifting excess denaturation points to a transcendence of bourgeois society. This transcendence would take place not through the return of ancient virtue nor merely in the perfection of the political state. Emile does not 'seek his freedom under the power of the laws' (E 437) and is not destined for citizenship, at least not in the sense that Rousseau habitually gives to the term.

The lifting of excess denaturation would, moreover, create the possibility of a dialectical reconstitution of the golden age. In the second *Discourse* Rousseau had hesitated over the source of historical alienation, over whether it was given in 'the spirit of society' or whether it issued from 'the establishment of property and laws.' The issue is finally decided only in Emile, who, not destined to occupy a particular slot in the division of labour or be a member of the system of needs, is no longer in need of private property. Whereas civil society has its foundations in private property in the productive resources of society, Emile has transcended the need for an enjoyment realized in possession, consumption, and acquisition: 'I can only be master of a cottage by ceasing to be master of myself' (E 437).[25] Removed at birth from acculturation within the system of needs, 'he can only appropriate things by personal enjoyment' (E 154). But this is not a moralistic plea for moderation or restraint in pursuing happiness; it is not a limitation on desire, imposed either voluntarily or socially. Just as primitive society knew common property without privation, Emile is capable of recognizing his own wealth in that of society:

If you would have pleasure without pain let there be no monopoly: the more you leave it free to everybody, the poorer will be your own enjoyment ... monopoly destroys pleasure. Real pleasures are those we share with the crowd; we lose what we try to keep to ourselves alone ... The demon of property spoils everything he lays hands upon. A rich man wants to be master everywhere, and he is never happy where he is; he is continually driven to flee from himself. I shall therefore continue to do in my prosperity what I did in my poverty. Henceforward, richer in the wealth of others than I ever shall be in my own wealth, I will take possession of everything in my neighborhood that takes my fancy; no conqueror is so determined as I ... I make what use I choose of the ground to walk upon, and you will never convince me that the nominal owner of the property which I have appropriated gets better value out of the money it yields to him than I

24 See also E 8.
25 See also ibid., 443.

do ... Pleasure is ours when we want it; it is only social prejudice which makes everything hard to obtain, and drives pleasure before us. To be happy is a hundredfold easier than it seems ... Emile knows this as well as I, but his heart is purer and more healthy, so he will feel it more strongly. (*E* 319-20)[26]

Free from the system of needs, Emile also stands for the possibility of a reduction of the dehumanizing effects of the division of labour, 'the plain foundation of all our institutions' (*E* 156). Whereas in the second *Discourse* the division of labour appeared as an alien power denying the individual his own self-realization, Rousseau now sees in it the source of the 'true advantages of human society' so long as each practices an occupation 'that suits him best' (*EMF* 198). It is not, however, merely a matter of fitting individual preferences and abilities to pre-established functions in the manner of Fourier, but of developing the individual in the direction of universality. As it stands in civil society, 'man is the cheapest commodity on the market, and among all our important rights of property, the rights of the individual are considered last of all' (*E* 211). The tendency of the system of needs is to multiply 'those stupid trades in which the workmen mechanically perform the same action without pause and almost without mental effort. Weaving, stocking knitting, stonecutting; why employ intelligent men on such work? It is merely one machine employed on another' (*E* 163). Although Emile will acquire a trade, his education does not aim at preparing him for a life subordinated to the division of labour: 'Fit a man's education to his real self, not to what is not part of him ... in striving to fit him merely to one station, you are unfitting him for anything else' (*E* 157).

Emile must bear his share of the burden of the necessary labour of society (*E* 158), but his freedom is to be found beyond this sphere: 'This ought to be, at least according to me, the man nourished in the order of nature but brought up for society. He will have none of the qualities that dazzle the vulgar; he will have acquired no particular talents; he will not at all be formed for this or that occupation, but he will possess the instruments that serve for all of them. He will not be a this or a that; he will be nothing but a man; he will be nothing, but he will be fit for everything' (*EMF* 237). According to Rousseau we cannot enjoy the pleasure of our existence unless it is in activities that are free of all external constraint (*RPS* 1052-3). When, therefore, necessary labour is accomplished, freedom is realized in an expansion of activity:

26 See also ibid., 388.

When our natural tendencies have not been interfered with by human prejudices and human institutions, the happiness alike of children and of men consists in the enjoyment of their liberty. (*E* 49)

Life is not breath, but action, the use of our senses, our mind, our faculties, every part of ourselves which makes us conscious of our being. (*E* 10)

Emile is meant to be able to 'work like a peasant and think like a philosopher' (*E* 156).

The possibility of a reduction in the humanly debilitating effects of the division of labour is premised, however, on a liberation from the system of needs. The key to the distinction between necessary and excessive denaturation lies there. Rousseau apparently came to believe that once scientific and technological reason had been liberated from the shackles of tradition, there would be no further requirement that they be developed within the social relations of the market society. And Emile himself is not subject to the needs of the technological apparatus emerging from the operations of a capitalist economy. To be sure, he will not strive after the tremendous wealth that that economy is capable of generating. The liberation from the system of needs might mean a slowing down in the rate of the human acquisition of power over nature, and it certainly does mean the rejection of the cheap consumer satisfactions that the system of needs promises (*LM* 1087). But Emile himself will not give up the accomplishments of human civilization. Book 3 of *Emile* is, after all, devoted to a scientific and technical education, and the pupil, upon reaching his majority, realizes quite clearly that, 'when you wished me to be free and at the same time without needs, you desired two incompatible things, for I could only be independent of men by returning to dependence on nature ... Rich or poor, I shall be free ... All the chains of prejudice are broken; as far as I am concerned I know only the bonds of necessity' (*E* 436). As we have seen, Rousseau does not insist upon a reduction in human powers; indeed, he maintains that an insistence upon self-limitation would leave 'part of our faculties idle.'

The 'reduction' of needs that would take place generally once the system of needs was abolished would not result in an impoverishment of human needs or human powers. It would simply mean the abolition of the alien compulsion that is present in bourgeois society to go on amassing wealth at the individual and social levels. Once that compulsion was eliminated it would be possible to go on extending human power in such a way that the equilibrium between power and desire might be maintained. Emile's needs are not poor and unrefined. When Rousseau attempts to distinguish between true and false needs, luxury and necessity, 'bodily' needs and 'vain desires,' he is not attempting to fix boundaries to the development of needs or powers, which develop in tandem, but to distinguish between structures of needs that can be satisfied without subjection to an alien and overpowering productive apparatus, and those that emerge from the needs of the productive apparatus itself. Thus, 'true needs themselves change according to the situation of men. There is a great deal of difference between the natural man living in the state of nature and the natural man living in the state of society. Emile is not a savage I would want to relegate to the wilds. He is a savage who ought to inhabit cities' (*EMF* 213).[27] Thus when Emile claims that, whether rich or poor, he is capable of being free, he foreshadows in a real sense Marx's early conception of the rich man:

It can be seen how the *rich man* and the wealth of *human* need take the place of the *wealth* and *poverty* of political economy. The *rich* man is simultaneously *in need* of a totality of vital human expression; he is the man in whom his own realization exists as inner necessity, *as need*. Given socialism, not only man's *wealth* but also his *poverty* acquire a human and hence *social* significance. Poverty is the passive bond which makes man experience his greatest wealth – the other man – as need.[28]

In the *Social Contract* Rousseau had sketched the outlines for the possible development of political life within the limits established by bourgeois social relations. Under these limitations political life appeared as the alienated communal life of society, while the substance of political life was found in the act of legislation in a formal and universal mode. The citizen of the *Social Contract* necessarily lived a division between the particularity of his will within the relations of civil society and the universality of will to which he could aspire in the State, in his capacity as a member of the Sovereign. State and Sovereign maintained their existence only through the mediation of the Prince. The supersession of the split between civil society and the state that Rousseau called democracy was seen as a limit situation. Although it did not seem 'possible to have a better constitution than that in which the executive and legislative powers are united,' this possibility was vitiated from the start, under the system of needs, because 'nothing is more dangerous than the influence of private interests in public affairs' (*SC* 54–5). In the *Social Contract*

---

27 See also *E* 167, 217.
28 Marx, *Economic and Philosophic Manuscripts*, in *Early Writings*, 356

the possibility of common ownership of productive resources was a subject that was dropped as quickly as it was broached. Rousseau knew that it was possible for men 'to unite one with another before they possess anything, and that, subsequently occupying a tract of country which is enough for all, they enjoy it in common' (*SC* 18). But that work was devoted to political life, given 'men as they are.'

In *Emile*, by contrast, men are presented as they might be. The essence of the social contract was the universality of will that had its germ in the system of needs itself. The general will was an organic development of the equality inherent in the relation of instrumental reciprocity. But for Emile the other is not an instrument to the satisfaction of a need, nor does he consider himself such an instrument. Still less is Emile directly a communal being, immediately identified with a reified status. None the less, Emile finds his individual existence fulfilled only within a community. He is 'dependent only on himself and on his like.' For Emile, however, communal existence does not have the divided character it does for the citizen of the *Social Contract*; the other is not at one and the same time an instrument to be mastered and an equal, a fellow citizen whose rights must be recognized in the act of legislation. The general will can now be founded upon the concrete recognition of the other within social relations themselves: 'Our most pleasant existence is relative and collective, and our true self is not entirely within us. In short, the constitution of man in this life, is such that one never succeeds in truly enjoying one's own self without the concourse of another.'[29] For Emile virtue is no longer obedience to duty imposed externally as law. Autonomy no longer means obedience to a superior force, entrusted with making the universal thrust of one's will a better bet in terms of self-preservation. For this was the key to the workings of 'the political machine' in the *Social Contract*.

Emile will not separate communal and individual, public and private life into antithetical spheres. Yet unlike the citizen of the polis, he has no need to set the *moi commun* above the man. Where the *Social Contract* was itself based on the private ownership of productive resources, resulting ultimately in communal life maintaining an ideal existence above the life of the particulars, the polity to which Emile seems to be destined

---

29 Quoted by Burgelin, *Existence*, 286-7. Cf 251, from 'Lettre à Sophie,' in *OCI* 136: 'Il est manifeste que je ne dois plus me regarder comme un être individuel et isolé, mais comme partie d'un grant tout, comme membre d'un plus grand corps, de la conservation duquel dépend absolumment la mienne, et qui ne sauroit être mal ordonné que je ne me resente de ce désordre.'

aims at the full communal control of economic life. This would in turn be a condition for the elimination of the system of needs and for a reduction in the division of labour. There are, between the time of the *Discourse on Political Economy* and that of the *Social Contract* and *Emile*, strong hints of a progression in Rousseau's thought away from the notion that, once it has been established, private property in productive resources remains a permanent necessity. In the second *Discourse*, although private property was seen as the root of evil, Rousseau was ambiguous as to whether once it had been established it could ever be abolished. In the *Discourse on Political Economy* the right of private property appeared as 'the most sacred of all the rights of citizenship' (*PE* 254) and was held to be the basis of political society: 'It should be remembered that the foundation of the social compact is property; and its first condition, that everyone should be maintained in the peaceful possession of what belongs to him' (*PE* 261). In the *Social Contract*, although the private right of ownership was subordinated to the will of the Sovereign and common ownership was held to be conformable with the notion of a general will, private property itself was only annulled 'politically.' Class distinctions were banished from the state. The equality of the state of nature returned as the formal equality of all citizens. Yet classes and economic inequality would in all likelihood persist.

In *Emile*, however, Rousseau makes it clear that private property in one's own person and goods is actually not the foundation of political community: 'If the sovereign power rests upon the right of ownership, there is no right more worthy of respect; it is inviolable and sacred for the sovereign power, so long as it remains a private, individual right; as soon as it is viewed as common to all the citizens, it is subject to the common will and this will may destroy it. Thus the sovereign has no right to touch the property of one or many: but he may lawfully take possession of the property of all' (*E* 425). Nor does Emile enter society as a proprietor of his own person or of productive resources. 'The man and the citizen, whoever he may be, has no property to invest in society but himself, all his other goods belong to society in spite of himself' (*E* 158). It is evident to a being such as Emile, who recognizes that 'every man owes all that he is' (*E* 158) to society, that the right of ownership is a communal one and not a private individual right. In such a community, where finally the private and the common good are not antithetical to one another, the democracy that appeared as a limit situation in the *Social Contract* becomes a real possibility. This possibility was also evoked by Rousseau in the *Social Contract*, but only 'as long as several men in assembly regard themselves as a single body:

A state so governed needs very few laws; and, as it becomes necessary to issue new ones, the necessity is universally seen. The first man to propose them merely says what all have already felt, and there is no question of factions or intrigues or eloquence in order to secure the passage into law of what everyone has already decided to do, as soon as he is sure that the rest will act with him.

Theorists are led into error because, seeing only States that have been from the beginning wrongly constituted, they are struck by the impossibility of applying such a policy to them. (SC 85)

We may then speculate that the lifting of excess denaturation would lead to a condition in which the general will would tend to merge with the will of all, and communal life would no longer take the form of an ideal existence manifesting itself in the form of laws. The law that Rousseau speaks of in the passage above has lost the onerous character of duty. It is once again much more like the law that governed the primitive community, where social life and politics are not separate and antithetical spheres.

In raising up Emile in his imagination, Rousseau has sought to indicate that a lifting of excess denaturation would make possible a society in which alienation could be overcome. In such a community men would no longer be subject to the blind mechanics of the laws of the market; scarcity, to the extent it existed, would be a force leading to the creation of a communal purpose rather than one enforcing inequality and toil; activity would once again, as was the case in primitive society, become self-expression, even in the necessary and unpleasant labour of society, which could be the occasion for the affirmation of community; and political life could concern itself with the articulation of common ends rather than with the subjugation of the *moi humain* to the *moi commun*, or of passion to virtue. In all these ways the community foreshadowed in *Emile* goes beyond even the austere democracy that was the ideal of the *Social Contract*.

But it is evident that in order for alienation to be overcome in fact, the conditions enforcing excess denaturation, civil society itself, must be transformed. As was the case with the Legislator, 'the effect would have to become the cause' (SC 34). The lifting of excess denaturation depends, in the individual, upon the avoidance of the instrumentalization of the self, which has been the primary demand of civilization. Necessary denaturation and the form of the social individual it is sufficient to sustain must remain a dream in the absence of prior political change. In the end, therefore, Rousseau is constrained to remain within the ambivalence that issues from the *Social Contract*. If the *Social Contract* defines the limits of foreseeable political change within the historically received social conditions, then, even though the ideal of social individuality proclaimed in the general will leads towards the type of community of individuals embodied metaphorically in *Emile*, this non-austere democracy must remain utopian. And *Emile* is utopian to a much greater extent than the *Contract*, in spite of its appearance as a practical manual of education. Yet if nature, or ontology, demands a transcendence of the limitations of the *Contract*, the dream of *Emile* cannot be relinquished. How might the two be joined? Rousseau does not say. And it would be a grave mistake to think that he would see in a Legislator an avenue out of this impasse. For one thing, such a figure has no place in the formation of an Emile.[30]

But might not this ambivalence redound to Rousseau's credit? To the extent that Rousseau is ignorant of history as an objective process unfolding of itself, he is immune to the temptation to hypostatize development and its laws. To the extent that the historical mediation of the real and the ideal is absent from his thought, he is true to the notion of history as praxis. To that extent the mediation of the real and the ideal cannot become automatic; it must be a function of the consciousness

---

30 The tutor's task is to 'keep the child dependent on things only.' This is because it is impossible and undesirable to identify the individual completely with the rule of custom. Human laws cannot have the unvarying content or force of the laws of nature; see *E* 49: 'If the laws of nations, like the laws of nature, could never be broken by any human power, dependence on men would become dependence on things; all the advantages of a state of nature would be combined with all the advantages of social life in the commonwealth.' The grammatical construction is contrary to fact because human laws cannot imitate nature in this way. The Legislator must aim precisely at this imitation of nature; in making human laws as much like the laws of nature as possible, the Legislator assumes the role of supreme ideologist. Unlike the tutor, the Legislator manipulates *amour-propre* to bring about the desired results. Consider in this respect the following passages from *GP* 7-8, describing the genius of Lycurgus and others: 'He fixed upon them a yoke of iron, the like of which no other people has ever borne; but he tied them to that yoke, made them, so to speak, one with it, by filling up every moment of their lives. He saw to it that the image of the fatherland was constantly before their eyes – in their laws, in their games, in their homes, in their mating, in their feasts. He saw to it that they never had an instant of free time that they could call their own. And out of this ceaseless constraint, made noble by the purpose it served, was born that burning love of country which was always the strongest – or rather the only – passion of the Spartans, and which transformed them into beings more than merely human ... All these legislators of ancient times based their legislation on the same ideas. All ... by constantly rekindling the spirit of emulation and the love of glory, raised Greek courage and Greek virtues to a level of strenuousness of which nothing existing today can give us even a remote idea – which, indeed, strikes modern men as beyond belief.' Cf R. Matthews and D. Ingersoll, 'The Therapist and the Lawgiver: Rousseau's political vision.'

of those who bear the historical process upon their backs. Thus Rousseau has the virtue of his faults, and this is the real problem he has left to posterity. He does not give us a Hegelian dialectic of master and slave, but neither are there immanent teleological processes, universal classes with imputed consciousness, laws governing the dialectic of the development of the productive forces and the relations of production, or providential unfoldings of divine reason. There are no guarantees. The perfectible animal is left entirely to his own devices and in their grip. But although in the end history and nature remain separated in fact, they do not remain essentially inseparable.

There is thus one more dimension of the existence of the hypothetical social individual that should be considered. In the history of the species so far, alienation and objectification have been inextricably fused. The question of the ultimate character of objectification, of the separation from nature itself, arises once again when the two conditions are seen as separable. In the second *Discourse* Rousseau looks upon human existence itself as a painful condition in which the self is divided and lost in otherness. Action and mediation, the very conditions of a human existence, seem to be at fault. Whatever added dimensions of alienation social inequality might introduce, the loss of immediacy, the descent into temporality seem to be final and irreversible sources of misery. In so far as labour and culture enforce the delay, deflection, and modification of desire, they seem to create the conditions of an existence given over to inner conflict.

For Emile, however, who symbolizes the possibility of overcoming the historical forms of alienation, objectification and action are not painful. The imposition *only* of necessary denaturation removes the causes of a great deal of inner conflict. In this situation desire, rather than being relegated to subterranean realms of fantasy, has access to the sphere of cultural activities. Not required to devote a large portion of his energy to defending against passions that would interfere with a culture dedicated to the domination of nature, Emile will experience his activity in the world as the fulfilment of desire. Activity as such is not, in the end, alienation. It is the human medium for the sense of existence that the animal experiences immediately: 'While we were weak and feeble the care of self-preservation concentrated our attention on ourselves; now that we are strong and powerful, the desire for a wider sphere carries us beyond ourselves, and hurls us as far as for us is possible' (*E* 130).[31] What characterizes Emile above all is his strength, but this strength is

31 Modified trans.; see also *EMF* 168.

in reality a relative absence of repression. Desire, for Emile, is not equivalent to a threat of annihilation, but the very source of self. And when desire is thus returned to the self, it is redirected outward, where it can find its realization precisely in externality: 'In every age, and especially in childhood, we want to create, to copy, to produce, to give all the signs of power and activity' (*E* 62). The imposition only of necessary denaturation thus is not only the condition for a reintegration of the self but of a rationally controlled union of self with other.

The very quality of existence itself tends towards transformation. Consider the following passage in which the sections inside Rousseau's brackets are his responses to the accusation of Christophe de Beaumont, archbishop of Paris, concerning *Emile*: 'In a treatise on the Inequality of mankind, he has reduced man to a level with the brutes (which of us elevates or debases him, in the alternative of being wicked or a brute?). In another production still more recent, he has insinuated all the poison of voluptuousness. (Oh! that I could but, indeed, substitute the real charms of voluptuousness for the false ones of debauchery!)' (*LCB* 352-3)[32] The lifting of excess denaturation is a return even beyond primitive human society to the voluptuousness that characterized man in his immediate unity with nature. Only this reunion with nature is not the fantastic striving for pure immediacy that Rousseau sees in himself and with which much of his autobiographical writing is concerned.[33] Nor is it purchased at the cost of rejecting reason and reflection, action and mediation. It is rather the human form of that happiness that Rousseau considers almost the birthright of man. The enemy of mankind is no longer time; Emile 'enjoys time without being its slave' (*EMF* 173). Similarly, the voluptuousness that would characterize civilization after the removal of excess denaturation is not a paradise without pain and death. Human life remains an inevitable encounter with contingency, a 'continual flux' where pure pleasure is an abstraction and annihilation is the inevitable end of each and all (*EMF* 83; *E* 185). For Emile, however, life itself is not governed by the fear of annihilation: 'Life is short, not so much because of the short time it lasts, but because we are allowed scarcely any time to enjoy it' (*E* 172). The pain of separation, of the alienation from nature, of necessary denaturation is in itself insufficient to instil such a fear. Thus for Emile the possibility of happiness is not affected by the human knowledge of death:

---

32 Modified translation
33 See, eg, Promenade 6 of the *Rêveries*, in *RW* 1050, 1059.

My master, you have made me free by teaching me to yield to necessity. Let her come when she will, I follow her without compulsion; I lay hold of nothing to keep me back ... If my hands fail me, I shall live if others will support me; if they forsake me I shall die; I shall die even if I am not forsaken, for death is not the penalty of poverty, it is a law of nature. Whensoever death comes I defy it; it shall never find me making preparations for life; it shall never prevent me having lived. (*E* 436)

Emile is fundamentally concerned with what nature permits the species to become. Through a lifting of excess denaturation, the possibililty emerges of overcoming both the social alienation and the pain of objectification that have characterized the species since its beginning. With *Emile*, what seemed like an equation between the perfectibility of mankind and a deepening of its misery and degradation is reversed. Emile represents the possibility of a reconciliation, in a higher synthesis, of self and other, history and nature, freedom and happiness, reason and passion. But it has become possible to envision this reconciliation only as a result of the depths of alienation into which the species had already descended. In earlier forms of society, social life was itself too embedded in second nature for the possibility to appear. Even the Enlightenment carried over this embeddedness into its idea of society, in its conception of a social science modelled on Newtonian natural science. In Rousseau for the first time a consciousness of the radical historicity of human nature and a sensibility attuned to if not fixated upon the experience of alienation are joined.

After Rousseau came others who conceived of history as a process of alienation and its overcoming. Yet the uniqueness of the Rousseauan vision and its fecundity ensure that his thought will for a long time escape being relegated to the status of a historical monument. Rousseau in some ways already anticipates Marx's critique of Hegel. For him history is not the unfolding of mind, in which alienation is overcome in the absolute knowledge attainable in the final analysis by the philosopher. It is rooted, rather, in the social praxis of sensuous, suffering beings. Consciousness is simply the consciousness of finite historical beings (or, if there is one, of a God who stands completely outside the historical drama). Alienation and objectification are not conflated, even though the historical process so far has fused them in practice. Yet, although for Rousseau the overcoming of alienation is predicated upon a change in economic systems and social and political institutions, he cannot conceive, like Marx, of a revolutionary consciousness developing within a virtually autonomous economic process. In 1761-62, when *La Nouvelle Héloïse*, the *Social Contract*, and *Emile* appeared almost simultaneously, the development of an industrial proletariat was only beginning; had Rousseau even looked for one, he could not have seen a class that felt the universal state of alienation as its own particular condition. Although he realized, as would Marx, that a 'radical revolution can only be the revolution of radical needs,' Rousseau could not but expect that 'the preconditions and seedbeds for such needs appear to be lacking.'[34] Emile represented the hope of a new golden age that would be better than the first because it would incorporate all the achievements of human reason. But the revolution that might inaugurate this change lacked a passive element: 'Men say the golden age is a fable; it always will be for those whose tastes and feelings are depraved. People do not really regret the golden age, for they do nothing to restore it. What is needed for its restoration? One thing only, and that is an impossibility; we must love the golden age' (*E* 438). Yet this absence of a passive element, of a universal class, in some ways brings Rousseau even closer than Marx to our own time.

If there is one thinker who has resurrected the Rousseauan project it is Marcuse. In *Eros and Civilization* the utopian project of the lifting of excessive denaturation is conceived of once again, as the abolition of surplus repression and as a concrete possibility. Yet this project is not the exclusive burden of a particular class. Where Marcuse does see the possibility of a rupture in the order of domination is in the reassertion of its rights of the non-rational – in imagination, myth, fantasy. When Rousseau says that it is an impossibility to love the golden age, we must suspect him of falsehood, for his whole art was directed at making it possible for men to love the golden age. Those who have condemned Rousseau for the socially and psychically regressive qualities in his work have never been able to see that the regression that led in his personal life to neurosis and to the denial of time, history, and society was still and always under the control of reason, that it was always, in his theoretical works, a regression in the service of the ego and of civilization. They have never been able to see that his condemnation of the rationality of domination and his defence of instinct were in reality the highest praise possible of reason itself. For reason in Rousseau's eyes is not, in the final analysis, equated with repression and domination. What Marcuse reserves as the highest praise for Freud could also be said of Rousseau:

---

34 Marx, introduction to *A Contribution to the Critique of Hegel's Philosophy of Right*, in *Early Writings*, 252

'His work is characterized by an uncompromising insistence on showing up the repressive content of the highest values and achievements of culture. In so far as he does this he denies the equation of reason with repression on which the ideology of culture is built.'[35]

---

[35] Marcuse, *Eros and Civilization*, 17

BIBLIOGRAPHY

Althusser, Louis. *Politics and History: Montesquieu, Rousseau, Hegel and Marx*. London: New Left Books 1977
Arendt, Hannah. *The Human Condition*. Chicago: University of Chicago Press 1958
Aristotle. *The Politics*. Ed. Ernest Barker. London: Oxford University Press 1973
Avineri, Shlomo. *Hegel's Theory of the Modern State*. London: Cambridge University Press 1972
Baczko, Bronislaw. 'Rousseau and Social Marginality.' *Daedalus* (Summer 1978): 27-40
Barber, Benjamin R. 'Rousseau and the Paradoxes of the Dramatic Imagination.' *Daedalus* (Summer 1978): 79-92
Barker, Sir Ernest. *The Political Thought of Plato and Aristotle*. New York: Dover Publications 1959
Becker, Carl L. *The Heavenly City of the Eighteenth-Century Philosophers*. New Haven: Yale University Press 1969
Berman, Marshall. *The Politics of Authenticity*. New York: Athenaeum 1970
Bloom, Allan. 'Jean-Jacques Rousseau.' In *History of Political Philosophy*, eds. L. Strauss and J. Cropsey. Chicago: Rand McNally 1963, 514-48
- 'The Education of Democratic Man: Emile.' *Daedalus* (Summer 1978): 135-153
Bowler, Peter J. 'Evolutionism in the Enlightenment.' *History of Science* 12 (1974): 159-83
- *Evolution: The History of an Idea*. Berkeley: University of California Press 1984
Brown, Norman O. *Life Against Death: The Psychoanalytic Meaning of History*. New York: Vintage Books 1959

Burgelin, Pierre. *La Philosophie de l'existence de Jean-Jacques Rousseau*. Paris: Presses Universitaires de France 1952
- 'Kant lecteur de Rousseau.' In *Jean-Jacques Rousseau et son oeuvre*, Comité pour la commémoration de Jean-Jacques Rousseau. Paris: Klencksieck 1964, 303–15
Burke, Edmund. *Reflections on the Revolution in France*. Harmondsworth: Penguin Books 1973
Burnyeat, M.F. 'Sphinx without a Secret.' *New York Review of Books* 32, no 9, (May 1985): 30–6
Cameron, David. *The Social Thought of Rousseau and Burke*. London: Weidenfeld and Nicolson 1973
Cassirer, Ernst. *The Philosophy of the Enlightenment*. Trans. F.C.A. Koelln and J.P. Pettegrove. Boston: Beacon Press 1955
- *The Question of Jean-Jacques Rousseau*. Bloomington: Indiana University Press 1967
Cell, Howard. 'Breaking Rousseau's Chains.' In *Trent Rousseau Papers*, ed. J. MacAdam, M. Neumann, and G. LaFrance. Ottawa: University of Ottawa Press 1980, 161–71
Chapman, J. 'Rousseau.' In *Critical Bibliography of French Literature* vol. 4 *Supplement*, ed. R.A. Brooks. Syracuse: Syracuse University Press 1968, 142–64
Cobban, Alfred. *Rousseau and the Modern State*. Rev. edn. London: George Allen & Unwin 1964
Cole, G.D.H. Introduction to *The Social Contract and Discourses*. New York: Dutton 1968, v–xv
Colletti, Lucio. *From Rousseau to Lenin: Studies in Ideology and Society*. New York: Monthly Review Press 1972
- Introduction to *Karl Marx: Early Writings*, ed. Quintin Hoare. New York: Vintage Books 1975, 9–56
Collingwood, R.G. *The Idea of Nature*. London: Oxford University Press 1972
Crocker, Lester G. *Rousseau's Social Contract: An Interpretive Essay*. Cleveland: Press of Case Western Reserve University 1968
della Volpe, Galvano. *Rousseau and Marx*. Trans. John Fraser. London: Lawrence and Wishart 1978
Derathé, Robert. *Le Rationalisme de Jean-Jacques Rousseau*. Paris: Presses Universitaires de France 1948
- *Jean-Jacques Rousseau et la science politique de son temps*. Paris: Presses Universitaires de France 1950
Diamond, Stanley. *In Search of the Primitive*. New Brunswick: Transaction Books 1974

Dottrens, Robert. 'Jean-Jacques Rousseau éducateur.' In *Jean-Jacques Rousseau.* Neuchâtel: Editions de la baconnière 1962, 101-26

Ehrard, Jean. *L'Idée de la nature en France dans la première moitié du xviiie siècle.* 2 vols. Paris: SEVPEN 1963

Ellenburg, Stephen. *Rousseau's Politicial Philosophy: An Interpretation from Within.* Ithaca: Cornell University Press 1976

Engels, F. *Herr Eugen Duhring's Revolution in Science.* New York: International Publishers 1939

Featherstone, Joseph. 'Rousseau and Modernity.' *Daedalus* (Summer 1978): 167-92

Fenichel, Otto. *The Psychoanalytic Theory of Neurosis.* New York: Norton 1945

Fetscher, I. *Rousseau's Politische Philosophie.* Neuwied: H. Luchterhand 1960

Findlay, J.N. *Hegel: A Re-examination.* New York: Oxford University Press 1958

Freeman, Michael. *Burke and the Critique of Political Radicalism.* Oxford: Basil Blackwell 1980

Freud, Sigmund. *Civilization and Its Discontents.* Trans. J. Strachey. New York: Norton 1962

- 'Civilized Sexual Morality and Modern Nervousness.' In *Sexuality and the Psychology of Love*, ed. P. Rieff. New York: Collier Books 1974, 20-40
- 'Contributions to the Psychology of Love.' In *Sexuality and the Psychology of Love*, ed. Rieff. 49-86
- *The Ego and the Id.* Trans. J. Riviere. New York: Norton 1962
- 'Five Lectures on Psychoanalysis.' In *Two Short Accounts of Psychoanalysis*, trans. J. Strachey. Harmondsworth: Penguin Books 1962, 31-87
- 'Formulations Regarding the Two Principles in Mental Functioning.' In *General Psychological Theory*, ed. P. Rieff. New York: Collier Books 1974, 21-8
- *A General Introduction to Psychoanalysis.* Trans. J. Riviere. New York: Pocket Books 1975
- 'Instincts and Their Vicissitudes.' In *General Psychological Theory*, ed. Rieff. 83-103
- *The Interpretation of Dreams.* Trans. J. Strachey. New York: Avon Books 1972
- *New Introductory Lectures on Psychoanalysis.* Trans. J. Strachey. Harmondsworth: Penguin Books 1973
- *An Outline of Psychoanalysis.* Trans. J. Strachey. New York: Norton 1969
- 'The Passing of the Oedipus Complex.' In *General Psychological Theory*, ed. Rieff. 176-182
- *The Problem of Anxiety.* Trans. H.A. Bunker. New York: Norton 1963
- *Three Essays on the Theory of Sexuality.* Trans. J. Strachey. New York: Avon Books 1962
- 'The Unconscious.' In *General Psychological Theory*, ed. Rieff. 116-50

Gauthier, David. 'The Politics of Redemption.' In *Trent Rousseau Papers*, ed. J. MacAdam, M. Neumann, and G. LaFrance. Ottawa: University of Ottawa Press 1980, 71-98

Gay, Peter. *The Rise of Modern Paganism*. Vol. 1 of *The Enlightenment: An Interpretation*. New York: Norton 1966

- Introduction to Ernst Cassirer, *The Question of Jean-Jacques Rousseau*. Bloomington: Indiana University Press 1976, 3-32

- *The Science of Freedom*. Vol. 2 of *The Enlightenment: An Interpretation*. New York: Norton 1969

Gayard-Fabre, Simone. 'J.-J. Rousseau ou les prémisses d'une révolution.' In *Trent Rousseau Papers*, ed. J. MacAdam, M. Neumann, and G. LaFrance. Ottawa: University of Ottawa Press 1980, 11-22

Gilden, H. *Rousseau's Social Contract: The Design of the Argument*. Chicago: University of Chicago Press 1983

Glas, B., O. Temkin, and W.L. Straus, Jr, eds. *Forerunners of Darwin: 1745-1859*. Baltimore: Johns Hopkins Press 1968

Goldschmidt, Victor. *Anthropologie et politique*. Paris: Librairie Philosophique J. Urin 1974

Gossman, Lionel. 'Time and History in Rousseau.' *Studies on Voltaire and the Eighteenth Century* 30 (1964): 311-49

- 'The Innocent Art of Confession and Revery.' *Daedalus* (Summer 1978): 59-77

Gouhier, Henri. 'Ce que le Vicaire doit à Descartes.' *Annales Jean-Jacques Rousseau* 35 (1959-62): 139-54

Gould, Carol C. *Marx's Social Ontology: Individuality and Community in Marx's Theory of Social Reality*. Cambridge: MIT Press 1978

Greene, John C. *The Death of Adam: Evolution and its Impact on Western Thought*. Ames: Iowa State University Press 1959

Grene, Marjorie. *Approaches to a Philosophical Biology*. New York: Basic Books 1968

Grimsley, Ronald. 'Rousseau and the Problem of Happiness.' In *Hobbes and Rousseau: A Collection of Critical Essays*, ed. M. Cranston and R. Peters. Garden City: Anchor Books 1972, 437-61

- *The Philosophy of Rousseau*. London: Oxford University Press 1973

Hampson, Norman. *The Enlightenment*. Harmondsworth: Penguin Books 1968

Hartmann, Heinz, and Rudolph M. Loewenstein. 'Notes on the Superego.' In H. Hartmann, E. Kris, and R.M. Loewenstein, *Papers on Psychoanalytic Psychology*. New York: International Universities Press 1977, 144-81

Hegel, G.W.F. *Phenomenology of Spirit*. Trans. A.V. Miller. Oxford: Clarendon Press 1977

- *Philosophy of History*. Trans. J. Sibree. New York: Dover Publications 1956

- *Philosophy of Right.* Trans. T.M. Knox. London: Oxford University Press 1967
Heller, Agnes, *The Theory of Need in Marx.* London: Allison and Busby 1974
Hobbes, Thomas. *Leviathan.* Ed. C.B. Macpherson. Harmondsworth: Penguin Books 1968
Horkheimer, Max. *Critical Theory: Selected Essays.* New York: Seabury Press 1972
- *Eclipse of Reason.* New York: Seabury Press 1974
Horkheimer, Max, and T.W. Adorno. *Dialectic of Enlightenment.* New York: Seabury Press 1972
Horowitz, Gad. *Repression: Basic and Surplus Repression in Psychoanalytic Theory: Freud, Reich, Marcuse.* Toronto: University of Toronto Press 1977
Hume, David. *A Treatise of Human Nature.* Ed. L.A. Selby-Biggs. Oxford: Oxford University Press 1978
Hyppolite, Jean. *Studies on Marx and Hegel.* Trans. J. O'Neill. New York: Harper Torchbooks 1969
Jacoby, Russell. *Social Amnesia: A Critique of Contemporary Psychology from Adler to Laing.* Boston: Beacon Press 1975
Jameson, Frederic. *Marxism and Form: Twentieth-Century Dialectical Theories of Literature.* Princeton: Princeton University Press 1971
Kant, Immanuel. *On History.* Ed. L.W. Beck. New York: Bobbs-Merrill 1963
Kaplan, David, and Robert A. Manners. *Culture Theory.* Englewood Cliffs: Prentice-Hall 1972
Kauffman, Walter. *Hegel: A Re-Interpretation.* Garden City: Anchor Books 1966
Kelly, G.A. 'Rousseau, Kant and History.' *Journal of the History of Ideas* 28 (1968): 347-64
Keohane, N.O. '"The Masterpiece of Policy in Our Century": Rousseau on the Morality of the Enlightenment.' *Political Theory* 6 (1978): 457-83
- 'Rousseau on Life, Liberty and Property: A Comment on MacAdam.' In *Theories of Property: Aristotle to the Present*, ed. A. Parel and T. Flanagan. Waterloo: Wilfred Laurier University Press 1979, 203-17
Kessen, William. 'Rousseau's Children.' *Daedalus* (Summer 1978): 155-66
Kettler, David. 'Herbert Marcuse: The Critique of Bourgeois Civilization and Its Transcendence.' In *Contemporary Political Philosophers*, ed. A. de Crespigny and K. Minogue. London: Methuen 1975, 1-48
Kojève, Alexandre. *Introduction to the Reading of Hegel.* Trans. J.H. Nichols, Jr. New York: Basic Books 1969
Kontos, Alkis. 'Domination: Metaphor and Political Reality.' In *Domination*, ed. A. Kontos. Toronto: University of Toronto Press 1965, 211-28
LaBarre, Weston. *The Human Animal.* Chicago: University of Chicago Press 1954

Lapassade, G. 'Sartre et Rousseau.' *Études Philosophiques* 17, no 4 (Winter 1962): 511-17
Laski, Harold J. *The Rise of European Liberalism: An Essay in Interpretation.* London: Unwin Books 1962
Layton, L. 'Rousseau's Political and Cultural Revolution.' In *Trent Rousseau Papers*, ed. J. MacAdam, M. Neumann, and G. LaFrance. Ottawa: University of Ottawa Press 1980, 199-210
Lee, Dorothy. *Freedom and Culture.* Englewood Cliffs: Prentice-Hall 1959
Lemos, R.M. *Rousseau's Political Philosophy: An Exposition and Interpretation.* Athens: University of Georgia Press 1977
Levine, Andrew. *The Politics of Autonomy: A Kantian Reading of Rousseau's Social Contract.* Amherst: University of Massachussetts Press 1976
Lévi-Strauss, Claude. 'Jean-Jacques Rousseau, fondateur des sciences de l'homme.' In *Jean-Jacques Rousseau.* Neuchâtel: Editions de la Baconnière 1962, 239-48
Locke, John. *An Essay Concerning Human Understanding.* Ed. A.D. Woozley. New York: New American Library 1964
- *Two Treatises of Government.* Ed. Peter Laslett. New York: New American Library 1963
Lovejoy, Arthur O. 'The Supposed Primitivism of Rousseau's *Discourse on Inequality.*' In *Essays in the History of Ideas.* New York: Capricorn Books 1960, 14-37
- *The Great Chain of Being: A Study of the History of an Idea.* Cambridge: Harvard University Press 1964
Löwith, Karl. *Meaning in History.* Chicago: University of Chicago Press 1949
- *From Hegel to Nietzsche.* Garden City: Anchor Books 1967
Lukács, Georg. *History and Class Consciousness: Studies in Marxist Dialectic.* Trans. Rodney Livingston. Cambridge: MIT Press 1968
MacAdam, J. 'Rousseau: The Moral Dimensions of Property.' In *Theories of Property: Aristotle to the Present*, ed. A. Parel and T. Flanagan. Waterloo: Wilfred Laurier University Press 1979, 181-201
McDowell, Judith H. Introduction to *La Nouvelle Heloise.* University Park: Pennsylvania State University Press 1968, 2-16
McManners, J. 'The Social Contract and Rousseau's Revolt against Society.' In *Hobbes and Rousseau: A Collection of Critical Essays*, ed. M. Cranston and J.S. Peters. Garden City: Anchor Books 1972, 291-317
Macpherson, C.B. *The Political Theory of Possessive Individualism: Hobbes to Locke.* London: Oxford University Press 1962
- *Democratic Theory: Essays in Retrieval.* Oxford: Clarendon Press 1973
- 'Human Rights as Property Rights.' *Dissent* (Winter 1977): 72-7

- *The Life and Times of Liberal Democracy.* Oxford: Oxford University Press 1977
- 'Liberal Democracy and Property.' In *Property: Mainstream and Critical Positions,* ed. C.B. Macpherson. Toronto: University of Toronto Press 1978, 199-207
- 'Property as Means or End.' In *Theories of Property: Aristotle to the Present,* ed. A. Parel and T. Flanagan. Waterloo: Wilfred Laurier University Press 1979, 3-9

Manuel, Frank E. *Shapes of Philosophical History.* Stanford: Stanford University Press 1965

Marcuse, Herbert. *Reason and Revolution: Hegel and the Rise of Social Theory.* Boston: Beacon Press 1960
- *One-Dimensional Man.* Boston: Beacon Press 1964
- *Eros and Civilization: A Philosophical Inquiry into Freud.* Boston: Beacon Press 1966
- *Negations: Essays in Critical Theory.* Boston: Beacon Press 1968
- *An Essay on Liberation.* Boston: Beacon Press 1969
- *Five Lectures.* Boston: Beacon Press 1970
- *Counter-Revolution and Revolt.* Boston: Beacon Press 1972
- *Studies in Critical Philosophy.* Boston: Beacon Press 1973
- *The Aesthetic Dimension: Toward a Critique of Marxist Aesthetics.* Boston: Beacon Press 1978

Marshall, T.E. 'Rousseau and Enlightenment.' *Political Theory* 6 (1978): 421-55

Martin, Kingsley. *French Liberal Thought in the Eighteenth Century.* New York: Harper Torchbooks 1963

Marx, Karl. *Early Writings.* Ed. Quintin Hoare. New York: Vintage Books 1975
- *Grundrisse: Foundations of the Critique of Political Economy.* Trans. Martin Nicolaus. New York: Vintage Books 1973

Marx, Karl, and Friedrich Engels. *The Marx-Engels Reader.* Ed. Robert C. Tucker. New York: Norton 1972

Masters, Roger D. *The Political Philosophy of Rousseau.* Princeton: Princeton University Press 1968
- 'The Structure of Rousseau's Political Thought ' In *Hobbes and Rousseau: A Collection of Critical Essays,* ed. M. Cranston and J.S. Peters. Garden City: Anchor Books 1972, 401-36
- 'Jean-Jacques is Alive and Well: Rousseau and Contemporary Sociobiology.' *Daedalus* (Summer 1978): 93-105
- 'Nothing Fails like Success: Development and History in Rousseau's Political Teaching.' In *Trent Rousseau Papers,* ed. J. MacAdam, N. Neumann, and G. LaFrance. Ottawa: University of Ottawa Press 1980, 421-55

Matthews, R.J. *The Radical Politics of Thomas Jefferson*. Lawrence: University Press of Kansas 1984

Matthews, R.J., and D. Ingersoll. 'The Therapist and the Lawgiver: Rousseau's Political Vision.' *Canadian Journal of Political and Social Theory* 4, no 3 (1930): 83-99

Melzer, Arthur M. 'Rousseau and the Problem of Bourgeois Society.' *American Political Science Review* 74, no 4 (Dec. 1980): 1019-33

Mercken-Spaas, Godelieve. 'The Social Anthropology of Rousseau's *Emile*.' *Studies on Voltaire and the Eighteenth Century* 132 (1975): 137-81

Midgley, Mary. *Beast and Man: The Roots of Human Nature*. Ithaca: Cornell University Press 1978

Montagu, M.F. Ashley, ed. *Culture: Man's Adaptive Dimension*. London: Oxford University Press 1968

Montesquieu. *The Persian Letters*. Trans. C.J. Betts. Harmondsworth: Penguin Books 1973

- *The Spirit of the Laws*. Trans. Thomas Nugent. New York: Hafner Press 1975

Moran, J.H. Afterword to *On the Origin of Languages*, ed. J.H. Moran and A. Gode. New York: Frederick Ungar 1966, 75-83

Muntéano, B. 'Les Contradictions de Jean-Jacques Rousseau.' In *Jean-Jacques Rousseau et son oeuvre*, Comité pour la commémoration de Jean-Jacques Rousseau. Paris: Klencksieck 1964, 95-111

Pateman, Carole. *Participation and Democratic Theory*. Cambridge: Cambridge University Press 1970

Peled, Yoav. 'Rousseau's Inhibited Radicalism: An Analysis of His Political Thought in Light of His Economic Ideas.' *American Political Science Review* 74, no 4 (Dec. 1980): 1034-45

Plattner, Marc F. *Rousseau's State of Nature: An Interpretation of the Discourse on the Origins of Inequality*. DeKalb: Northern Illinois University Press 1979

'Political Thought and Political Action: A Symposium on Quentin Skinner.' *Political Theory* 2 (1974): 251-303

Poulet, Georges. *Studies in Human Time*. Trans. Elliot Coleman. New York: Harper Torchbooks 1959

Radin, Paul. *The World of Primitive Man*. New York: E.P. Dutton 1971

Reich, Annie. 'Pathological Forms of Self-Esteem Regulation.' *The Psychoanalytic Study of the Child* 15 (1960): 215-32

Rycroft, Charles. *A Critical Dictionary of Psychoanalysis*. Harmondsworth: Penguin Books 1968

Ryklin, M. 'Rousseau, Rousseauism and the Fundamental Concepts of Structural Anthropology.' *International Social Science Journal* 30, no 3: 605-17

Sahlins, Marshall D. *Tribesmen*. Englewood Cliffs: Prentice-Hall 1968

Schmidt, Alfred. *The Concept of Nature in Marx*. Trans. Ben Fowkes. London: New Left Books 1971
Schwartz, Benjamin I. 'The Rousseau Strain in the Contemporary World.' *Daedalus* (Summer 1978): 193-206
Shklar, Judith. *Men and Citizens: A Study of Rousseau's Social Theory*. Cambridge: Cambridge University Press 1969
- 'Jean-Jacques Rousseau and Equality.' *Daedalus* (Summer 1978): 13-25
Skinner, Q. 'Meaning and Understanding in the History of Ideas.' *History and Theory* 8 (1969): 3-53
- 'Motives, Intentions and the Interpretation of Texts.' *New Literary History* 3 (1972): 393-408
Spuhler, J.N., ed. *The Evolution of Man's Capacity for Culture*. Detroit: Wayne State University Press 1965
Starobinski, Jean. *Jean-Jacques Rousseau: La transparence et l'obstacle*. Paris: Presses Universitaires de France 1957
- 'Jean-Jacques Rousseau et les pouvoirs de l'imaginaire.' *Revue Internationale de Philosophie* 14, no 51 (1960): 43-67
- 'Rousseau et Buffon.' In *Jean-Jacques Rousseau et son oeuvre*, Comité national pour la commémoration de Jean-Jacques Rousseau. Paris: Klencksieck 1964, 135-47
- 'The Accuser and the Accused.' *Daedalus* (Summer 1978): 41-58
Strauss, Leo. *Natural Right and History*. Chicago: University of Chicago Press 1953
Talmon, J.L. *The Origins of Totalitarian Democracy*. London: Sphere Books 1970
Toulmin, Stephen, and June Goodfield. *The Discovery of Time*. Harmondsworth: Penguin Books 1967
Vaughan, C.E. Introduction to *The Political Writings of Jean-Jacques Rousseau*, ed. C.E. Vaughan. Cambridge University Press 1915, 1-117
Wokler, Robert. 'Perfectible Apes in Decadent Cultures: Rousseau's Anthropology Revised.' *Daedalus* (Summer 1978): 107-34
Wright, E.H. *The Meaning of Rousseau*. London: Oxford University Press 1929

Index

Adorno, Theodor W. 50, 135
Alembert, Jean Le Rond d' 40
alienation: and civil society 112, 119-28; as consequence of history 30; and inauthenticity 25-6; and objectification 209-10, 249-51; political 24, 167-8, 183, 188-93, 210-11; in relation to repression 32, 128; and 'self-contradiction' 219-20; of sovereignty 171-3, 184; transcendence of 206-16, 241-8; universal 190-1; *see also* Denaturing, History, Repression
Althusser, Louis 9n, 22, 190-1
ambivalence 229-40; *see also* Conflict, inner
amour-de-soi: and *amour-propre* 93, 128, 227-8; as basis of compassion 236-8; and conscience 143; and proto-human drive structure 68; *see also* Eros
amour-propre: absence of in savage man 72; in bourgeois society 110-11, 125-7; and conscience 142-3, 157; and domination 230; and excess denaturation 236; not an essence 121; and history 128, 209, 220; as mediator between biology and culture 132; and money 94; and primitive society 93-5, 99, 224; and the self 213; and virtue 104-5, 238; *see also* Competition
anachronism 9n, 10
anamnesis 154-5
Arendt, Hannah 88n, 106n
Aristotle 13, 106, 123
arrested development 220-2; *see also* Conflict, inner; Repression
artifice: in civilization 21, 216-18; and convention 171; not identified with nature 51, 117, 128; and legislation 103-5, 210-11, *see also* History, Nature
associations 22n, 200, 202
authenticity 25-8, 88
autonomy: and conscience 143-5; and drives 70, 238-40; as essence of morality 43; and renunciation of will 172-3; *see also* Negativity
Avineri, Shlomo 108n

Baczko, Bronislaw 189
Barber, Benjamin 6n
Barker, Sir Ernest 13
Beaumont, Archbishop Christophe de 250
Bentham, Jeremy 101
Berman, Marshall 26-7
biologism 82-5
Bloom, Allan 19-20, 226n, 237n
Bonald, Viscount Louis de 18
Bonnet, Charles 57
bourgeois society: see Civil society
Bowler, Peter J. 55-6
Buffon, Georges-Louis Leclerc, comte de: his deism & evolutionary theory 56; and dynamic view of nature 53; his hypothesis of unitary evolution 54; and question of transformism 58-9; Rousseau's use of his theory of speciation 66-7; his theory of the solar system 41; Starobinski's comparison of him with Rousseau 62
Burgelin, Pierre 9, 11n, 24, 146
Burke, Edmund 9, 10n, 18

Cameron, David: 7; on Rousseau's ambiguity 11n, 15n; on Rousseau and historicity 28n, 87n; on Rousseau as transition to idealism 8n
Cassirer, Ernst: 16; on discontinuity in Rousseau's writings 191n; on humanity as moral perfectibility 28n; his interpretative method 9; on Rousseau's ethics 140-1; on Rousseau's failure 27
citizenship: in civil society 24, 120, 174, 187-9, 193-5; and 'inner conflict' 218-20; and the polis 104-7; in the polis compared with civil society 168-71; primitive society and problem of 91-2; Rousseau

compared with Aristotle on 13; see also Civil society, Community
civil religion 15, 24, 44
civil society: and alienation 119-28, 133, 189-93; and *amour-propre* 124-7; and class division 113-14; contrasted with primitive society 92; definitions of 108-9; and equality 183-5; and law 119; as market society 26; in the moral sciences 101; and money 113-15, 121-3; and the state 115-19, 183-5, 193-5, 198-200; see also Nature, state of
civilization: problem of 4, 21, 135-9, 206-25 *passim*; problem of and historicity 32, 128-34; Rousseau's apparent refusal of 27-8
class division 113-14, 116, 119, 200-1; see also Civil society, Competition
Cobban, Alfred 14
Colletti, Lucio: comparing Rousseau to Marx 21; on Rousseau as ahistorical pessimist 45n; on Rousseau as critic of civil society 23-4, 108n, 111; on Rousseau's philosophy of history 28n; on Rousseau as theorist of alienation 191
Collingwood, R.G. 36n
community: in civil society 119; in *Emile* 245-7; and the general will 167, 186; and the polis 104-7, 169; and primitive society 94-5; and the social contract 184-5; and the state 189-92; and universality in Kantian interpretation 44
compassion: see *Pitié*
competition: and primitive society 93-6; and civil society 110-16, 119, 177-83; see also Division of labour, Needs, Property
Condillac, Etienne Bonot de: and chal-

lenge of empiricism to natural law 47; compared with Rousseau 83-5; on the family 77; and sceptical implications of his epistemology 41-2, 136; use of resolutive-compositive method 51
conflict, inner: distinguished from 'self-contradictions' 219-20, 224-5; and excess denaturing 218-25; in *La Nouvelle Héloïse* 147-56, 158-62; see also Alienation, Denaturing, Repression
conscience: and civilization 137, 139-46; development of 227-30; and free agency 71; and historicity in the Kantian interpretation 63; and the super-ego 162; as the voice of nature 42-3; see also Duty
Constant, Benjamin 13
contractarianism 11n
contract theory: and civil society 118-19; and democracy 173; and popular sovereignty 174-6, 185; Rousseau's use of 11n, 33-4, 97, 183-4
Crocker, Lester G. 13-14

Darwin, Charles 33, 53-4, 74
deism 39-40, 55-6, 62, 73n
democracy: as limiting concept 203-6; and civil society 195; and contract theory 173; in *Emile* 240-8; as utopian concept 248; see also General will
denaturing: necessary and excessive 213-15, 218-40 *passim*, 250-1; and virtue 146-65 *passim*
Derathé, Robert: as critic of Cassirer 17; on Rousseau and Cartesianism 86n; on Rousseau as natural-law theorist 8n, 171n; on Rousseau's two moralities 140

Descartes, René: contrasted with Rousseau 44, 63-4; Derathé's comparison of with Rousseau 86n; and problem of correspondence 38; and Rousseau's overthrow of the Cogito 65-6n; Rousseau's premises compared to 18; Starobinski's comparison of with Rousseau 62-3
dialectical regression 5n, 131, 241, 252
dialectical theory 5, 89-90
Diamond, Stanley 95n
Diderot, Denis 41n, 53, 55
Dilthey, Wilhelm 9
division of labour: and needs 109-10; in primitive society 96-7; reduction in 242-3; see also Competition
drives: their displaceability as consequence of labour 84; and human nature 51-2, 68-70, 78-9, 212-13; and human sexuality 78; see also *Amour-de-soi*, Eros, Passions, Sexuality
dualism 16, 60, 63-6
duty: and conflict with interest in civil society 120-1; and tension with happiness 44, 105-7; see also Conscience, Happiness

education: of the Legislator versus the Tutor 248n; negative 222-5, 236; in the polis 104-5; see also Denaturing
ego development 226-35
egoism: see *Amour-propre*
Ehrard, Jean 36-7n
Ellenburg, Stephen 28n
Engels, Friedrich 5, 21
equality: in civil society 114-15, 183-4, 200-1; as foundation for law 181-2, 185; and ideology, 117-19; illegitimacy of moral or conventional 50; and property 196-7, 200-2

eros 6n, 106-7, 157, 162; see also *Amour-de-soi*, Drives, Passions
essence, human: not ahistorical 71; definition of as freedom 19; as negativity 31; and social labour 33-4; see also Historicity, Nature
essentialism 5n, 47-8
evolution: in eighteenth century 53-62; question of in Rousseau 54-5, 62-7, 72, 74-5; see also Transformism

family: and the polis 104, 106-7; and political authority 170; and primitive society 97-8; Rousseau's theory of 77-8
Fenichel, Otto 159n
Fourier, Charles 242
free agency: and ontological dualism 64-6, 75; and development of from pre-human to human 70-5; see also Negativity
freedom: in civil society 126-7, 170-1, 199; flight from 27; and history 129-34; and *l'homme sauvage* 67, 70; as negativity 72, 92-3; in the polis 102-3, 107, 169-70
Freeman, Michael 10n
Freud, Sigmund: his concept of civilization compared to Rousseau's 6, 6n, 162-5; as critic of rationalism 33; on neoteny and neurosis 77n; in relation to Rousseau 4, 4n, 158; on the super-ego 160-1

Gauthier, David 15n
Gay, Peter 7, 8n, 37n
general will: and civil society 185-6, 194-5; and community 187; development in Rousseau's idea of 187; differing interpretations of 204; in *Emile* 245, 247; in the Kantian interpretation 43-4; and popular sovereignty 175, 182; and the 'will of all' 202; see also Civil society, Equality, Reciprocity
German idealism 13, 15, 82
Gierke, Otto von 23
Goldschmidt, Victor 19n, 61n, 81n
Gossman, Lionel 28-30, 45n
Gouhier, Henri 65n
Gould, Carol C. 23n
Greene, John C. 54
Grene, Marjorie 71n
Grimsley, Ronald 16n
Grotius, Hugo 170, 171, 172, 173

Hampson, Norman 41n, 54
happiness: as dynamic equilibrium 232-3; and *l'homme sauvage* 67, 93, 131-2; in the Kantian interpretation 210; and virtue 16, 144-6, 239-40
Hegel, G.W.F.: on alienation 25; on civil society 108, 110; on the 'cult of beautiful souls' 146-7; on needs and *l'homme sauvage* 92-3; on the polis 169n; on the 'revenge of the family' 106-7; on the *Social Contract* 198-200; as successor to Rousseau 5, 13; on the 'finite-teleological viewpoint' 72-3
Heller, Agnes 23n
Helvétius, Claude-Adrien 42, 101
historical anthropology 33, 49, 80-7
historical materialism 18, 206
historical method 29
historicity: absence of in Kantian interpretation 17; and evolution 31; and forms of virtue 100-1; and free agency 65-6, 70-3; and human nature 168, 191; importance to Rousseau 28-35; of moralities 98-9,

120-1; of the passions 79; of the self 124; and the state of nature 177-83; *see also* Essence, human; Nature, human

history: as alienation 30, 190-1, 213-16, 249; as collapse of nature and artifice 51-2, 81; and conscience 141-6; as degradation 23, 88; in deist outlook 39; and evolutionary theory 29, 61, 72-84; as mediation versus innocence 25; and necessity 80; as praxis 81-2, 99-100, 251; as process 117, 128; and repression 130-4, 217-24; Rousseau's pessimism about 29-30; and social individuality 129-34, 136-9; as social vicissitudes of the drives 78-9; in Starobinski's interpretation 62-3

Hobbes, Thomas: and absolutism 171, 173, 176; his contract compared with Rousseau's 184; and enlightened self-interest 40, 101; on obligation 174; and Rousseau's critique of his concept of human nature 52, 116-17, 124-5, 179; Rousseau's premises compared to 18-19; his state of nature contrasted with Rousseau's 183; his use of resolutive-compositive method 51

Holbach, baron d' 42

l'homme sauvage: in comparison with animals 69-75; Hegel's notion of 92-3; as ideal of freedom and happiness 67, 129-30, 131-2; and openness to historicity 73; in Rousseau's evolutionary theory 62-3, 66-73; as symbol of biological core of human nature 85; as symbol of primary narcissism 227

Horowitz, Gad 6, 77n

Hume, David: compared with Rousseau 64; completing scepticism of Condillac 42, 136; on natural religion 57; and Rousseau's moral alternative 44

ideology: critique of in the *Social Contract* 191-2, 204-6; and duty 157; and the static conception of human nature 116-17

imagination: and compassion 237-8; and fantasy 229; and displacement of drives 78-9; and problem of civilization 137-8, 157; and 'thought experiments' 50, 214-16; *see also* Magical thinking

imported concepts 11

incest taboo 98

induction 38, 49

instincts: defence of 165, 252; 'open' and 'closed' 69-70, 72; and Rousseau's opposition to sensationalist psychology 68; *see also* Drives, Eros

interpretation: approaches to 7-12; conservative 18-20; disagreement among contextualists 8, 8n; existentialist 24-30; Kantian 42-6, 210-11; Marxist 20-4, 27; problems of 7, 9n, 15-16, 87-90, 96-8, 101; problems of in relation to *Emile* 207-16; problems of in relation to *La Nouvelle Héloïse* 146-7; problems of in relation to the *Social Contract* 166-8

Jameson, Fredric 6n

Kant, Immanuel: on culture as 'second nature' 212; on foundations of morality 24, 144-5, 181-2; on 'imported concepts' 11; in relation to Rousseau's evolutionary theory

63; on Rousseau as critic of utilitarianism 16
Kelly, George Armstrong 17n
Kettler, David 4n
Kojève, Alexandre 106n

labour: and development of language 76-7; and development of needs 109; and history 31, 128; and human phylogenesis 31, 74-6; and humanization 92-3; and perfectibility 80; and Rousseau's critique of biologism 82-5
La Mettrie, Julien Offroy de 55
language 70, 76-7
Laski, Harold 9n
law: function of in civil society 119; and the general will 185-7; in the modern state compared to the polis 170; in the polis 103; rule of 14-15; source of 18; view of state in liberal tradition of 23; *see also* General will, Natural law
Legislator 44, 167, 197-8
Lemos, R.M. 8n, 28n, 61n, 211n
Levine, Andrew: on alienation 5n, 190; on Rousseau's ambiguity 10, 11n; on Rousseau's historicization of the individual 22n; on Rousseau's liberalism 15n
Lévi-Strauss, Claude 48-9, 65-6n
liberal democracy 14, 15n; *see also* Democracy, Totalitarian democracy
Linnaeus, Carl von 59
Locke, John: and challenge of empiricism to natural law 47; on consent 174; contrasted with Rousseau on property 95-6; his epistemology and 'essentialism' 47-8, 64; on ethics and experience 40, 80; on the family 77-8; influence of on the Enlightenment 37-8; on innate knowledge of moral truth 15; and limited government 171; on the money economy 115; and the 'plain historical method' 41; on property and the 'hidden harmony' 40; Rousseau's critique of his concept of human nature 52, 124; his sensationalist psychology and equality 39; on sovereignty 173; his use of resolutive-compositive method 51
Lovejoy, Arthur O. 54
Löwith, Karl 36n
Lukács, Georg 21
Lycurgus 107, 218

Machiavelli 20
McManners, J. 15-16
Macpherson, C.B. 22, 52n, 125n
magical thinking 229; *see also* Imagination
Maillet, Benoît de 55
Maistre, Joseph de 18
Malebranche, Nicolas de 86n
Manuel, Frank E. 36n, 88n
Marcuse, Herbert 4, 4n, 23n, 252-3
market society: *see* Civil society
Marx, Karl: 4, 86, 207; on civil society 108-9; on human phylogenesis 75n; on ideology 116n; on the 'inverted world' 123n; on meaning in history 73n; on money and need 122n; on need and division of labour 110n; on the 'political annulment of private property' 196; on political emancipation 191-2, 206; on 'radical needs' 251-2; in relation to Rousseau 5, 5n, 20; on social individuality 82n; on the state 23, 166, 189-90, 195n; on the Terror 199; on universal alienation 127n; on

wealth and poverty under socialism 244
Masters, Roger D. 9n; on Rousseau's ambiguity 11n; on Rousseau's concept of nature 19n; on Rousseau as critic of modernity 20; on Rousseau as precursor of the philosophy of history 28n
materialism 42, 63-6; *see also* Historical materialism
Maupertuis, Pierre-Louis Moreau de 53
mediation: absence of in *l'homme sauvage* 69, 72; absence of in Rousseau's utopianism 88; and conscience 157; Rousseau's non-rejection of 30-1, 198-200, 222, 239-40, 250; and selfhood 26, 200; Starobinski's concept of 25
micro-evolution 59-60; *see also* Evolution, Transformism
Midgley, Mary 69n
mimesis 70, 74
money 94, 113-15, 121-3
Montaigne, Michel de 29
moralism 29
Muntéano, Basil 24n, 45n

narcissism 25, 227
naturalism 64-5, 74-5
natural law: in Enlightenment philosophy 39; and ideology 116-17; Rousseau's critique of 31, 46-7, 52, 64-5, 67, 176, 179; Rousseau's critique of on the family 77-8; and the state in Locke 40; *see also* Law, Nature
natural man: see *L'Homme sauvage*
natural sociability 178
nature: and artifice 31-2, 48, 106-7, 127-8, 216-18; and conscience in the Kantian interpretation 42-6; as dynamic process 67; feeling and subjection to 16; as immanent totality 29n; as limit 32; Lukács on concept of 21; and opinion 157-8; in the philosophy of the Enlightenment 36-42; as physical maturation 223; and repression 138-9, 162-5, 211-15, 221-2; rhetorical use of opposition to artifice 50-1; revenge of 133-4; Rousseau's concept contrasted with that of the Enlightenment 46-9, 80-2; in static opposition to society 17; and virtue 105-6, 139-43
nature, human: and biological drives 51-2, 219-20; and empirical ethnography 49; as historical process 52, 65, 71, 88-90; and the Legislator 198; and mediation 220; problem of first and second 28n, 52n, 212-13; Rousseau's concept of 31, 80-2; Strauss on Rousseau's historicization of 18
nature, state of: distinction between historical and juridical use of 115, 181; as inverse of despotism 119; and parallel to primary narcissism 235-6; Rousseau's contrasted with natural-law theory 48; Rousseau's use of 32, 87, 117; in the *Social Contract* 177-83; and state of war 91
needs: and civil society 109-12, 122-3, 178-81, 183; in the polis 105-7; and primitive society 92-6; and principle of dynamic equilibrium 232-3; reduction in 243-4; see also *Amourpropre*, Competition, Division of labour
negativity 31, 72, 74, 129-30; *see also* Free agency

neoteny 77, 77n, 222
neurosis 153-4, 162
Newton, Isaac 38, 40-1, 47

Oedipal conflict 159-62; *see also* Conflict, inner
ontology 62-7, 206
original sin 25, 38-9, 210, 213-15

passions: and conscience 143-6; and negative education 232-40; in opposition to reason 18-20; and the self 250; see also *Amour-de-soi, Amour-propre*
pathological narcissism 14
perfectibility: and *amour-propre* 128-9; and evolutionary theory 59-62, 73-5, 212; and labour 76-7, 80, 86; as result versus origin 75-6; and virtue 211
Physiocracy 39
pitié 179
Plato 4n, 11n, 20, 218, 240-1
Plattner, Marc F. 8n, 61n, 115n
pleasure principle 69, 235
Plessner, Helmuth 71n
political emancipation 189-90
politics: as articulation of common ends 247; and eschatology 88-9; and historical anthropology 86-90; in the Kantian interpretation 43-4, 210; in primitive society 91-2, 206; *see also* Civil society
polyvalence 10, 10n
popular sovereignty: *see* Sovereignty
primitive society 91-100
progress 40, 101
property: in civil society 112-13, 242; in *Emile* 245-6; and the general will 195-7, 200-2; Macpherson on Rousseau's doctrine 22; in the polis 103; in primitive society 95-6, 99
providence 54, 56-8, 77, 142
psychoanalytic theory 6, 131, 154-5
Puffendorf, Samuel 112n, 171, 178

radical individualism 26
reality principle 69
reciprocity 113-15, 117-19, 124-5, 181-3
regression: economic 22; and intellectual progress 26; in *La Nouvelle Héloïse* 159; pathological 32-3; in the service of the ego 26, 252-3
Reich, Annie 162n
reification 21, 168, 197-8
representation 23, 173
repression: and denaturation 221-2; and history 130-4; necessity of for individuation 33; in *La Nouvelle Héloïse* 147-65 *passim*
resolutive-compositive method 51-2
Robespierre 13

Sahlins, Marshall 91n, 95n, 99
Saint-Just 13
savage man: see *L'Homme sauvage*
Schiller, Friedrich 5
Schmidt, Alfred 65n, 72n
science 101, 105, 243
second nature 28n, 52n, 212-13
self: and *amour-propre* 213; and authenticity 26-7; its autonomy in relation to conscience 43; and civil society 217-22; as comparative relation 93; and intersubjectivity 222; not an origin 124, 128; and repression 230
self-esteem 93; see also *Amour-propre,* Denaturing
self-love: see *Amour-propre*
Service, E.R. 95n

sexuality: and compassion 238; and malleability of drives 78; and stages of development 226, 236-7
Shklar, Judith 14, 87n, 88n, 100n, 189
Skinner, Quentin 10n
Smith, Adam 108
Socrates 5, 157
sovereignty: inalienability of 172-4, 184-5; in natural-law theory 171-2; popular 174-6
Sparta 13, 74, 102, 106-7
species and varieties 58-9, 63; *see also* Evolution, Transformism
spontaneous generation 55
Starobinski, Jean 9, 215; his comparison of Rousseau with Buffon 62-7; on *La Nouvelle Héloïse* 146-7; on Rousseau and Freud 158; on Rousseau's failure 28; on Rousseau's inauthenticity 25-6, 30, 88, 100n; on the division of labour 110n
state: as instrumentality in Locke 40; and relation with civil society 115-19, 193-5
state of nature; *see* Nature, state of
state of war 179-81
Stoicism 121, 131, 144, 238-9
Strauss, Leo: on Rousseau's ambiguity 11n; on Rousseau as critic of modernity 18-19, 21, 101n; on Rousseau and historical materialism 206; on Rousseau and modern natural right 8n; on Rousseau's failure 27; on the specificity of human nature 72
sublimation 104-5, 161; *see also* Drives, Imagination
substance 63-5, 71
super-ego 157-65, 240; *see also* Conscience

Taine, Hyppolite 13

Talmon, J.L. 13
time 30, 223-5, 249-50
totalitarian democracy 13-16
transformism 34, 55, 58-61

uniformitarian geology 41, 53
utilitarianism 143-4
utopia 14, 25, 88, 186, 248-9

Vaughan, C.E. 8n
virtue: in conflict with happiness 16, 144, 163-5, 239-40; and conscience 139-46; and the *moi commun* 14, 245; and neurosis 133-4, 137, 143-4, 160, 238-9; in opposition to *bonté* 17, 100, 141, 163n; and the polis 100-7
Voltaire 39, 40

Washburn, S.L. 61-2, 62n
wealth 114, 123, 241-2
Weil, Eric 6
will: as basis of civil society 169-70; and custom 177; and ego development 227-31, 236-7; Hegel on Rousseau's view of 5; and *l'homme sauvage* 129; particular 187-9, 193-5; in relation to virtue 16, 103; and sovereignty 171-6; *see also* Autonomy, Civil society, Negativity
Wright, E.H. 52n

WITHDRAWN
FROM STOCK
QMUL LIBRARY